OCEANA

OCEANA

OUR ENDANGERED OCEANS
and what
WE CAN DO *to* SAVE THEM

TED DANSON

with MICHAEL D'ORSO

RODALE

Rodale books may be purchased for business or promotional use or for special sales. For information, please write to:
Special Markets Department, Rodale Inc., 733 Third Avenue,
New York, NY 10017.

Printed in the United States of America
Rodale Inc. makes every effort to use acid-free ⊖, recycled paper ◉.
This book was printed on paper containing 30 percent postconsumer waste.

Book design by Headcase Design • www.headcasedesign.com
Infographics by Headcase Design
Illustrations on pages 22–23, 60–61, 82–83, 128–129, 142–143, 158–159, 188–189, and 226–227 by Don Foley

Credits for photos can be found on page 304.

The graph on page 101 is reprinted by permission from Macmillan Publishers Ltd: R.Watson and D. Pauly. 2001. Systematic distortions in world fisheries catch trends. Nature 414 (Nov. 29): 536–538.

The figure A map on page 159 is reprinted courtesy of the Sea Around Us Project: A. Kitchingman and S. Lai. 2004. Seamounts: Biodiversity and Fisheries. Edited by Telmo Morato and Daniel Pauly. Fisheries Centre Research Reports 12 (5): 10.

Library of Congress Cataloging-in-Publication Data
Danson, Ted
    Oceana : our endangered oceans and what we can do to save them /
    Ted Danson with Michael D'Orso.
        p.   cm.
    Includes bibliographical references and index.
    ISBN 978-1-60529-262-5 (hardcover)
    1. Marine ecology.   2. Marine pollution.   3. Marine resources conservation.
    4. Environmental degradation.   5. Environmental policy.   6. Environmental
    protection.   I. D'Orso, Michael.   II. Title.
    QH541.5.S3D34   2011
    333.95'616—dc22   2011001685

Distributed to the trade by Macmillan
2 4 6 8 10 9 7 5 3 1 hardcover

We inspire and enable people to improve their lives and the world around them.
www.rodalebooks.com

———— *To my family* ————

M a r y , **Kate** , L i l l y , C h a r l i e , *and* K a t r i n a

———— The companions of my life and my heart ————

CONTENTS

LAGUNA BEACH, 1953—*two years before the very scary dream*

PREFACE

I WOKE UP SCREAMING. It was late—two or three in the morning. The whole house was asleep, and I could hear the sound of surf outside the open windows of the little vacation beach house we had rented. I was soaked with sweat, terrified, not sure if I was awake or dreaming. I was seven years old.

Clutching my stomach, my face a mask of pain and confusion, I stumbled into my parents' bedroom. My mom and dad rushed me into the bathroom, splashed water on my face, and did their best to calm me down.

Soon enough I was back to normal, a sleepy, exhausted kid who just wanted to go back to bed. Everything was fine.

But the next night it happened again. And the next. And the one after that.

The same, terrible dream.

And here's how it went:

I'm sitting on a beach, the middle of a glorious day, and a voice speaks to me out of the clear blue sky. God's voice.

"Ted," it says.

A bucket appears in the sand beside me.

And then a spoon filled with holes appears in my hand.

"You have one hour to empty the entire ocean into this bucket," says the voice, "or the world will explode. And it will be your fault."

Now, clearly this dream represents your basic, run-of-the-mill messiah complex, not uncommon among us actor types. But if you're in the mood to grant me a little poetic license, you could say this was the awakening of my concern for our world's oceans. And if so, then while I've spent the past twenty-five years actively working on the various issues facing our oceans, if you count the scary dream, my concern for the seas has actually been stirring inside me for more than a half century—for almost my entire life.

By the way, around the time I had that dream, there were this many of the "big fish"—the lions and tigers of the sea—in the ocean:

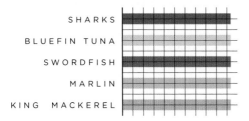

Fifty-five years later, as I'm writing this preface, only this many remain:

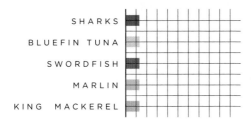

I grew up about as far away from the ocean as you can get—first in the hills outside Tucson, Arizona, then among the Ponderosa pines of the northern part of that state, just outside of Flagstaff.

My father was an archaeologist and later became the director of the Museum and Research Center of Northern Arizona. Our home, just an hour south of the Grand Canyon, was routinely visited by some of the world's leading scientists in the fields of geology, paleontology, anthropology, and, of course, archaeology.

My mother was very involved in our church and led a spiritual life, not just inside that Episcopal chapel but out in the foothills and forests that surrounded our home. She loved nothing more than going out for a walk. She took us—me and my sister—with her all the time, and when you went for a walk with my mother, you better not be in a hurry. Because she took in everything, she saw beauty everywhere, and she always stopped to relish it.

The more you look, the more you see. That's something my mom taught me. She was the great appreciator. My father was much more the scientist—studying things, dissecting them, taking them apart, sorting them out, putting them back together, understanding what made them tick.

And, although I wasn't aware of it at the time—I was busy playing with my friends, in the canyons and ravines around our house, just being a kid—I have no doubt that what my parents' lives stood for back then somehow sunk in, providing a foundation for the advocacy work that I do today.

I strongly believe that science and spirituality go hand in hand, and any conversation we have about the environment has to take both into account. Unless all our actions to save the oceans are based on science, we will end up doing more harm than good. And unless we acknowledge our spiritual connectedness to one another and to this planet we live on—unless we realize that almost everything each of us does has an impact on somebody else—we may never rise above our self-interests in order to gather the collective forces we need to face the environmental challenges that now surround us.

BOULDER, COLORADO—on the way to Tucson

Speaking of self-interest, I was pretty much consumed by it until my mid-thirties. It was then, around my fourth year of playing Sam Malone on the TV show *Cheers*, that I noticed being a celebrity was not very different from being a five-year-old in a room full of adults. Everyone is focused on you. All the attention and energy in the room is directed your way. I realized that if I wasn't careful, my life could easily spin out of control, and I'd run the danger of becoming the five-year-old who's stayed at the grownups' party too long. I knew that I needed to do something constructive with all that energy before it really screwed me up. I needed to focus it on something outside of myself.

That something, it turned out, became the oceans.

In 1984, my family and I moved to Santa Monica Canyon, about ten blocks from the Pacific.

One day I was walking on the beach with my two young daughters, Kate and Alexis, and we came upon a sign that said "Beach Closed, Water Polluted." Kate, who was eight at the time, was puzzled as to why—and how—a beach could be closed. Frankly, I was just as puzzled as she was. When she asked me for an answer, I didn't have one.

So I began looking for them. I started asking some questions myself.

Not long after that, I went to a neighborhood meeting that had been called in an attempt to stop Occidental Petroleum from drilling sixty oil wells near Will Rogers State Beach, right there beside Santa Monica and other surrounding communities.

The meeting was organized by a lawyer named Robert Sulnick, an environmental activist who'd been involved in these kinds of fights for many years. In the beginning, I was completely unaware of the complex web of forces threatening our oceans. I didn't know any more about industrial bottom trawling, habitat destruction, ocean acidification, or government fishing subsidies than Sam Malone, the affable high school dropout turned bartender, did.

But I learned fast. Bob and I joined forces, ultimately stopping those wells from being drilled, and became great friends in the process. Flushed with success, a little naïve but full of passion, we created an organization called American Oceans Campaign. Our focus was on coastal pollution and maintaining the national moratorium on offshore oil drilling. I was full of a novice's enthusiasm—eager to convert people to the cause and quick to spar with those who dared contradict me. I was quickly schooled by several conservative talk show hosts and rightfully learned my lesson. For a while, Howard Stern had a daily "Danson's Countdown to Doom." Rush Limbaugh took me to task when a rash prediction I made for the end of the oceans as we know them came and passed—and the oceans still looked pretty much the same . . . at least to the untrained eye. So here's what I learned: Stick to the science. Tell people what's going on, turn them toward the experts who *really* know what's happening, and then let the people themselves decide what to do about it. Don't make speeches just to impress the audience with how much you've learned. Because there's always so much more to know, whether you're just starting out, or you've been at it a while. That's why we need the experts, and we need to listen to them. Because they *do* know. I never let myself forget how lucky I've been to be able to meet many of these experts . . . and to be able to help get their message out.

By the way, I should say right here that I love seafood. I'm not here to tell you not to eat it. Just the opposite, in fact. I want there to be oceans full

of healthy fish so that we—and our children and grandchildren—can continue to turn to them for pleasure, for sustenance, and in many cases, for sheer survival. The oceans are a vital resource for all of humanity, and they need to last forever. Right now, there are more than a billion people on this planet who rely on the oceans as their primary source of animal protein. And it's been estimated that 200 million people make their living by fishing, directly or indirectly.

In 2001, American Oceans Campaign joined forces with several other nonprofits to form a new global marine organization called Oceana, the biggest international group in the world solely focused on ocean issues. And I have to confess, when that merger occurred, I thought, *Great! Now I've got a back door, a way out.* I was tired of asking my friends for money, frustrated trying to raise awareness about something that seemed so basic, and not sure I was really making a difference.

But it turned out I wasn't quite ready to throw in the towel. The new organization upped the ante to a whole new level, pulling together such an astounding array of great, committed, and inspiring people that I found myself happily working even more for this cause, not less. You'll meet some of these people in the pages that follow—marine biologists, fishermen, activists, politicians, even chefs and restaurateurs—along with a whole host of other people whose lives are, in one way or another, deeply tied to this cause.

The fact is—and this is the fundamental reason I've written this book—that all our lives are intertwined with and, in the end, dependent upon the health of the seas that surround us. We know that—or we should. And the health of those seas is declining, *rapidly.* The stakes for the oceans have become that high. If you like eating seafood—and who doesn't?—here's something you should know: Just a few years ago, scientists discovered that the world's fish catch peaked in 1988—just around the time I started working on ocean policy. Until that year, it had never declined. But each year since then, the number has decreased. No one ever imagined that there might be a limit to the number of fish in the sea. It was unthinkable. The oceans have always been considered an inexhaustible resource. We now know that this simply isn't true. By some definitions, one-third of the world's fisheries are currently in collapse—unable to regenerate their populations fast enough to keep pace with the rate at which they are being caught or killed. And as I mentioned earlier, recent studies show that the number of "big fish" (swordfish, marlin, bluefin tuna, king mackerel, and sharks) that inhabit the world's oceans today has dropped 90 percent since the year of my scary dream—1955.

Okay, you might think. So the number of wild fish out there is declining. Big deal. What about *farmed* fish? Well, here's another surprising fact. Farmed fish make the problem worse, for reasons that you'll learn in Chapter 7. And overfishing is only one of the ways in which our oceans are in dan-

ger. We're also contaminating our seas with trash and toxic chemicals and radically changing their pH in a process called *ocean acidification*. We all know by now about the dangers of too much carbon being released into the atmosphere, accelerating the process of global warming. But not many of us are aware that the oceans are endangered by this same process as well. For millennia, the oceans have absorbed carbon, helping to keep our air breathable and also helping to regulate the climate. But as we've burned more and more fossil fuels, the oceans have become increasingly saturated with carbon. You'll learn more about this in Chapter 2 and see how it is destroying our reefs, which are the very base of the oceans' food web. The tiny creatures that call those coral reefs home, from phytoplankton to shellfish, are destroyed along with them, disrupting the food web above them, leaving the next layer up with little to eat. And, as the top of the food web is disappearing due to the overfishing of the "big fish," the bottom of the web is disappearing as well. The entire system is being squeezed from both ends. That's a recipe for disaster.

Speaking at the National Press Club in 2008

Yet another issue is energy—specifically, oil. The oceans have provided us with energy for decades in the form of oil from offshore drilling. We've always known we run a risk with any kind of oil drilling—the risk of leaks, spills, or other kinds of accidents. The 1989 *Exxon Valdez* tanker spill was the hallmark for such risks in terms of oceanic destruction—until last year, when a state-of-the-art oil rig in the Gulf of Mexico exploded, killing eleven workers and rupturing an underwater pipeline. The resulting spill was the worst oil disaster in the history of the United States, by far overshadowing the damage done by the *Exxon Valdez*—damage that Alaskans are still dealing with today, more than two decades later. No one can say how long it

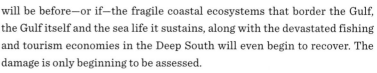

will be before—or if—the fragile coastal ecosystems that border the Gulf, the Gulf itself and the sea life it sustains, along with the devastated fishing and tourism economies in the Deep South will even begin to recover. The damage is only beginning to be assessed.

Clearly, offshore drilling is a practice we need to get away from. There is a way that oceans can provide a rich source of clean, renewable energy—not from the oil that lies beneath them, but from the winds that blow above them.

I know the list above might look daunting. But the good news is that experts believe we still have the time and the means to tackle each of these problems, to solve them, and to bring back our oceans. This battle is not over, by any means. This is a fight we can win. Actually, "fight" is the wrong word. It's going to take cooperation, people on both sides of these issues working together, to avoid the catastrophes looming ahead of us. If the conservationists and the fishing industry can find a way to work together—and I absolutely believe that they can—then everyone wins. If they don't, everyone loses.

By making policy changes nation by nation, enforcing the laws that are already on the books, halting destructive fishing practices, and using good plain common sense to limit the amount of pollution that ends up in our oceans and in our bodies because of the fish we eat, we can turn things around.

These steps, many of them simple, will save our oceans. Again, 90 percent of the "big fish" that existed in the 1950s are now gone. As for the rest of the 30,000 known species of fish in the world's oceans, we could conceivably "fish them out" in the next fifty years. That's within some of our own lifetimes, certainly within the lifetimes of our children.

No more fish. It's hard to imagine. Almost inconceivable. But it's true. And right now we're moving closer to that reality every day.

The purpose of this book is to help make sure that doesn't happen. In the pages that follow, I'd like to share what I've learned over the course of the past twenty-some years, and to introduce you to a number of gifted, deeply intelligent people who have devoted their lives to the cause of saving our oceans.

It's been an amazing journey for me. The more I understand, the more certain I am that it's not too late to take action. I'm not going to pretend that it will be easy or quick. But it can—it *will*—be done. The most important thing I've learned from the men and women I've been fortunate enough to work with over all these years is to remain hopeful.

That's what my own journey has taught me, and I have no doubt that, armed with the information contained in the pages that follow, you'll feel the same way I do. By the time you've finished reading this book, you'll not only know what needs to be done to save our endangered oceans, but you'll know *how* to do it, and you'll be determined to turn what you know into action.

I still have the occasional nightmare, but by and large I am optimistic about our oceans. After two decades of talking and thinking about these issues, I can now see that the political will that is necessary to address these problems is building fast. I felt that way before last year's Gulf disaster, and feel ever more strongly today. If there's anything good that can possibly come out of something as horrific as that blowout, it's that a lot of people who might not have paid attention to our oceans before are paying attention now.

And this is our message: Time is short. But with your help, we can do it. We can save our oceans. The oceans have been good to us. It's time for us to do something for them. If we act now, we can see abundant and healthy improvement in as little as a decade.

The oceans make up 70 percent of our planet's surface. They are a permanent gift to the future of all people—a legacy to our children, and to our children's children.

We've started to turn the tide.

Now let's finish the job.

CHAPTER ONE

TOUGH OIL

OUT OF SIGHT, OUT OF MIND

There's no phrase that better explains how our planet's oceans have reached a point where they are so direly threatened on so many fronts and yet so few of us have any idea of the danger they're in.

On one level, this makes perfect sense. Humans are terrestrial creatures. We live on the land, not in the sea. When we refer to the "environment," we're typically talking about *our* environment—the land, air, rivers, lakes, and coastlines where we live, work, and play. It's no surprise that a study of charitable giving in America showed that of all donations directed toward environmental concerns, 99 percent went to agencies and organizations focused on terrestrial issues, while 1 percent went to groups working to protect the oceans and the sea life within them.

Protect them from what?

That would be the typical question asked by anyone on the street. And again, at first glance, this makes sense. We're all taught in school that 71 percent of the Earth's surface is covered by oceans, and much of that is so deep that only a handful of humans have ever gotten close to the bottom. It would probably come as a shock to most people to learn that less than 1 percent of the living space on the Earth is on land—the other 99 percent is in the oceans, which contain many unique, and undiscovered species.

So what kinds of hazards could possibly threaten that many animals in that much water?

This has been the prevailing attitude ever since men first began pulling fish from the sea. Until the past half century or so, the oceans have always been seen as an inexhaustible resource, far too vast and abundant for us to even conceive of any danger that could possibly threaten them.

It's only when a disaster of one kind or another hits close to home—meaning close to our shorelines—that we consider the health of our high seas.

So it makes sense to begin this book with just such a disaster—the April 2010 explosion at BP's Deepwater Horizon oil drilling rig, some fifty miles off the coast of Louisiana, a blast that killed eleven workers, injured seventeen others, and, as I've mentioned, triggered the biggest oil disaster in the history of the United States.

OCEANS:

71%

of the Earth's surface

250,000

named marine species

1.75 MILLION

named terrestrial species

LAND:

29%

of the Earth's surface

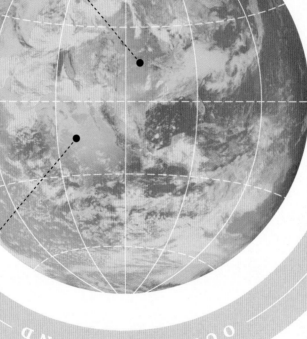

OCEAN *vs.* LAND

Source: Census on Marine Life, Millennium Ecosystem Assessment

APRIL 2010
EXPLOSION at BP's
DEEPWATER HORIZON

THERE SEEMS to be **A CYCLE** to these **OCEAN DISASTERS—** and it's **A CYCLE WE SIMPLY CANNOT AFFORD** to **LET CONTINUE.**

TIMELINE: THE EVOLUTION OF US OFFSHORE DRILLING REGULATIONS

January 28, 1969:
Santa Barbara
oil spill

1970:
Clean Air Act
(includes some
drilling provisions)

1982:
Congressional
moratorium on
offshore drilling
leases enacted.

March 24, 1989:
Exxon Valdez spill

1990:
President
George H. W.
Bush enacts
executive ban on
offshore drilling.

IT WAS TRAGIC, HORRIFYING, ALMOST BEYOND COMPREHENSION . . .

And, sad to say, it wasn't surprising at all—not to anyone familiar with the ever-increasing dangers of offshore drilling.

It's almost eerie to look at the similarities between the situation our American Oceans Campaign (AOC) group in Santa Monica faced back in the 1980s, when we began our fight against drilling near the coast of Southern California, and the situation our entire nation faces today in the wake of the Gulf tragedy. There seems to be somewhat of a cycle to these ocean disasters—and it's a cycle we simply cannot afford to let continue.

At the time that Bob Sulnick and I formed the AOC and launched our antidrilling campaign in the Pacific, it had been roughly twenty years since an offshore platform off the coast of Santa Barbara—just up the coast from us—suffered a blowout the likes of which, at that time, had never been seen in America. By the time that well was capped nearly twelve days later, a hundred thousand barrels of crude oil (4.2 million gallons) had spewed into the surrounding waters, creating an eight-hundred-square-mile surface slick, shutting down the region's fishing industry, coating seabirds and mammals with chocolate pudding–like petroleum, and blackening the area's beaches with tar balls.

March 31, 2010: The Obama administration proposes opening up the Atlantic from Delaware to the central coast of Florida to offshore drilling and expresses interest in drilling in the Alaskan Arctic and the still-protected southeast Gulf Coast.

July 14, 2008: President George W. Bush rescinds executive ban on drilling, opening up thousands of miles of US coastline to leasing and drilling

April 20, 2010: The Deepwater Horizon oil rig explodes in the Gulf of Mexico.

December 1, 2010: The Obama administration announces that no new drilling will be allowed in the eastern Gulf of Mexico or off America's Pacific and Atlantic coasts for five years

AGREE TO DISAGREE

ROBERT SULNICK

Cofounder of the American Oceans Campaign

In 1985 I was the president of No Oil Inc., an organization fighting to stop Arm & Hammer and Occidental Petroleum from drilling oil wells adjacent to the Will Rogers State Beach in Pacific Palisades, California.

On a cold rainy night, we held a poorly attended fundraiser in the basement of the Presbyterian Church in Santa Monica. After my speech to the nine people there, a tall thin man walked up to me and said that he liked what I had to say. When he left, the other No Oil folks asked if I knew who that was. I said no. At the time, I thought *Cheers* was a bar somewhere in Los Angeles. So began one of the most amazing friendships I have ever had. In 1987 Ted Danson and I founded American Oceans Campaign (AOC).

The environmental community, as necessary and vital as it is, cannot solve environmental problems on its own; it does not have the resources or infrastructure to do so. Industry, of course, has the resources

and the infrastructure. AOC decided to approach the oil industry with the proposition that we agree to disagree about offshore oil drilling and agree to agree about things like conserving energy and re-refining used oil.

By reaching out to the oil industry, we were able to accomplish things that otherwise would have been out of reach. During the 1980s, we had a constant dialogue with big oil, which led, among other things, to California's first re-refined oil program. Those relationships also helped BP Solar establish solar energy in California and the Western States Petroleum Association (WSPA) support California's first used-oil re-refining law.

I will always believe that agreeing to disagree with an opponent while being able to work with them on other mutually beneficial issues is the right approach for environmental problem solving.

These days, unfortunately, we're all too familiar with those kinds of images. But back then, just one month into the year of 1969, they were shocking, unprecedented. The entire nation looked on with a mixture of outrage and disgust. This was a landmark turning point for America's oil industry, which, until then, had enjoyed almost completely unchecked expansion. In the explosive decade of street protests and demonstrations that followed the Santa Barbara spill, people responded by burning their gasoline credit cards and marching with placards calling for the government to step in and take action so something like this would never happen again.

Which the government did, with a vengeance. Its response to that spill reached far beyond oil. With cities across the nation smothered in smog, rivers so polluted they actually caught fire (as Cleveland's Cuyahoga River famously did later in 1969), bodies of water as large as Lake Erie declared "dead" because of oxygen-sucking algal blooms caused by decades of chemical runoff from industries and farms, and, finally, the Santa Barbara disaster, US lawmakers at all levels passed an avalanche of landmark environmental legislation, including, in 1972, the Clean Water Act and the statutes creating the Environmental Protection Agency.

Dozens of federal and state laws were enacted, restricting and regulating what Americans, both as individuals and as corporations, were allowed to dump into our water, our soil, and our air. A little more than a year after that Santa Barbara spill, the first Earth Day was celebrated. Eventually, a moratorium was placed on all new leases for gas and oil exploration in federal waters for the lower forty-eight states (outside of existing areas in the Gulf of Mexico) which, of course, included those waters off the coast of Southern California.

And here's where the cycle set in.

You would think—you would hope—that that outrage and those laws would stand strong forever. But the very success of that moratorium seemed to lull people to sleep. As years passed with virtually no disasters to speak of—certainly nothing on the scale of those events of '69—public concern over environmental issues faded. People became complacent. All the while, the oil industry was pushing behind the scenes for legislators to lift those restrictions and allow them to begin drilling again—on land and, even more critically, at sea.

By the late 1980s, it looked like those efforts would pay off. A movement among congressional supporters of the oil industry to lift that offshore drilling moratorium began picking up steam. This was my first taste of a high-stakes, toe-to-toe battle on behalf of the environment, and our AOC joined with like-minded organizations around the country to push back against the bill proposing the change. I traveled around the country, speaking at rallies, appearing on radio and television, even testifying before Congress.

When we finally prevailed in 1995, with a House committee voting to keep the ban in place, I was euphoric, just like the rest of my fellow activists. But just like them, I also knew that this deal was far from done, with so much at stake for the oil industry, and with its advocates in Congress, led by some pretty fierce political brawlers—like Texas representative Tom DeLay—bound and determined to tear down that ban.

When Andy Palmer, our spokesman for AOC at the time, spoke to the press after that vote, he shared our mixed feelings.

"Those who treasure America's fragile coastal ocean waters can breathe a little easier today," he said. "However," he added, "it would be a serious mistake to assume this fight is over."

He was right.

If Americans needed a wake-up call on this issue, they got it just past midnight on March 24, 1989—almost precisely twenty years after the Santa Barbara spill—when the *Exxon Valdez*, an oil tanker bound for Long Beach, California,

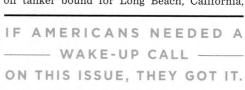

IF AMERICANS NEEDED A ——— WAKE-UP CALL ——— ON THIS ISSUE, THEY GOT IT.

struck a reef while avoiding some icebergs as it was leaving a port on Alaska's southern coast. To this day, estimates of how much crude oil gushed out of that vessel range from 11 million gallons to more than 30 million (the ship had been carrying 53 million gallons of oil). To this day, no one knows the precise amount that escaped. The generally accepted figure is that low-end number of 11 million. At the very least, it was well over twice the size of the Santa Barbara spill.

Once again the nation was battered with images of wildlife smothered in oil, of surface slicks spreading for miles, and of black, gooey crude washing up on one of the most ecologically productive coastlines on the planet. Once again the public was horrified and irate. Once again there were calls for more legislation, for tighter rules and restrictions. Once again the oil industry was forced to retreat and circle its wagons.

And once again the years went by.

And the outrage faded.

And by the turn of this century, the oil industry was on the offensive again, pushing for exploratory wells in the tundra of Alaska's Arctic National Wildlife Refuge wilderness and off both US coasts, as well as in the Gulf of Mexico. With the arrival of the George W. Bush administration and its numerous ties to big oil, the industry had

FINDING THE MIDDLE GROUND

MAYOR EDWARD ITTA

Barrow, Alaska

I went up to the village of Barrow, Alaska, to talk to the mayor of the North Slope Borough, Edward Itta. The North Slope Borough is above the Arctic Circle; the area has been home to Itta's people, the Inupiat Eskimos, for thousands of years. In his two terms as mayor, he has found himself smack in the middle of the debate over oil. North Slope contains the largest oil field in the country: The area of Prudhoe Bay and just offshore, in the Chukchi and Beaufort seas, is thought to be the next major source of oil and natural gas. Itta spoke to me about his position on oil and how he is trying to balance environmental concerns about drilling with the tremendous growth energy development has brought to his part of Alaska.

MAYOR ITTA: Since Prudhoe Bay was discovered in 1968, we have been worried that the oil development would interfere with our way of life up here. As hunters and whalers, we know that smelt, the very lowest of the food chain, are the organisms that feed the krill, who feed the cod fish, who feed the seal, who feed the polar bears, which feed everything else. If that's gone, no kind of Endangered Species Act is ever going to matter.

When I was growing up, we had no electric switches, diesel, or natural gas. We had virtually no airports, runways, landfills, or health clinics and just a small hospital. We now support eight outlying villages that all have airports, health clinics, and schools. Obviously our revenues come from being able to tax Prudhoe Bay and the Trans-Alaska Pipeline within our borders, but oil is decreasing, so our revenues are going down as well.

Five years ago, my position on drilling in the Chukchi and Beaufort seas was "Hell no, over my dead body." But one of my responsibilities as mayor is the economic well-being of our people—ensuring that our children and grandchildren will have an economic base. So I've been negotiating with the oil companies and the government, pushing for baseline science, pipelines, stricter regulations, and an examination of the cumulative impact.

We are inseparable from the land and sea because we cannot live as Inupiat Eskimos without them. One lesson from our past and current elders: "You as Inupiat Eskimos were here long before oil, so whatever happens, you do your best to ensure you're going to be here after the oil."

strong support in the White House. Over the course of the next eight years, it took extraordinary resources to fight back just to hold the fort and preserve that moratorium. By then, our AOC had merged into the largest oceans conservation organization in the world—Oceana.

You can imagine our disbelief when President Bush, in one of his last acts in office, as he was literally headed out the door of the White House following the election of 2008, opened up the Atlantic and Pacific coasts to drilling, and Congress, for the first time in more than 20 years, failed to renew its moratorium as well. Shock was followed by a sense of relief when Barack Obama took the oath of office in January 2009—twenty years after the *Exxon Valdez*—and suspended the Bush decision. But that relief turned to disappointment when, in March 2010, President Obama made his first moves toward allowing oil and gas exploration in the formerly protected areas.

Naturally, the oil industry geared up to finally sink those wells they'd been waiting so long to drill, especially out there in the oceans' deep water.

And then—again, right on cue—a mere month after Obama's decision to move forward with new offshore leasing, came the blast in the Gulf.

DEEPWATER HORIZON EXPLOSION:

2 MILLION GALLONS OF RAW CRUDE A DAY

X 85 DAYS

171 MILLION GALLONS OF OIL RELEASED INTO THE GULF (*estimated*)

WHICH BRINGS US TO THE PRESENT, WHEN WE FIND OURSELVES in yet another post-spill uproar, with the White House reassessing its decision to allow drilling, with the oil industry's PR machine kicking in with its same old game— sharing our sorrow over such a tragic event and swearing to make things right, while continuing to insist that the very future of our nation depends on continuing to drill, pushing as far as possible to find and extract every drop of "our" oil that we can in order to protect our energy independence and preserve the American way of life as we know it. That's the party line.

Within weeks of the Deepwater Horizon explosion, even as raw crude from the still-uncapped well continued to gush into the Gulf at a rate of more than 2 million gallons a day (roughly the entirety of the *Exxon Valdez* spill every four days), oil industry executives were already busy in Washington, working to convince Congress that this "accident" should not stall any efforts to allow them to drill new offshore wells wherever they possibly can.

They were still there the day the well was finally capped—eighty-five days after the explosion occurred. Estimates of the total amount of oil released into the Gulf over that time were all over the place. The final official federal estimate was nearly 171 million gallons.

That's more than fifteen *Exxon Valdez* spills.

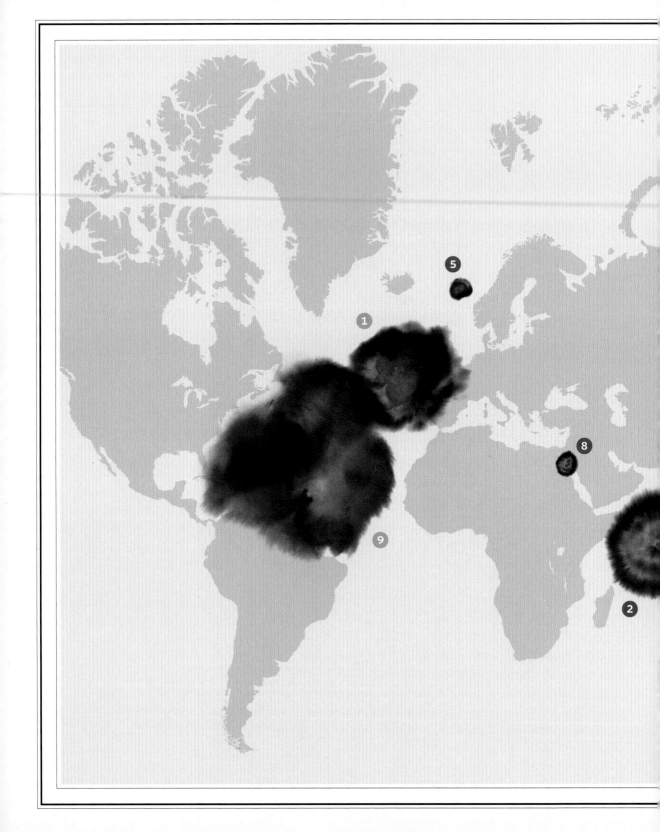

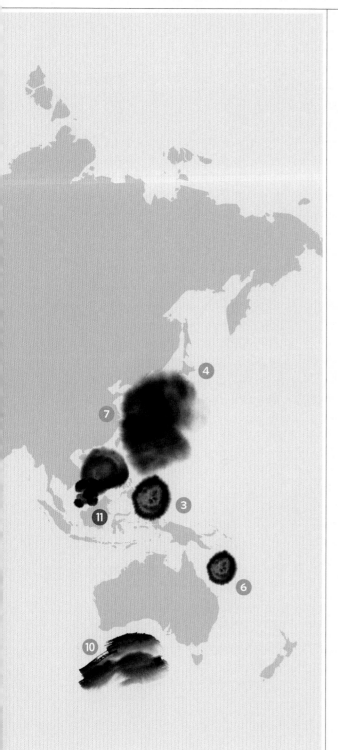

OIL DISASTERS

#	Amount	Location	Date	Description
1	**23.7** MILLION gallons	Spain	11/13/2002	Tanker destroyed
2	**8.6** MILLION gallons	Pakistan	7/28/2003	Tanker destroyed
3	**530,000** gallons	Philippines	8/11/2006	Tanker destroyed
4	**3.7** MILLION gallons	South Korea	12/7/2007	Tanker collision
5	**3,079** gallons	United Kingdom	10/31/2008	Offshore rig leak
6	**22,000** gallons	Queensland	3/11/2009	Cargo ship leak
7	**8.6** MILLION gallons	Vietnam	6/17/2009	Tanker exploded
8	**16,320** gallons	Suez Canal	8/28/2009	Tanker spill
9	**171** MILLION gallons	Gulf of Mexico	4/20/2010	Offshore rig blowout
10	**1.3** MILLION gallons	Australia	4/20/2010	Offshore rig blowout
11	**115,400** gallons	Vietnam	4/27/2010	Tanker sunk

And yet the BP machine was still working overtime, churning out its own images to put its own spin on the spill, emphasizing how inconsequential this amount of oil is when you look at the big picture.

For example, the company compared the spill at the time it was capped to the size of the body of water that surrounds it. If a water-filled Cowboys Stadium in Dallas represented the Gulf of Mexico, the spilled oil would equal one twenty-four-ounce can of beer. Heck, they pointed out, the Mississippi River empties as much freshwater into the Gulf every fifty-six *seconds* as the amount of oil the Deepwater Horizon spill took three months to release.

All true. But these facts simply illustrate the amount of the oil itself. They do nothing to change the nature and extent of the damage done by that oil.

Yes, it's the same old song and dance being kicked into gear once again, the same old cycle. The industry minimizes the effects of an accident while pushing forward to punch even more wells into the ocean floor.

WHEN IT COMES to the **RISKS** and **RAMIFICATIONS** of **DRILLING FOR OIL**, **EACH WAKE-UP CALL** is **MORE DEVASTATING THAN THE LAST.**

And we simply cannot afford to let it continue. Not anymore.

We can't afford to fall asleep for another twenty years, until the next wake-up call comes. Because, as the past four decades have shown us, when it comes to the risks and ramifications of drilling for oil, each wake-up call is more devastating than the last. Each of these disasters raises the stakes in terms of the damage that's done, to the point where we're not even able to assess it anymore.

We're still dealing today with the long-term impacts of the *Exxon Valdez* collision. We have absolutely no idea how long it will be before we can even begin to quantify and repair the damage done by the Deepwater Horizon spill—if indeed it can ever be repaired. How many more times are we willing to roll the drilling dice until we're finally tapped out?

I have no doubt that if the American people knew all the facts, if we really understood the specifics and the severity of the damage wrought not just by these headline oil disasters, but by the petroleum industry's everyday offshore operations as well, our minds would never again be changed by the propaganda and myths perpetuated by the industry to convince us to "Drill, baby, drill."

Don't get me wrong. There's no question that none of us would be where we are today without oil. I totally get that. Its most critical value, of course, has been as a source of energy in the forms of the gasoline, jet, and diesel fuel that have literally powered our nation over the course of the past century.

Then there's the energy provided by the petroleum and natural gas that generate a significant amount of our nation's electricity.

THE FUTURE OF ENERGY

PETE SLAIBY

Royal Dutch Shell Exploration and Production

On a visit to Alaska, I sat down with Pete Slaiby, the vice president of Shell Oil's Alaska Venture. He manages the company's exploration and production activities and works with stakeholders in the region, including the government and the Inupiat people, to build support for drilling in the Beaufort and Chukchi seas, offshore from the North Slope Borough. Slaiby spoke to me about oil and the future of energy.

PETE SLAIBY: We're open books here. There's no man behind the curtain on anything we do, including here in Alaska. Shell was one of the first oil companies, if not the first, to acknowledge climate change. Ask any oil executive if we believe in climate change—of course, we all do. We are all students of climate change. It's our view that it will take a several-pronged approach to manage the issue to the extent it's possible.

When we look at energy, we see demand increasing by 50 percent by 2030 and doubling by the year 2050—so Shell does a huge amount of planning around that. Energy needs can be met by a plan or they will be met by a scramble. Our fear is that without a policy, we will stumble into something chaotic and unpleasant.

Historically, new energy sources take a number of years to develop. We're big into biofuels. We're also growing in wind: We have a little over 1.5 gigawatts, which is our share of wind power installations in the United States, Canada, and Western Europe.

We like those technologies, but they grow at a slow rate. Right now, solar and wind account for less than 1 percent of US energy needs. It could take 20 years to grow that to 2 percent.

We as Americans need to address energy policy. And we have to make sure there's a robust transition into these plans and ensure that markets are protected with respect to manufacturing jobs and our overall way of life. Shell has been out front saying we need an energy policy in the United States that incorporates renewables, solar, and sustainable biofuels. It also involves things that are potentially unpopular—like nuclear. It involves major investment

in infrastructure. We're going to find solutions through sensible policy—holding all of our politicians on both sides of the aisle accountable, coming together and putting aside their differences and coming up with policies that will work and are sustainable.

WE as **AMERICANS NEED** to **ADDRESS ENERGY POLICY.**

Oil's innumerable uses as a lubricant are obvious.

Less obvious, but no less pervasive, are the tens of thousands of products made from petroleum that permeate our everyday lives, both inside and outside our homes. That businessman who pulled the young Dustin Hoffman aside in *The Graduate* and told him the future could be summed up in one word—"Plastics"—knew what he was talking about. Think about the fact that almost every object you touch every day includes at least one component that is made of plastic. Then think about the fact that almost all plastic is made from petroleum.

As is the asphalt that covers our roads.

And the synthetic rubber tires that roll over that asphalt.

Think about the fertilizers, pesticides, and herbicides used on our farms and in our gardens, almost all of which use petroleum as part of their manufacturing process.

ALMOST EVERYTHING that TOUCHES our DAY-TO-DAY LIVES INVOLVES PETROLEUM PRODUCTS.

As do many detergents we use for our laundry. And the film for our cameras—for those of us who haven't gone digital.

The point is, almost everything that touches our day-to-day lives involves, in one way or another, petroleum products. Which seemed all well and good at one time in our history—through, say, the first two-thirds of the twentieth century, as America ascended to its place as the world's preeminent superpower and the American people (most of us) came to enjoy an incredibly high quality of life.

But that time has passed, and with it has gone the luxury of basing virtually our entire culture—particularly our energy use—on a foundation of fossil fuels, with little concern for the future.

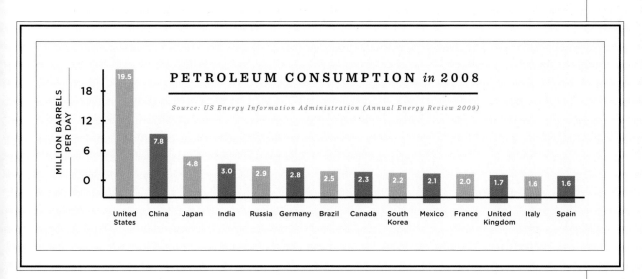

PETROLEUM CONSUMPTION *in* 2008

Source: US Energy Information Administration (Annual Energy Review 2009)

MILLION BARRELS PER DAY

United States	China	Japan	India	Russia	Germany	Brazil	Canada	South Korea	Mexico	France	United Kingdom	Italy	Spain
19.5	7.8	4.8	3.0	2.9	2.8	2.5	2.3	2.2	2.1	2.0	1.7	1.6	1.6

THE US CONTROLS

25%

MORE OCEAN THAN LAND.

IT'S EASY TO SEE HOW WE WERE LULLED INTO THIS way of thinking. When the first big oil strike in American history—the Drake well—burst up through a wooden derrick near Titusville, Pennsylvania, in August of 1859, the black crude that seeped out from the not-quite-seventy foot hole barely produced 20 barrels a day. Compare that with our wells today, the deepest of which are more than thirty thousand feet down (deeper than Mount Everest is tall).

In those early heydays, oil reservoirs from Pennsylvania to Texas to California were so shallow that their contents just about bubbled up through the earth's crust. That scene in the opening credits of the old *Beverly Hillbillies* TV series, where Jed Clampett is out hunting in the Ozarks and strikes oil with a bullet meant for a rabbit—that could actually have happened back in 1901.

But not in 2001. By then, America's shallow, easy-to-reach oil was long gone. Even those thirty-thousand-foot wells were down to a trickle. By then, we were into the era of hunting for oil in some of the most remote, hard-to-reach spots on the planet, where drilling is both extremely expensive and extremely dangerous. The scientists call the era we're now in one of "extreme energy." The wildcatters who actually wield the machinery call it simply "tough oil." And the toughest of that oil lies in the petroleum hunters' last frontier, the final place on the planet where significant gushers might still be found—deep under the seabed.

This may come as a surprise (it certainly surprised me when I first learned it), but the United States controls 25 percent more ocean territory than it does land. This has been true only since the end of World War II. Before then, the territorial boundary of every coastal nation on Earth was recognized as three nautical miles from its shorelines. The reason for that distance was primitively simple—at the time when this general agreement was made, in the 1700s, three miles was the maximum length of an effective cannon shot.

It wasn't until the 1970s, when the UN Convention on the Law of the Seas (UNCLOS) established national marine boundaries at 200 miles from shore, that the offshore drilling industry really began to grow. While the United States has not formally ratified UNCLOS, it does assert jurisdiction over the seafloor out to 200 nautical miles, and it is there that America's oil industry began drilling in earnest as its land-based deposits began running dry.

MOST OF US KNOW LITTLE or NOTHING ABOUT the DEVASTATION THAT OCCURS out there UNDER THE SURFACE.

OIL DRILLING

and

ALL THE THINGS THAT

COULD GO WRONG

Oil is lethal to wildlife. A quarter of a million seabirds were killed after the *Exxon Valdez* disaster. Because the Deepwater Horizon blowout occurred 70 miles from shore, we will never know exactly how many birds, sea turtles, and other wildlife were killed. The effects on seafood will take years to understand. For example, the Gulf of Mexico is one of only two spawning grounds for endangered Atlantic bluefin tuna—and the fish were reproducing just as the nearly 200 million gallons of oil were staining the Gulf's waters. Offshore drilling, and the disasters it can cause, will always have catastrophic results for marine ecosystems.

The Deepwater Horizon blowout was not an isolated event. The exploding rig was especially tragic, but the truth is that the oil industry produces pollution every day. In fact, the little spills associated with oil extraction, transportation, and consumption add up to about 195 million gallons every year. That's as much as one Deepwater Horizon gusher.

- As we saw in the Gulf of Mexico in 2010, extracting oil from the seafloor is dangerous business. BP and Transocean's Deepwater Horizon were drilling for entry to a new oil reserve when it exploded into an enormous fireball. Everyday drilling and extracting—that is, bringing the oil to the surface—result in chronic leaks adding up to 11 million gallons of oil pollution annually.

- Transporting oil is also a major source of pollution. Sometimes ships intentionally discharge what's known as oily ballast water—the thousands of gallons of dirty water used to keep a giant transport ship stable. Otherwise, despite all the best attempts to keep the black gold on board, moving oil around inevitably results in spills to the tune of 44 million gallons a year.

- Lastly, just using oil as fuel pollutes the oceans. Oil is burned by cars, boats, airplanes, power plants, and heating units. The resulting air pollution eventually precipitates—turns into rain—and returns to the waterways and to the oceans. This tiny trickle, repeated worldwide, results in 140 million gallons of oil pollution in the oceans each year.

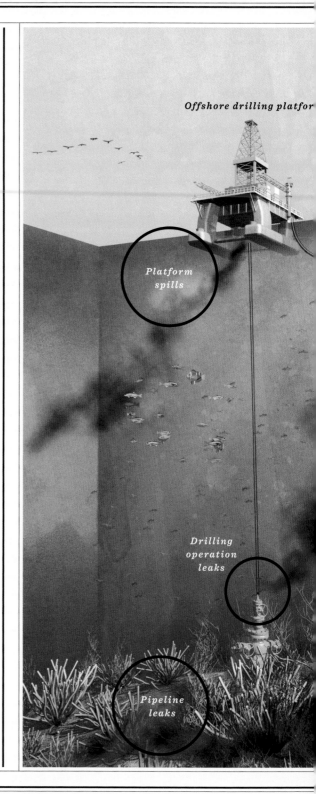

Offshore drilling platform

Platform spills

Drilling operation leaks

Pipeline leaks

It didn't take long, with modern technology, for the relatively shallow waters of our continental shelves in places like Southern California and the Gulf of Mexico to become studded with oil platforms, many easily visible from shore in places like Long Beach, California, and Grand Isle, Louisiana. As those shallow offshore reservoirs began to be depleted and technology developed, the industry pushed its rigs farther out, beyond the shelves, into the dark, icy "deep water" that lies beyond the horizon, where the seafloor sits more than a mile beneath the surface (compared to the three-hundred-or-so-foot depths of the continental shelf waters), and the oil deposits themselves lie as many as six or more miles beneath that.

It's not hard to see how wells drilled at such depths and such distances from shore, along with the more extensive infrastructure needed to support them (the rigs, the pipelines, the transport and supply vessels, and, yes, the manpower), add up to a recipe for "minor" mishaps at the very least and, at the worst, for disasters on the scale of the Deepwater Horizon.

Those "minor" mishaps, which the industry considers normal in the day-to-day operation of deepwater rigs—leaks and "small" spills at well sites; seepage from the surrounding seafloor; leaks and spills that occur in transporting the oil to shore; discharges of toxic ballast water from ships' tanks that had been filled with crude—when coupled with everyday chemical runoff from land sources, add up to 15 million gallons of oil entering North America's oceans each year, just as the result of "business as usual." That's enough to fill 4,500 residential swimming pools.

That's not to mention the contaminated drilling fluid, "produced water" (polluted water occurring naturally in a field), and heavy metals found in the rock cuttings that are generated by the operation of an

"minor

m i s h a p s

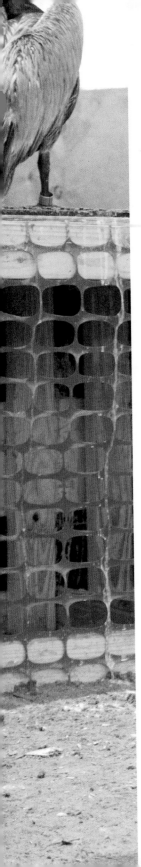

OCEAN HERO

JAY HOLCOMB

Executive Director of the International Bird Rescue Research Center (IBRRC)

JAY HOLCOMB has dedicated almost three decades of his life to rescuing and rehabilitating oiled wildlife, especially seabirds. Beginning as a volunteer responding to California oil spills in the 1970s and '80s, Holcomb has worked with seabirds, land birds, and birds of prey, leading more than two hundred oil spill responses around the world.

During the *Exxon Valdez* oil spill in Alaska in 1989, Holcomb directed the wildlife search and rescue program in Prince William Sound. The effort provided care for more than sixteen hundred birds and included a six-month rehabilitation for the wildlife. In South Africa, in 2000, he managed the largest and most successful oiled bird rehabilitation program ever mounted. Caring for twenty-one thousand oiled African penguins, one-third of the entire world population of that species, Holcomb's program successfully returned more than 90 percent of the penguins to the wild.

After the Deepwater Horizon blowout in 2010, he led the IBRRC rescue efforts to clean up thousands of oiled birds in the area. Working out of a makeshift warehouse in Venice, Louisiana, Holcomb and his team received 8,183 birds, many of them brown pelicans, the state bird of Louisiana. Though many of the birds died in captivity or were dead on arrival, 1,246 birds were brought back to health and released into the wild. His unwavering commitment to rehabilitating oiled wildlife is truly inspiring.

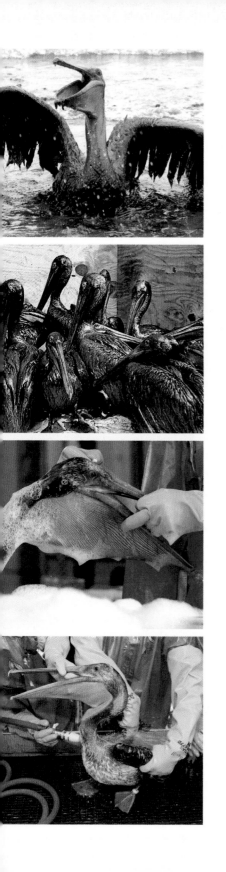

offshore rig, all of which are routinely released into the surrounding sea. Studies in the Gulf of Mexico have shown that over the course of its lifetime, a single rig dumps more than ninety thousand tons of these toxic materials into the surrounding seawater— that's six times the weight of the Brooklyn Bridge.

Consider the fact that there are nearly six hundred active offshore drilling rigs operating in the world today and that adds up to a lot of "routine" contamination. While most of the Gulf of Mexico's oil is shuttled to the shore through underwater pipelines, much of the world's oil must cross the ocean in huge—and sometimes leaky—tankers.

Did you know that oil accounts for more than one-third of the total tonnage of all sea cargo worldwide?

OVER THE COURSE OF ITS LIFETIME

1 RIG

D U M P S

90,000

TONS OF TOXIC MATERIALS

INTO THE SEAWATER

And that the global level of oil consumption is projected to increase by 20 percent (!!) over the next twenty years?

Or that in the Gulf of Mexico alone, besides those active wells, over the course of the past seventy years more than twenty-seven thousand abandoned oil and gas wells have been "sealed" using the same questionable materials and under the same questionable oversight that led to the Deepwater Horizon explosion? They're sitting out there right now like ticking time bombs, any number of them very possibly leaking— or about to spring leaks at any moment.

You'd think facts like these might warrant some headlines.

And maybe they'd get them if we, the public, demanded it. If we all understood the full extent and specifics of the damage oil does when it enters our oceans, I think it would be hard for any of us to sit still and do nothing.

So let's take a look at what exactly oil is, and what exactly it does when it is released into the ocean.

PROJECTED OIL
CONSUMPTION:

UP
20%
OVER
20
YEARS

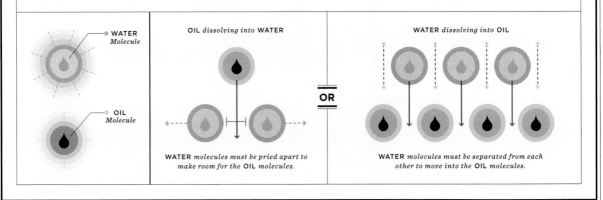
WE ALL KNOW THAT CRUDE OIL, WHEN RELEASED INTO OUR environment, whether on land or in water, is a dangerous thing. But what harm, specifically, does it do? Unless you're a chemist—or an oilman—chances are you can't really say. I certainly couldn't, not until I was taught by some of the marine scientists I've been fortunate enough to work with over the past quarter century.

Essentially, crude oil is a mixture of hydrocarbon compounds created over the course of some 600 million years by enormous pressure and heat acting on the decayed remains of ancient plant and animal life. Many of crude's components, alone and in various combinations, are highly toxic. These components include benzene, kerosene, nitrogen, sulfur, trace metals, light gases, and polycyclic aromatic hydrocarbons, which are carcinogenic. At one hundred parts per million, oil is classified as a hazardous waste. Studies showed that more than twenty years after the *Exxon Valdez* spill, oil at one hundred parts per million could still be measured in some intertidal sediments in the region affected by that spill. If that's not cause for concern, I don't know what is.

Okay, so that's what crude oil *is*. Where it *goes* when there is a spill, and what it does when it gets there, are questions whose answers might surprise you. Again, they surprised me when I first learned about them.

Forget for a moment those images we see when a blowout occurs—the oil-soaked wildlife, the blackened water and beaches, the devastated fishermen and local business owners. We all have a pretty good sense of the damage an oil spill does to these visible victims. On the other hand, most of us know little or nothing about the devastation that occurs out there *under* the surface, within the sea itself.

Maybe that's because we relate more to our fellow mammals and birds—the wildlife that capture the spotlight every time there's a spill—than we do to the scaly, slimy, often repulsive fish and other weird, moon-eyed creatures with tentacles and claws that live at or near the bottom of the sea.

Or maybe it's simply another example of "out of sight, out of mind"—damage we can see captures our attention far more effectively than damage we can't.

Whatever the reasons, rarely does anyone besides marine scientists and commercial fishermen pay much attention to the underwater destruction wrought by oil spills. It wasn't until more than a month after the Deepwater explosion that mainstream media reports finally began to look beyond what was happening on the surface of the Gulf—the spread of the slick; the despoiled wildlife, wetlands, and beaches; the destruction of local

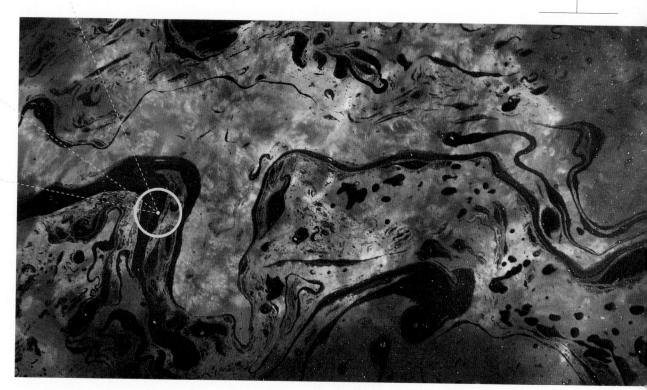

OIL SWIRLING through the once-clean water in SPAIN

economies—and began to examine what was happening out there beneath the waves, in the mile-deep columns of water that are home to tens of thousands of species of sea life ranging from majestic sperm whales to microscopic phytoplankton. One scientist put it plainly to a *Newsweek* magazine reporter: "I'm not too worried about oil on the surface," he said. "It's the things we don't see that worry me the most."

That was in a story published nearly two full months after the spill began. By then reports had arisen of several disturbingly large oil "plumes"—one measuring twenty-two miles in length, six miles wide, and three thousand feet thick—spreading "like Medusa's locks" beneath the Gulf surface, as the *Newsweek* reporter poetically put it.

—— A SUBSURFACE SPILL like the ——
DEEPWATER HORIZON, and the PLUMES
that it GENERATES, can ENDANGER the
—— ENTIRE OCEANIC FOOD WEB. ——

This discovery caused officials to rush back to their calculators and revise their estimates of the size of the spill, since their numbers until then had not taken subsurface plumes into account. While BP's spokespeople stubbornly denied that such plumes even existed—insisting, "Oil floats!"—these undersea clouds of crude oil and methane continued to billow away from the site of the ruptured well.

The extent of the devastation caused by such plumes was powerfully and succinctly described by Philippe Cousteau Jr.—grandson of Jacques and cofounder of EarthEcho International—when he appeared on MSNBC that June to discuss the spill.

"There are a lot of animals that live within the water column," he explained. "It's a very important habitat, and, in fact, the largest migration of all animals that occur on the planet occurs every night in the oceans, when deepwater animals rise to the surface and then descend back, swimming through this toxic soup."

Experts have pointed out that while a *Valdez*-type surface spill has little effect on the creatures that live in the deep, a subsurface spill like the Deepwater Horizon, and the plumes that it generates, endanger the entire oceanic food web, from tiny shrimp larvae and plankton to massive sharks, marlin, and the precious and endangered bluefin tuna—the latter of which we'll look at more closely when we get to the subject of overfishing. This king of the tunas, the Atlantic bluefin, currently breeds only in the Mediterranean Sea and the Gulf of Mexico. We won't know for years how badly bluefin tuna were affected by the Deepwater Horizon spill, but their larvae, recently hatched, were incredibly vulnerable when the oil rig exploded.

OIL GUSHES from BP's ruptured well, summer 2010.

TED and PHILIPPE COUSTEAU JR. testified before Congress against offshore drilling in 2009.

Besides the effects of the depleted oxygen levels within these plumes—oxygen without which the fish and other creatures that make their homes in the water column will suffocate—the "toxic soup" Cousteau refers to is a mixture of oil and methane that can kill the fish and other sea life that come in direct contact with it by clogging their gills.

Making matters even worse with a spill like this are the chemical dispersants often sprayed on the surface—and in this spill released at the wellhead, too—to break up the oil and make it easier for microbes to digest it. This was one of the first things BP did in response to the spill.

These dispersants are toxic themselves, being composed of petroleum distillates and propylene glycol, the chemical that is the main ingredient in automobile anti-freeze and in the deicing solution used on aircraft. How dangerous is propylene glycol? Government health agencies warn factory workers to avoid skin contact with it for fear of its causing brain, liver, and kidney abnormalities.

These dispersants change the chemistry and physics of the oil by breaking it up into countless tiny droplets, which tend to disperse underwater rather than on the surface. Some of the more cynical observers of the Deepwater spill suspect that this is actually what BP intended, in order to get as much of the spill as it could out of sight as quickly as possible.

A final—fatal—possibility about the crude oil and dispersants that spread throughout the deep waters where offshore eruptions like this one occur is that the lives of

FUEL SPILL in Ibiza, Balearic Islands, Spain, in July 2007.

these toxic materials may well be prolonged in the near-freezing waters near the sea-floor. Much as a refrigerator keeps produce and milk from spoiling, we may find that the icy-cold depths of the ocean—or in this case, the Gulf—keep the oil and dispersants from degrading as quickly as they would in the warmer water at or near the surface.

None of these deadly consequences is intended by the companies that hunt for oil beneath the oceans. There's no question that these corporations are sincerely concerned about mishaps, and that they are truly devastated when a disaster as severe as the Deepwater Horizon spill occurs.

But the reasons for the oil corporations' distress when an accident occurs are somewhat different from everyone else's. And those reasons are rooted in the funda-mental reason that these companies continue, in the face of great risk and repeated destruction, to keep up the hunt for "tough oil."

That reason, purely and simply, is profit, which is not a problem in itself, but when it comes at the cost of the kinds of destruction we're seeing—well, that *is* a problem.

Let's take BP as an example.

JUST SEVEN MONTHS BEFORE THE DEEPWATER HORIZON DISASTER, BP proudly issued a press release announcing that it had begun drilling the deepest offshore oil well on the planet, in the Gulf of Mexico above a deposit called the Tiber, more than thirty-five thousand feet below the Gulf floor.

BP trumpeted this news as a triumph of technology. It didn't mention all that could go wrong with a venture like this, nor did it mention all that had gone wrong

with past BP operations. BP isn't the only oil company that qualifies as a "repeat offender." It's just a good example.

In 2005, an explosion at a BP refinery in Texas killed fifteen workers. In the wake of that tragedy, the company vowed to address the safety shortfalls that caused the blast. Four years later, the federal agency that enforces workplace-safety rules, the Occupational Safety and Health Administration, found more than seven hundred violations at that same refinery, many of them related to the same safety problems that had contributed to the 2005 explosion.

In 2006, a year after the Texas "incident," a badly corroded BP pipeline in Alaska's Prudhoe Bay ruptured and spilled more than 250,000 gallons of crude oil into the icy tundra. Again, BP officials were contrite, promising to tighten their safety procedures.

In 2007, the company settled a series of criminal charges by paying $370 million in fines and pledging to improve its "risk management."

Apparently they didn't improve it enough. Two years after that, a BP refinery in Toledo, Ohio, was fined $3 million for "willful" safety violations. Among those violations were many of the same ones said to have contributed to the 2005 Texas blast.

With a record like this, it's not surprising that BP officials ignored one of the company's engineers just six days before the Deepwater Horizon explosion, when he warned that that rig's operational condition was "a nightmare."

The common denominator in all of these accidents is the same motivation that drives any corporation with shareholders looking over its shoulders—the need to deepen the pockets of its investors, which should be questioned when those profits

come at such a high environmental price. In these times of "tough oil," that need has created what many analysts call a culture of risk. Driven by the pressure to meet quarterly earnings targets, the big players in the oil business not only push their rigs and pipelines into uncharted territory rife with danger, but also are tempted to cut corners once they get there.

Representatives Henry Waxman, chairman of the House Committee on Energy and Commerce, and Bart Stupak put it succinctly in a letter to BP following the Deepwater Horizon explosion. "Time after time," they said, "it appears that BP made decisions that increased the risk of a blowout to save the company time or expense."

EarthEcho leader Philippe Cousteau Jr., in discussing the Deepwater Horizon blast, explains the issue in even broader terms—terms that cover the entire oil industry's attitude toward safety versus its eagerness to make a profit.

"Technology to get at the oil has outraced our knowledge and abilities to deal with mishaps like this. And in fact, it invites them by pushing into much riskier situations and settings, without care and preparation for the possibilities of accidents just like this one."

This kind of breakneck approach to deepwater drilling results in what a spokesman for the US Fish and Wildlife Service recently called "one giant experiment." Experiments, as we all know, are supposed to be conducted in controlled environments that limit the risk of danger, damage, and, certainly, death as much as possible. The recent history of the oil industry's oceanic "experiments" gone awry should

TECHNOLOGY TO GET AT OIL has **OUTRACED OUR KNOWLEDGE** and **ABILITIES TO DEAL** with **MISHAPS LIKE THIS.**

be enough to convince us—the American public—to insist that not only should the moratorium on all new deepwater offshore drilling be maintained, but also the entire industry of oil and gas production needs to be reassessed, as well as our own addiction to and reliance upon fossil fuels in our daily lives.

If disasters like the Deepwater Horizon and the others I've mentioned aren't enough to sound the alarm, consider the fact that in recent decades, dozens of other major nautical oil spills have occurred that most of us haven't even heard about because they've taken place in parts of the planet that don't grab many headlines in US newspapers—certainly not front-page headlines.

As bad as the *Exxon Valdez* disaster was, in the past thirty years there have been more than thirty-five spills worldwide that each unleashed far more petroleum into foreign oceans, gulfs, and bays than the 11 million gallons the *Valdez* poured into Prince William Sound.

CLEANING UP the beach in Ibiza, 2007.

GRAND ISLE,
LOUISIANA,
after the
Deepwater
Horizon spill

For example, just two years after the *Valdez* spill, a tanker containing almost 40 million gallons of oil exploded and sank off the coast of Italy, emptying its entire load into the Mediterranean. The same year, another tanker—this one carrying more than 71 million gallons of crude—exploded off the Angolan coast, spilling its contents into the Atlantic. Yet another tanker caught fire off the coast of South Africa in 1983, was abandoned by its crew, and then sank, dispersing more than 69 million gallons of oil into the waters off that nation's Saldanha Bay.

The point here is that accidents like these, in which toxic loads are spilled far from American shores, receive little, if any, attention in the American media. Most of the world's worst spills in the past generation have gone largely unnoticed by the American public. But they are no less damaging to the waters and sea life where

---

ACCIDENTS far from **AMERICAN SHORES RECEIVE LITTLE ATTENTION** —— in the **AMERICAN MEDIA. MOST** of the **WORLD'S WORST** —— **SPILLS** have gone **LARGELY UNNOTICED** by the **AMERICAN PUBLIC.**

---

they take place than "ours" are. And, in fact, there really is no separation between "our" water and "theirs"—not when it comes to the oceans. The seas are oblivious to the territorial lines and national boundaries we draw on our maps. We give different names to different oceans, but in fact they are all one massive body of water encircling the planet.

Taken individually, each of the global oil industry's "mishaps" is a tragedy. Considered cumulatively, and with the knowledge that the repercussions of these spills last for decades, they add up to nothing less than an epidemic, a worldwide web of oceanic disasters that are becoming more numerous and more severe as the planet's consumption of fossil fuels pushes the extractors deeper into the deadly realms of "tough oil" and that oil is transported by aging fleets of tankers and through tens of thousands of miles of vulnerable, untended pipelines that are aging as well.

——————

SO WHAT CAN WE DO ABOUT ALL THIS? PLENTY, BELIEVE ME.

But before we get to that, there's one last aspect of oil and the damage it does that we haven't discussed yet. And, as hard as this might be to believe, it's something even more destructive and insidiously widespread than anything we've talked about so far. It's called ocean acidification, and it gets much less attention, for essentially the same reason cited in the first six words of this chapter: *Out of sight, out of mind.*

OUT of SIGHT,

OUT of MIND

WHAT YOU CAN DO

TAKE ACTION

- **EDUCATE AND ACTIVATE YOUR COMMUNITY TO HELP STOP NEW OFFSHORE DRILLING.** Visit www.oceana.org to sign up to be an activist.

- **SPEAK OUT TO MEMBERS OF CONGRESS, STATE AND LOCAL ELECTED OFFICIALS, AND COMMUNITY LEADERS** about the need to protect our oceans, shorelines, and coastal communities from the dangers of new offshore drilling.

- **TELL PRESIDENT OBAMA TO INVEST IN OFFSHORE WIND, NOT OFFSHORE OIL.**

  Visit: www.change.org/petitions/view/offshore_wind_not_offshore_oil

REDUCE YOUR OWN OIL *and* OTHER FOSSIL FUEL CONSUMPTION

- **DRIVE A HYBRID OR ELECTRIC CAR.** Find out more: www.hybridcars.com

- **TAKE MASS TRANSIT.** Plan your next trip at google.com/transit.

- **MAINTAIN YOUR VEHICLE APPROPRIATELY**—proper inflation of tires, among other things, can improve efficiency tremendously.

- **COMMUTE** by bicycle, inline skates, or skateboard, especially for shorter trips. (This has added benefits for your health!)

- **SHOP FOR AND BUY** petroleum-free cosmetic and personal care products.

- **INVESTIGATE AND SIGN UP FOR CLEANER ENERGY OPTIONS.** Check out these two good URLs to start:

  www.ehow.com/about_4683585_green-energy-options.html
  www1.eere.energy.gov/femp/pdfs/purchase_green_power.pdf

- **CHANGE YOUR CAR'S** motor oil every 50,000 rather than 30,000 miles.

- **AVOID UNNECESSARY IDLING** of your vehicles and, better yet, ask your local shuttle bus drivers and delivery truck drivers to stop idling their vehicles to save fuel costs.

  Visit: http://oee.nrcan.gc.ca/transportation/idling/wastes.cfm?attr=8

CHAPTER TWO

THE QUIET
TSUNAMI

GLOBAL "WEIRDING":

**RAINSTORMS,
DROUGHTS,
HURRICANES,
SNOWSTORMS**

SO WE NOW HAVE A PRETTY CLEAR NOTION

of how much damage is directly inflicted upon the oceans by unleashed oil and other fossil fuels, and the toll it takes when we drill for oil under the ocean floor. But as devastating as that damage is, most marine scientists agree that our oceans are suffering even worse destruction from the *indirect* effects of oil, coal, and gas—the emissions these fossil fuels create when burned.

You'd have to live in a cave not to be aware of the current debate in the country surrounding the issue of climate change. No one can deny that we're living in an age of weather abnormalities. Boiled down to its basics, the argument is over whether these climatic disruptions are caused by emissions from humans burning fossil fuels or by nothing more than a natural temperature surge in Earth's eons-old climate cycle, no more man-made than the Ice Ages.

As environmental activist and former vice president Al Gore and many others have pointed out, the scientific evidence points to humanity's involvement in climate change. But as long as scientific uncertainty remains, which it always will, hard-core deniers will twist the evidence to support their claims that humans have no role in global warming, and even that it doesn't exist.

I actually prefer the term "global *weirding*," used by Tom Friedman, the outstanding *New York Times* columnist. That one word, "weirding," accounts not just for the heat-related phenomena caused by climate change, but also for the dozens of other off-kilter, crazy weather events we've experienced in recent years, ranging from unprecedented rainstorms, to record droughts, to off-the-chart hurricanes, to—notably—the freaky snowstorms that the deniers love to point to as proof that global warming is a hoax. How can Earth be getting warmer, they ask, if it's snowing in June? As scientists have demonstrated, that snow is actually more proof that serious climate disruption is afoot.

In any event, despite the fact that just about every sector of the world's scientific community agrees that the evidence for global warming is unequivocal, surveys show that more Americans than at any time since the late 1970s believe that global warming is either a hoax or nowhere near as serious a threat as the scientists say. This just goes to show the power of propaganda in an age when there are so many outlets for "information"—most notably, of course, the Internet—and so many people are willing to believe what they are told without carefully considering the source (or sources).

In the case of global warming, in the past thirty years opponents of environmental reform have raised a virtual army of lobbyists, foundations, "think tanks," and political operatives overwhelmingly financed by corporations and individuals whose industries and fortunes depend in one way or another on the consumption of fossil fuels. The mere mention of environmental reform or regulation is enough to quicken their pulses.

One of the primary tactics of these antireformers and antiregulators is to manipulate public opinion by spreading misinformation—distorted facts and outright lies—in order to raise doubts about the scientific research that supports the existence and causes of climate change. The brilliant investigative journalist Jane Mayer wrote an extensive article titled "Covert Operations," published in the *New Yorker* in 2010, that delved into the shadowy world of organized global warming deniers and the billionaire industrialists who support them. Mayer wrote that the primary strategy of opponents of environmental reform is to "question the science, a public-relations strategy that the tobacco industry used effectively for years to forestall regulation."

This strategy has been remarkably effective in raising doubts about atmospheric global warming. But with the *oceans*, such tactics are useless, because there is absolutely no question that the oceans are in trouble. When it comes to the effects of carbon dioxide (CO_2) overload in the oceans, the evidence is empirical, drawn from irrefutable test results and analyses. All science; no speculation.

And here's what the science says.

MELTING ICE CAPS, Norway

THE PIONEERS OF
CLIMATE CHANGE SCIENCE

Ever since the ancient Greeks noticed that rainfall seemed to decrease in regions where they had cut down the forests, people have pondered the question of how human activity might affect the Earth's climate. But it wasn't until the nineteenth century that the issue was studied seriously by scientists.

The first of note was a Frenchman named Joseph Fourier—an orphan who rose to prominence both as a mathematician and as a governor of Egypt appointed by Napoleon. In 1824, Fourier published a study of how warmed air trapped in the atmosphere radiates energy back to the Earth's surface. This was the first description of what would come to be called the "greenhouse effect."

In 1896, a Swedish scientist named Svante Arrhenius brought carbon dioxide into the equation by predicting, with the advent of the Industrial Revolution, that the CO_2 gas emitted by the world's new fossil fuel–burning factories would raise the planet's average temperature. Indeed, over the next four decades, a steady rise in temperatures was recorded, particularly in North America, where the United States' industrial might was fueled by its many factories. But most

scientists attributed the temperature change to natural planetary climate cycles, not to human activity.

One man—a British steam engineer and amateur meteorologist named Guy Stewart Callendar—insisted that Arrhenius and Fourier and their colleagues had been on the right track. Gathering data from around the globe, Callendar found that over the previous century, atmospheric CO_2 levels had increased by 10 percent—a substantial amount. His conclusion—which came to be called the "Callendar effect"—published in 1938, was that this CO_2 increase was directly linked to the subsequent worldwide rise in temperature.

Oddly, Callendar was obsessed with the past, not the future. His research was focused on explaining the Ice Age. His conclusion excited him because he believed mankind could use this knowledge to prevent what he called a "return of the deadly glaciers"—another Ice Age.

Today, however, the "Callendar effect," after being dismissed for decades, has come to be regarded as a fundamental principle of global warming research.

SINCE THEIR FORMATION EONS AGO, THE OCEANS HAVE PLAYED a critical role in regulating Earth's temperature by absorbing and "cleaning" a significant amount of the CO_2 from our atmosphere. Before humans built the first internal combustion engine, there was a harmonic balance in the cyclical journey of the CO_2 released into our planet's air by emissions from animals and natural disruptions such as volcanic eruptions. About 50 percent of that carbon dioxide was absorbed by the atmosphere. Roughly 20 percent was taken in by the land. And the remaining 30 percent was soaked up by the oceans. Those percentages remain the same today—but the *amount* has increased exponentially.

The critical term in the paragraph above is "balance." Left to itself, over millions of years, Earth took care of carbon dioxide quite nicely. In fact, a certain amount of CO_2 is important for life on Earth: Plants breathe it and in return provide us with oxygen, and it warms the planet to a habitable temperature. But then, in the eighteenth century, the Industrial Revolution kicked in, and everything began changing.

Once man-made machines powered by coal, oil, and gas began belching smoke, soot, and carbon dioxide from the factories that began filling the cities, from the farmlands where mules and plows were replaced with engine-powered tractors and combines, from the coal-powered railroad engines spewing black billows of virtually pure carbon as they crisscrossed the country, and, ultimately, from the automobiles and trucks churning out carbon emissions from their tailpipes—once all that man-made CO_2 was introduced into the system, all balance was lost.

When we put it all together, the studies show that in the roughly two and a half centuries since the Industrial Revolution began—just a blink of an eye in geologic time—humans have added a total of nearly 1.5 trillion metric tons of CO_2 to the atmosphere. Don't worry about straining to comprehend that number. Just consider the fact that the oceans have absorbed roughly a third of that amount, some 500 billion metric tons. If we want to play the "How much is that?" game, a Volkswagen Beetle weighs about one metric ton. Picture—or try to, anyway—500 billion Beetles dumped

SCIENTISTS measure the damage caused by pollution and excess CO_2.

SEA SURFACE
TEMPERATURES
·RISE·

1%

ANNUALLY

at sea. That's how much carbon dioxide, by weight, mankind has unloaded into the oceans since roughly the time of the American Revolution.

But here's something else to think about. As bad as things have become in terms of climate disruption and weather-related disasters, think how much worse it would be without the oceans soaking up so much of that CO_2 and, in the process, also absorbing 80 percent of the heat that has been added to the climate system. It's no stretch to say that the high seas have sacrificed themselves for us by softening the climatic blows that are hitting us now.

And they have paid a high price.

One of the most visible effects of climate change has been a significant rise in seawater temperatures. The print media have picked up on the more dramatic effects of warmer seas with headlines such as "Ocean 'Deserts' Expanding" and "Oxygen Starvation Robs Waters."

1 🚗 = 1 Metric Ton **× 500** BILLION **= CO₂** *mankind has unloaded into the oceans since roughly the time of the American Revolution*

OCEAN HEROES

DAVID and SUE ROCKEFELLER

David Rockefeller Jr., a longtime sailor and advocate for the oceans, is president of Sailors for the Sea. Sue Rockefeller is on the board of Oceana and is an environmentalist and filmmaker.

DAVID: I was lucky enough to grow up near the ocean and to become a keen sailor when I was ten years old. In those days, we didn't worry about the health of the ocean. We just played upon it or basked beside it on the beach. The ocean was vast, beautiful, and invulnerable to human impact. Or so we thought. But I learned differently when I served as a member of the Pew Oceans Commission. This motivated me to take action, and I founded Sailors for the Sea, modeling it on successful groups like Trout Unlimited and Surfrider. The idea was to engage the recreational users of the ocean in learning about the challenges to ocean health. Come join us! Please visit us at SailorsfortheSea.org.

SUE: My friend Barbara Ettinger had me read the *New Yorker* article "The Darkening Sea," by Elizabeth Kolbert. We couldn't believe that as environmentalists we knew so little about the effects of carbon dioxide on our oceans. We embarked on a journey with Barbara's husband, Sven Huseby, and made a documentary called *A Sea Change*. We learned that if we didn't stop the present escalation of CO_2 in our waters, our oceans could be devoid of fish. Imagine a world without fish! The film has been shown all over the world and has been a great tool to raise awareness about acidification. Making the film motivated me to become even more engaged as an ocean advocate. I want to leave a legacy of healthier oceans.

Those headlines are all true. Sea surface temperatures have been rising in recent years at an annual rate of about 1 percent. That might not sound like much, but it's been enough to wreak havoc by causing disruptions in the natural system of seawater circulation in various regions all over the world.

In deeper waters, out toward the edges of the continental shelves and beyond, abnormally warm surface water forms a cap of sorts, blocking the natural pattern of rising and sinking underwater currents. These cyclical currents are critical for seawater to become oxygenated. When this "capping" occurs, the currents are interrupted and the water takes up too little oxygen, and among the results are "ocean deserts" with the same lifeless conditions as shallower "dead zones." In both cases, fish and other sea life that are able to flee the area do so. Those that cannot escape die.

It's happening all over the planet. Oxygen levels in the seawater off the coast of Southern California, for example, have dropped nearly 20 percent over the past twenty-five years. A recent study by the National Oceanic and Atmospheric Administration found dead zones in roughly 20 percent of the world's oceans, particularly in equatorial regions.

So that explains one aspect of the damage global warming is inflicting upon our high seas.

———————————

ABOUT 4 MILLION PEOPLE LIVE ABOVE THE ARCTIC CIRCLE, from Canada to Russia, Sweden to Greenland, Norway to Alaska. Among them are the artisanal fishermen and hunters of the Far North—the Inuit and other indigenous tribes of the Arctic—whose lives have depended for centuries on the creatures that live in the oceans and on the ice that surrounds them, from whales to Arctic cod to sea lions to polar bears. They don't need laboratories or sophisticated instruments to prove global warming. They simply point to the sea ice that is thinning and receding more each year, taking with it a significant part of the diet of the larger fish and other animals in that region—creatures such as the tiny shrimplike crustaceans called krill, whales' favorite food, which, in the Arctic, breed in the cracks and crevasses of sea ice. Every year these peoples have to roam farther and search harder for the whales, seals, and polar bears they depend upon for everything from the food on their tables to the boots on their feet. Even here—*especially* here—in one of the harshest climate zones on the planet, the same disruption of the oceanic food web is occurring that is happening everywhere else on Earth. But it's occurring at a remarkably faster rate.

Although the same system and cycles that exist in any oceanic environment on Earth operate in these areas, there is one way in which the Arctic ecosystem is unlike any other—it is much more fragile. Nature, both on land and at sea, is more delicate in the polar regions, and it is impacted swiftly and severely by the slightest changes in climate. We would do well, say the experts who study the seas, to watch and listen closely to the people who live in the Arctic, because when it comes to the pace and the rate of global warming, they are like the canary in the coal mine. By listening to them, we will get a preview of what the rest of the planet is headed for in the decades to come.

YET ANOTHER CONSEQUENCE OF WARMER OCEANS IS RISING sea levels. One fundamental reason for this is the basic Science 101 principle of thermal expansion—when water gets warmer, its volume expands. In the case of Earth's oceans, the expansion forces the seawater surface to rise.

Sure enough, the global sea level today is eight inches higher than it was a century ago. Scientists have suggested that by the year 2080, whole island nations, such as the Maldives in the Indian Ocean, will disappear from the map, and hundreds of millions of people now living in low-lying coastal regions all over the planet will be forced to move inland. Eventually—inevitably—at the current rates of ocean warming and sea rise, metropolises such as New York, London, Tokyo, and Bangkok will face the same fate.

Left: ICEBERGS IN GREENLAND; *right:* solid pack ice with surface melt water in the Arctic Ocean.

ATMOSPHERIC CO$_2$ *from* 1958 *to* 2006

Measured at Mauna Loa Observatory

The chart shows the rising concentration of carbon dioxide measured above Hawaii, from the longest record of direct measurements of CO$_2$ in the atmosphere. The study, started by C. David Keeling of the Scripps Institution of Oceanography in 1958, and still running today, now also includes a data set of NOAA measurements, begun in 1974, which confirms the Scripps record.

The black curve represents seasonally corrected data. Data are reported as a dry mole fraction defined as the number of molecules of carbon dioxide divided by the number of molecules of dry air multiplied by one million (ppm).

Source: Dr. Pieter Tans, NOAA/ESRL
(www.esrl.noaa.gov/gmd/ccgg/trends/)

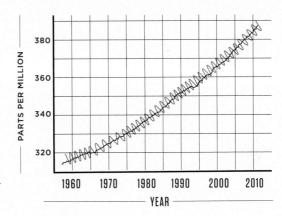

PROJECTED U.S. CO$_2$ EMISSIONS *vs.*
EMISSIONS TRAJECTORY *for* 350 PPM

The current level of atmospheric carbon dioxide is much higher than it has been at any time in the course of human civilization, approximately 385 parts per million and rising. Many scientists and environmental groups are saying that if we can't get under 350 parts per million of CO$_2$, and soon, the damage we're already seeing, including the devastating loss of coral reefs, will continue.

Source: Oceana, based on EIA (2008)
and IPCC (2007)

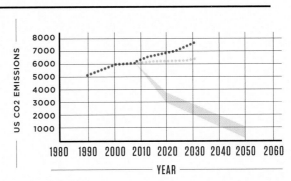

•••••• PAST EMISSIONS
•••••• PROJECTED EMISSIONS HIGH GROWTH
•••••• PROJECTED EMISSIONS LOW GROWTH

US EMISSIONS MUST FALL WITHIN THIS ZONE TO MEET 350 PPM GOAL

ICE CAPS MELTING
IN SUMMER
Svalbard, Arctic Ocean

Along with warmer water temperatures, the other contributor to rising sea levels is melting ice. Again, we only need to look to the polar regions to see what's headed our way to the south. By studying the shrinking, receding glaciers and ice fields of the Arctic and Antarctica, we can get a good idea of what other climatic and ecological changes loom as warming proceeds.

Sure enough, studies show that over the past hundred years, the Arctic has warmed at a rate twice as fast as the global average. This is truly taking its toll. Alaskan winters, for example, are on average five to seven degrees Fahrenheit warmer than they were sixty years ago. At the same time, the great ice sheets that cover much of Greenland and Antarctica have shrunk to less than half the size they were a mere thirty years ago.

SCIENTISTS HAVE SUGGESTED that by the **YEAR 2080, WHOLE ISLAND NATIONS WILL BE OFF** the **MAP.**

This has happened too slowly for anyone to notice with the naked eye. But field scientists have used time-lapse photography to monitor the recession of those glaciers and ice fields. The result is a horror film far more unnerving than those apocalyptic weather flicks Hollywood has been making. Those blockbusters pale in comparison to the scientists' time-lapse images for one basic reason.

The scientists aren't making it up.

ICE BREAKING in the Canadian Arctic

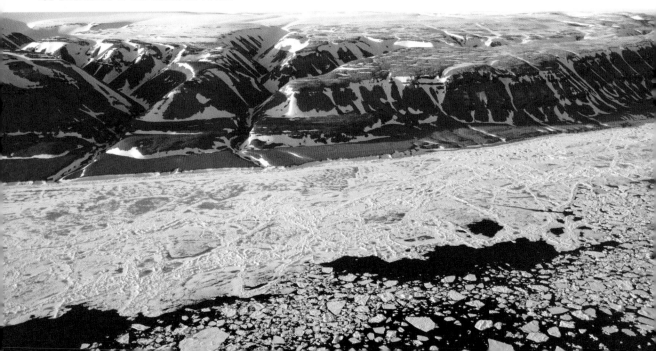

CLIMATE CHANGE *in the* ARCTIC

CALEB PUNGOWIYI

Senior Advisor and Arctic Rural Liaison, Oceana

Caleb Pungowiyi is a Native Alaskan who works with the Oceana organization as its Arctic Rural Liaison and senior advisor. A Yup'ik Eskimo, he "appeared on the Earth during the moon of Aqumuq" (November) in 1941. He was born and raised in the village of Savoonga, on St. Lawrence Island in the Bering Sea.

CALEB: I was born on St. Lawrence Island, in a small camp about sixty miles east of the village of Savoonga. Back in the '50s, we had no electricity in the village, no telephones, no TV; we had no runway so the mail came in from another village about forty miles away. We lived strictly off the sea, except for plants, roots, and berries, hunting walruses, whales, and other food from the sea, because the island has no large land mammals.

The community has been there since time immemorial. Our legends say that the island was made by the creator, Qiaghniq, who reached down into the waters of the northern Bering Sea, squeezed out the water from the mud he grabbed, and placed the island between the two continents, and so our island is called Sivuqaq, which means "the land that the water was wrung from."

You have to have some historical knowledge of things that happened in the past to connect the changes to climate change. You can't go visit and say "Oh, that has changed." You have to have some knowledge and historical connection. Probably the most direct effect of climate change is that erosion is really eating away at some of the communities—Shishmaref and Kivalina are virtually falling into the ocean due to erosion. The other impact is that the timing and the length of spring hunting season for seals and walruses is shorter than it used to be in the past because the ice melts so rapidly in the springtime.

As far as the community, there is not a whole lot you can change with regard to living off the land. If you are dependent on the migration of the animals, the timing of the migration, the number of animals that are available, and then your ability to harvest them and store them for future uses—those are things you can't mitigate. With the price of energy so high, the cost of groceries is four times what it costs in the lower forty-eight; people simply can't live off of buying things from the grocery stores.

I think that we as people of the United States, of North America, of the world, need to understand that things that are harmful to the Arctic—climate change and other things—are going to impact everyone. They are just happening here sooner.

THE RISE AND FALL OF A
CORAL REEF

Coral reefs cover around 1 percent of the world's continental shelves, yet they provide habitat and food to at least a quarter of all species in the oceans, including four thousand species of fish. These beautiful, diverse habitats also provide food, income, and coastal protection for some 500 million people.

Coral reefs and other species in the oceans have lived in levels of acidity that have remained relatively unchanged for at least the last 20 million years. But thanks to human-produced carbon dioxide emissions, the oceans are now 30 percent more acidic than they were prior to the industrial revolution and more acidic than at any point over the past 20 million years. Corals and other species are unlikely to be able to adapt to this rapid, sizable change in acidity and are likely to suffer severe decline.

By the middle of this century, if carbon dioxide emissions continue unabated, coral reefs could erode due to natural processes faster than they can grow their skeletons because of the combined pressures of increasing acidity and global warming. Reefs may become nothing more than eroded rock platforms, greatly changed from the vast three-dimensional structures that so many species rely upon. Corals face severe declines and even extinction, which will in turn threaten the survival of many marine species as well as the seafood and diving spots that people have come to love.

ANATOMY OF A POLYP

(Fig. A)

Coral reefs are built by tiny, soft coral animals, or *polyps*. These polyps are relatives of jellyfish and have evolved to secrete calcium carbonate skeletons that provide the polyp with structure and protection. Colonies of hundreds to thousands of polyps live together as corals and can build huge reef structures over many years. Not only are coral reefs some of the most diverse habitats on Earth, but they are also some of the oldest. Corals grow only millimeters to centimeters per year, and it can take tens to hundreds of thousands of years for large reefs to form.

Fig. A

ANATOMY
OF A POLYP

Tentacle
Mouth
Stomach

Reef crest
Inner reef
Shore
Outer reef
Reef limestone

ANATOMY OF A CORAL REEF

2080 AD
Coral reefs possibly extinct

Present day

2000 AD

1000 AD: *The First Crusades*

0: *Beginning of the Common Era*

1000 BC
Iron Age begins

2000 BC
The Great Pyramids are built

3000 BC
Development of writing

4000 BC
Development of plowing

5000 BC
Early use of copper

6000 BC
Invention of bricks, linen

8000 BC
*Polyps begin to form the
Great Barrier Reef*

OCEAN
ACIDITY
HAS RISEN
↑30%
• since the •
INDUSTRIAL
REVOLUTION

AS DESTRUCTIVE AS THE EFFECTS OF WARMER OCEANS and higher seas are, there is one other form of oceanic disruption caused by CO_2 overload that tops everything else in terms of its extent and impact. It's happening right now, right under our noses, and it's visible in the coral reefs, ocean beds, and bottom-dwelling shellfish all over the planet: They are literally being eaten away by a chemical process called acidification.

The catastrophic effects of this assault on the very foundation of the ocean's food web are immeasurable. But when was the last time you saw a headline about it?

Once again—out of sight, out of mind.

To explain the process without getting too technical, I'll say that the oceans process much of their 30 percent share of the planet's carbon dioxide load by creating something called carbonic acid, which increases the seawater's acidity.

In effect, the oceans clean the carbon dioxide in much the same way that CO_2 scrubbers installed on spacecraft recycle the air that the astronauts breathe: By removing the carbon from each breath the men and women exhale, the scrubbers provide them with a continuous stream of renewed fresh air to inhale.

In a spacecraft, the carbon that is separated from the craft's air by the scrubbers is removed from the system. In the oceans, however, that carbon becomes part of the system in the form of carbonic acid. The result is an increase in the acidity of the seawater—acidification.

Again, for ages before the Industrial Revolution kicked in, there was a beautiful natural balance in this oceanic scrubbing system. But in the more than two hundred years since then, those extra 500 billion metric tons of CO_2 the oceans have absorbed have pushed the undersea filtering system to its limits. The balance has been completely lost as the levels of acidity in the seawater all over the planet have risen substantially. Here are just a few numbers that show how severely things have shifted.

The acidity of the planet's oceans has risen by nearly 30 percent since the advent of the Industrial Revolution.

The current rate of ocean acidification is at least a hundred times faster than the maximum rate over the previous hundreds of thousands of years.

If we continue on our current emissions trajectory, by the end of this century the acidity of the planet's oceans could be more than double what it was prior to the Industrial Revolution.

The next question is "So what?" What exactly does ocean acidification do? Why have marine scientists come up with such ominous epithets for it as the Quiet Tsunami and the Final Warning?

A MASS EXTINCTION EVENT

— J. E. N. VERON —

Top Coral Reef Scientist

J. E. N. (Charlie) Veron spent a career studying coral reefs as the chief scientist at the Australian Institute of Marine Science. A few years ago, when his book, A Reef in Time: The Great Barrier Reef from Beginning to End, was published, he resigned in order to concentrate on the effects of climate change on coral reefs. He now devotes himself to educating the public about the looming crisis of ocean acidification.

Oceana editor Suzannah Evans had the opportunity to speak with Charlie Veron about what he calls "a mass extinction event."

CV: If we continue to emit carbon dioxide at the rate we are going, by 2030 we won't have any reefs that an experienced diver would call a coral reef. It will be mostly rubble, and what corals there are will be in deeper water.

SE: **Is that the worst-case scenario—or is there something even worse?**

CV: The worst-case scenario is when ocean acidification kicks in. There will be no refuges then; there will be nowhere that corals will be able to grow. By 2030, or even 2020, we'll have passed the point of no return, so this is incredibly serious.

SE: **What can be done, and do you feel at all hopeful?**

CV: I am hopeful because humans are very good at moving en masse when they feel motivated and when they really understand that a crisis of this proportion is upon us. We can make it happen. I think it's just a case of mass action on the part of people.

All governments now are pretty much aware of major consequences of climate change. They're not so much aware of acidification because it's quite new in the scientific arena. But they are aware of the main issues. Governments will act as long as they believe the people are behind them.

So I think education of the public has become the most critical thing. Once we do that, then the enormous range of technologies we now have can kick in, and we can fix it.

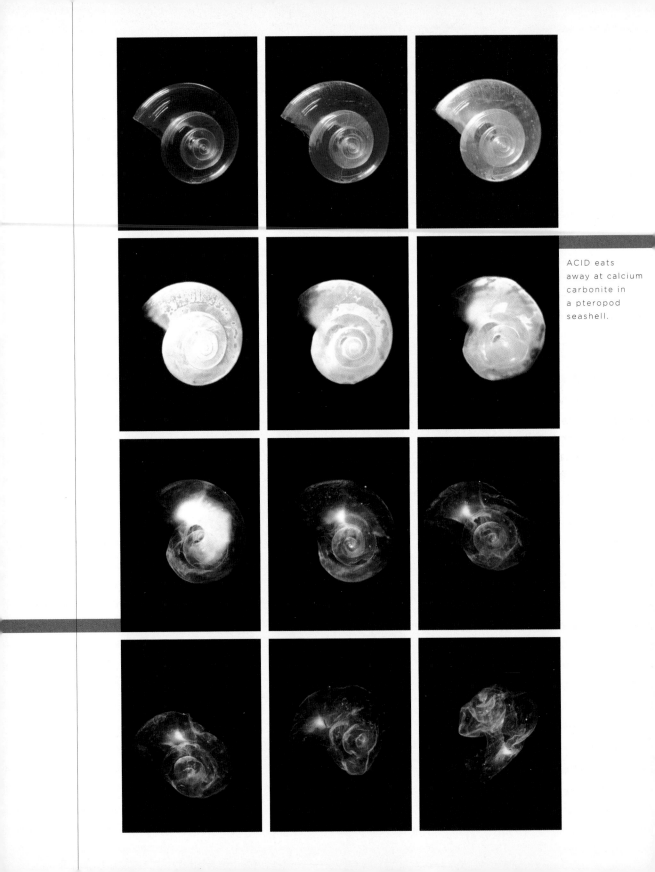

ACID eats away at calcium carbonite in a pteropod seashell.

The problem lies in the carbonic acid that's created by the CO_2 overload. When its presence in seawater reaches a certain point, the oceans' thousands of species of calcifying organisms—creatures that build structures such as shells and skeletons out of calcium carbonate—are unable to build the very structures they rely upon for their survival. The result is an epidemic of oceanic osteoporosis, with the shells and skeletons of organisms ranging from mussels, clams, sea stars, and sea urchins to smaller, near-microscopic organisms such as pteropods (sea snails) and phytoplankton weakening, or even failing to form. We are already seeing the consequences of this disaster in the making. Massive die-offs of oyster hatchlings along the US Pacific coast have been tied to ocean acidification. But it's not just the larger species that we need to be worried about. The damage being done to tiny organisms such as the pteropods will have catastrophic consequences within a matter of mere decades if nothing changes.

> **THE DAMAGE BEING DONE** to **TINY ORGANISMS SUCH** as the **PTEROPODS** —— will have **CATASTROPHIC** —— **CONSEQUENCES** within a **MATTER** of **MERE DECADES** if **NOTHING CHANGES.**

The reason, once again, is the fundamental fact that these tiny creatures form the base of oceanic food webs all over the planet. When these organisms begin disappearing, the fish and other sea life that feed on them suffer, which in turn affects the creatures that feed on *them*, and so on up the predatory chain, all the way up to the top of the line—the swordfish, bluefin tuna, and king mackerel that are already targeted as man's favorite prey.

We can look to the geologic history of the oceans to find out just how devastating ocean acidification can be for the organisms that make up coral reefs and for other marine calcifiers. About 55 million years ago, an ecological crisis called the Paleocene-Eocene thermal maximum (PETM) occurred. A huge release of carbon into the atmosphere caused the oceans to become significantly more acidic, and that resulted in mass extinctions. Many, many calcifying organisms died out during the PETM. If we continue to use fossil fuels, the amount of CO_2 the oceans absorb will likely be on a par with the PETM—and potentially even more catastrophic because the current rise in emissions is happening at a much faster rate, leaving the creatures no time to adapt. It took millions of years for the populations of calcifiers to recover from the acidification of the PETM. We simply can't afford to let these kinds of mass extinctions happen again.

ATMOSPHERIC

OCEAN ACIDIFICATION

The chemical composition of seawater normally buffers against large shifts in pH. However, large and rapid additions of carbon dioxide can cause changes in pH and reduce the availability of carbonate, and even make the seawater corrosive to calcium carbonate structures.

①

Atmospheric carbon dioxide gets absorbed by the ocean.

CO_2

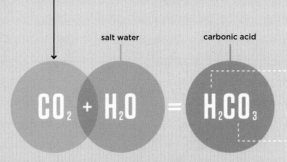

salt water   carbonic acid   hydrogen ion

$$CO_2 + H_2O = H_2CO_3$$

H^+

HCO_3^{1-}

② There it bonds with seawater, forming carbonic acid.

bicarbonate ion

③ The carbonic acid then releases a hydrogen and bicarbonate ion.

→ THE OCEANS CURRENTLY ABSORB 30 MILLION METRIC TONS OF CO_2 DAILY

HEALTHY

HIGH LEVELS OF CARBON DIOXIDE IN SEAWATER LOWERS CARBONATE AVAILABILITY

Water reacts with carbon dioxide absorbed from the atmosphere to form bicarbonate ions and, in the process, depletes carbonate ions. Carbonate and bicarbonate are in equilibrium with one another in the oceans, so an increase in the abundance of one causes a decrease in the abundance of the other. Carbonate is needed by marine animals to make their calcium carbonate shells and skeletons. At typical pH levels, most of the ocean's inorganic carbon is stored in the form of bicarbonate ions but there is still enough carbonate available for the formation of calcium carbonate. When carbon dioxide absorbed by the oceans reacts with water, it forms a bicarbonate ion and a hydrogen ion. This hydrogen ion can then bind with a carbonate molecule that would otherwise be available to make calcium carbonate (see figure). This tips the balance of the system away from carbonate ions, reducing the availability of this important molecule, which is vital to sea life.

Some of the species that will likely be affected by a decrease in the availability of carbonate ions include; corals, starfish, oysters, crabs, shrimp, mussels, lobsters, coccolithophores (a type of phytoplankton), pteropods (sea snails) and foraminifera (plankton related to amoebas).

Source: Ellycia Harrould-Kolieb and Jacqueline Savitz, "Acid Test: Can We Save Our Oceans from CO2?" (June 2009) http://na.oceana.org/en/ news-media/publications/reports/acid-test-can-we-save-our-oceans-from-co2

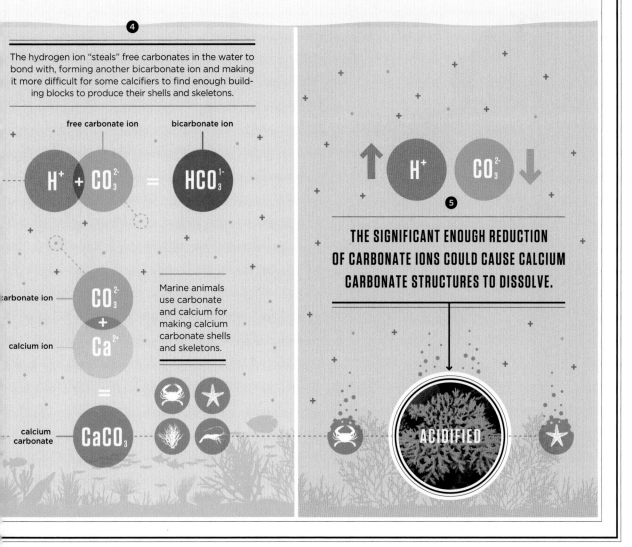

④

The hydrogen ion "steals" free carbonates in the water to bond with, forming another bicarbonate ion and making it more difficult for some calcifiers to find enough building blocks to produce their shells and skeletons.

free carbonate ion   bicarbonate ion

$$H^+ + CO_3^{2-} = HCO_3^{1-}$$

carbonate ion

$$CO_3^{2-} + Ca^{2+} = CaCO_3$$

calcium ion

calcium carbonate

Marine animals use carbonate and calcium for making calcium carbonate shells and skeletons.

⑤

$$\uparrow H^+ \quad CO_3^{2-} \downarrow$$

THE SIGNIFICANT ENOUGH REDUCTION OF CARBONATE IONS COULD CAUSE CALCIUM CARBONATE STRUCTURES TO DISSOLVE.

ACIDIFIED

HEALTHY CORAL and SEA ANEMONE

Acidification is just as destructive to coral reefs as it is to individual calcifying organisms. Besides their magnificent beauty (ocean lovers call them the jewels of the sea), coral reefs are treasured for their critical role as marine habitat. This is why oceanographers also call them the nurseries of the sea. Despite the fact that their total mass constitutes just over 1 percent of the oceans' continental shelves—about half the size of France—more than 25 percent of all marine life depends on coral

CLOSE to 30 PERCENT of the WORLD'S TROPICAL REEFS HAVE VANISHED SINCE 1980.

reefs. The disappearance of these reefs, say scientists, would be akin to wiping out the world's rain forests.

Contrary to their appearance as brittle, lifeless rocks, corals are actually alive, composed of tiny animals called polyps that secrete a hard calcium carbonate exoskeleton that provides the polyps with both protection and support. These

DAMAGED, DEAD, and BLEACHED CORAL

exoskeletons also provide homes to algae, which grow inside them and supply food to the coral polyps.

In the best of times—without the effects of acidification—coral has to struggle continuously against natural bioerosion caused by the various creatures that live among the reefs and are constantly breaking and damaging the corals' skeletons.

In overly acidic conditions, those skeletons are eroded and dissolved in the same way as the shells of shellfish are. Beyond that, the warmer seawater stresses the polyps, which then expel the algae living inside the coral tissue. This is a condition called bleaching, which causes the brilliantly colored coral to turn a sickly pale white and become even more fragile than it already was, because the polyps have lost the nourishment coming from the algae. The polyps are weakened. Many cannot survive the stress and simply die.

The current rate of destruction and death among the world's coral reefs due to a multitude of threats including trawling and bleaching is—there's no better word for it—horrifying. Close to 30 percent of the world's tropical reefs have vanished since 1980, including more than half of the reefs in the Caribbean. At this rate,

25%

— OF ALL —
MARINE LIFE
DEPENDS ON
CORAL REEFS

CORALS

ALL
CORAL
REEFS
COULD BE GONE
BY THE END OF THE
—— CENTURY ——

scientists forecast that Australia's Great Barrier Reef may be dead by the year 2050, and *all* tropical reefs on the planet could be gone by the end of this century.

That leaves the cold-water corals that grow in the oceans' greater depths. Only within the past century were these corals discovered. Some are more than one hundred feet tall, which, when you consider how slowly they grow—roughly one centimeter a year—tells you how ancient some of these coral beds are. Carbon dating has found cold-water corals as old as eight thousand years. That's roughly four times the age of the oldest California redwoods, to which these reefs are often compared in terms of their size and longevity.

Simply their age and their wondrous beauty would make the loss of these deep-water corals a tragedy. But beyond that, cold-water corals are a precious resource. Like their tropical cousins, they provide habitat for thousands of deep-sea species of fish and other organisms. And further, various species of cold-water corals are currently being studied as possible sources of breakthrough medical treatments for human diseases ranging from cancer to arthritis to Alzheimer's.

WE SIMPLY CAN'T AFFORD to LET THESE KINDS of MASS EXTINCTIONS HAPPEN AGAIN.

Like those in the tropical reefs, however, these cold-water corals are projected to disappear by the end of this century. If this happens, the consequences could be catastrophic in terms of the ocean food web whose base is rooted in these reefs. The cascading effects set in motion by the disappearance of the world's coral reefs could, according to some studies, cause the complete collapse of the world's marine ecosystems.

The end of the line.

Yes, the picture is grim, the forecasts are dark. But, as I promised in this book's opening pages, there is still time to turn the tide on each and every threat our oceans face.

WHAT YOU CAN DO

TAKE ACTION

- **TAKE ACTION TO HELP WITH OCEAN ACIDIFICATION.**
Visit at: www.aseachange.net/take_action.htm

- **IF YOU'RE A TEACHER OR STUDENT, DOWNLOAD AN OCEAN ACIDIFICATION LAB KIT:**
www.nrdc.org/oceans/acidification/files/labkit.pdf

- **ASK YOUR ELECTED OFFICIALS TO TAKE ACTION TO REDUCE CO_2.** Visit: www.stopglobalwarming.org/

- **SET UP A SCREENING IN YOUR NEIGHBORHOOD** for a viewing of *A Sea Change,* a documentary about ocean acidification. Visit: www.aseachange.net/upcoming_screenings.htm

- **JOIN A GROUP COMMITTED TO REDUCING CO_2** such as 350.org, 1sky.org, and repoweramerica.org.

REDUCE YOUR OWN CO_2 FOOTPRINT

- **TO FIND OUT WHAT YOUR CARBON FOOTPRINT IS,** go to www.carbonfootprint.com.

- **TO FIND OUT HOW TO REDUCE YOUR CARBON FOOTPRINT** (by doing things as simple as changing your lightbulbs and filling the air in the tires for your car), go to: http://repoweramerica.org/take-action/minimize-your-impact-save-money/

- **REDUCE YOUR USE** of oil, coal, and other fossil fuels, support and elect to use clean, renewable energy. Visit: www.dom.com/dominion-virginia-power/customer-service/energy-conservation/green-power.jsp

- **RESOURCES FOR HOMEOWNERS** interested in renewable energies? Go to: www.nrel.gov/learning/homeowners.html

- **REPLACE YOUR OLD (MORE THAN 15-YEAR-OLD) HOUSE-HOLD APPLIANCES** (especially refrigerators and washing machines) with EnergyStar-rated appliances.

- **INVEST IN RENEWABLE-ENERGY COMPANY STOCKS.**

- **VOTE WITH YOUR DOLLARS!** Support companies that are working aggressively to reduce their carbon footprint and send them an e-mail or letter communicating why you buy from them.

- **RECRUIT YOUR LOCAL SEAFOOD RESTAURATEUR OR MARKET** owner to write to his/her member of Congress about ocean acidification concerns.

- **SHOP LOCAL FARMERS' MARKETS** for produce, cheese, meats, and other consumable goods. This will create a robust market for food that travels fewer miles and conserve fossil fuels, reduce packaging, and improve your health.

- **REDUCE THE NUMBER** of leisure air-travel trips you take each year. Try a stay-cation or local hiking trip with family or friends.

- **SUPPORT AND RIDE AMTRAK AND LOCAL LIGHT-RAIL MASS TRANSIT SYSTEMS.**

- **MEASURE YOUR HOUSEHOLD'S OR ORGANIZATION'S** carbon footprint and act to offset it. The best resource: www.carbonconcierge.com/

CHAPTER THREE

JELLYFISH
SOUP

BACK WHEN I WAS WORKING WITH THE

American Oceans Campaign, we staged a banquet honoring Sylvia Earle, PhD, for her life's work on behalf of the planet's oceans.

For those of you who don't know, Sylvia Earle is to oceanography what Amelia Earhart was to aviation. She has spent more than seven thousand hours underwater and led more than four hundred diving expeditions worldwide, including a historic two-week stay in a laboratory at the bottom of the Caribbean Sea in 1970 that earned her and her four-woman crew a ticker-tape parade and a presidential reception at the White House.

In 1990, Dr. Earle became the first woman appointed chief scientist of the National Oceanic and Atmospheric Administration. When the Library of Congress announced a list of "Living Legends" in the spring of 2000, Sylvia Earle was included, along with the likes of novelist William Styron, boxer Muhammad Ali, choreographer and dancer Merce Cunningham, and journalist and activist Gloria Steinem. Dr. Earle is currently an explorer-in-residence with the National Geographic Society.

WE *NEED* FISH.

Friends kid her about her prestige by addressing her as "Your Deepness" or "the Sturgeon General." She's got a great sense of humor, but I pushed it a little too far that night at the banquet.

I emceed so many dinners back in those days that I had the routine pretty much down pat. If I could come up with one irreverent ocean joke to kick off the evening, the rest of the night would be fine. On this particular occasion, I can't remember exactly what the entrée was (chicken's always a good bet), but I know it wasn't seafood. So that's what I zeroed in on as I began my remarks.

"You'll notice we're not having fish tonight," I said. "But I can assure you that next year we'll be serving seafood, because I believe our motto should be 'Why save 'em if you can't *eat* 'em!'"

I can't recall how the rest of the room reacted, because all I could see was Sylvia Earle's face, and she did not look amused. I got the message loud and clear. No fish jokes—at least not when Dr. Earle is in the room.

The point of this little story is to speak to the misconception that many people have about ocean conservation groups—that we're a bunch of bleeding-heart "fish huggers," holier-than-thou oceangoing activists out to protect the precious life of every creature that swims in the seas, from the largest blue whale down to the tiniest minnow.

BLUEFIN TUNA in the Mediterranean Sea

Sure, everyone who works on behalf of ocean conservation appreciates, to one degree or another, the beauty and sanctity of the oceans and the wondrous, enormously complex ecosystems that they support. No doubt there are a few who, for any number of reasons, wouldn't dream of eating any sea life. But most of us—and I'm a typical example—enjoy seafood as much as the next person. That was part of the point of my joke.

I guess it didn't help our reputation that one of the early catchphrases of the movement was "friends of fish," which gave the impression that our mission was to defend the life of every finned animal on the planet. A more appropriate, more accurate motto would have been "friends of *fishermen*." Because, although ocean conservation groups certainly care about the creatures that inhabit the sea, there's a much more fundamental and practical reason that we've committed ourselves to this struggle:

We *need* fish.

"We" being the billions of people around the world, most of them poor, whose lives or livelihoods depend directly upon the bounty of the seas. Unlike these multitudes, I could survive without seafood. You probably could, as well. But these billions of men, women, and children cannot.

And their struggle to survive is becoming more difficult every year. Global seafood consumption has doubled in the past two generations. Over the past twenty-three years, the annual worldwide catch of seafood has steadily declined, year after year.

Considering those facts alone, it's easy to see that we're not simply headed toward a crisis of global proportions, we're already *in* one.

Consider this warning, issued three years ago by a group of 125 scientists from twenty-seven nations, assessing the state of Earth's oceans and fisheries:

> There is no longer any question—we have reached a critical state. The world's ocean ecosystems are at a tipping point, and overfishing represents one of the greatest threats to their productivity. . . . There are only decades left before the damage we have inflicted on the oceans becomes permanent. We are at a crossroads. One road leads to a world with tremendously diminished marine life. The other leads to one with oceans again teeming with abundance, where the world can rely on the oceans for protein, and enjoy its wildlife. The choices we make today will determine our path for the future.

WE'RE NOT SIMPLY HEADED TOWARD A CRISIS OF GLOBAL PROPORTIONS, WE'RE ALREADY IN ONE.

Which brings us back to that phrase I mentioned earlier: "friends of *fishermen*."

We need to define our terms here—or, more specifically, one term. When we talk about "fishermen," we're talking for the most part about the small-scale, *artisanal* captain and crew of a boat or a small fleet of boats. We're talking about the men—and in recent years women as well—who fish responsibly and have the same relationship with the oceans as their fathers and grandfathers did. Who take pride in doing one of the toughest, most dangerous jobs in the world. Who care for, love, and protect the oceans they fish in. Who want nothing more than for their sons and daughters and *their* children to carry on the tradition, to make their livings just as their families always have on the same seas filled with tuna and mackerel and cod.

While there are small-scale fishermen who overfish, many artisanal fishermen carefully make sure that the size of their catch will leave enough fish in the sea to reproduce at a rate that maintains or even increases their populations. That is essentially the definition of sustainable fishing.

Whether the artisanal fisherman knows it or not, he or she and ocean conservation groups, far from being enemies, are actually on the same side. Though many fishermen and their advocates don't see conservation groups as natural allies, we share many of the same concerns and the same basic goals, and we face common adversaries. The artisanal fisherman's profession and way of life are being washed away by the massive fleets of *industrial* fisheries and their unsustainable fishing practices: Factory trawlers the size of supertankers pillage the oceans, bulldozing the seafloor and indiscriminately hauling in vast net loads of fish as fast as they can with little concern for tomorrow, thinking only of the hunger for profit that drives them today. Even many of the smaller industrial ships—the trawlers and driftnetters with only a couple of people on board that produce huge hauls—do tremendous damage to the oceans. Their practices are the very antithesis of sustainable fishing.

OVERFISHING REPRESENTS ONE OF THE GREATEST THREATS to their PRODUCTIVITY. ... There are ONLY DECADES LEFT BEFORE the DAMAGE WE HAVE INFLICTED on the OCEANS BECOMES PERMANENT. WE ARE AT A CROSSROADS.

It's an ironic tragedy that the artisanal fisherman is now a species just as endangered as the fish that are vanishing. Ironic as well is the fact that those ravaging juggernauts—the large industrial fisheries—by causing the collapse of the species of fish that they plunder, are causing their own collapse as well.

OVERFISHING

A CONVERSATION WITH CHARLES CLOVER

When I was asked to narrate a documentary film version of British journalist Charles Clover's book about overfishing, The End of the Line, *I leaped at the opportunity. We finally got the opportunity to speak last year.*

TD: Do you remember what first piqued your interest in the topic of overfishing?

CC: Yes, I do. I walked into the wrong press conference in the Hague in 1990. I meant to attend a conference on ocean pollution, but wound up walking into the wrong room. The presentation was in Dutch, which didn't help, but I remember they showed slides of trawling, and it was sufficiently comprehensible for me to realize this was really interesting. This was the first time that I'd ever seen what a beam trawler does to the bed of the ocean. I wound up getting a splendid scoop out of it, so I thought I'd stay ahead on this issue from then on.

TD: What would you say are the one or two most effective ways that we can change how we are fishing our oceans?

CC: I think you have to attack it from both ends. First, I think it's incredibly important that we set aside areas of the ocean large enough for biologically representative populations of fish and other marine organisms to survive healthfully and turn those areas into "no-take" zones. No fishing allowed. I think you need a minimum of 20 percent of the oceans to do that.

Secondly, I'm one of those people who thinks the consumer has a huge amount of power. A lot of people pooh-pooh the idea, but it's worked tremendously with farming, for example. People became worried about the countryside, about pesticides, and the industry responded. It's all about telling your suppliers what you want and what you won't stand for. I don't see why it won't work with sustainable fishing. If you insist on sustainable fish, they'll go and produce some.

WHAT IS
TRAWLING?

Bottom trawls, enormous fishing nets that are dragged across the sea floor, clear-cut everything living in their path. The mouths of the largest nets are big enough to swallow a Boeing 747 Jumbo Jet, and trawls and dredges can destroy century-old reefs in mere moments. While beam trawling in shallow waters has been used by fisherman for centuries, they had stayed away from rocky, complex habitats where structures such as corals, boulders, or pinnacles might snag the trawl net. But in the mid 1980s, new high-tech materials changed bottom trawling dramatically. Large, heavy roller and rockhopper gear, in combination with more powerful fishing boat engines, sonar, fish-finders, and other technical innovations, now allow bottom trawls to access virtually all areas of the continental shelves and deeper continental slopes, ravaging the living habitats they crush.

HOW EXTENSIVE IS THE DAMAGE?
(Fig. A)

- The largest deep-sea bottom trawling ships—"supertrawlers" —are 450 feet or longer (the length of 1½ football fields).

- A large trawler can drag over a ½-acre swath of seabed with one pass.

- High-seas bottom trawlers can destroy 580 million square miles of seabed each day.

- Each year, the world's fleet of bottom trawlers disturbs a seabed area twice the size of the contiguous United States.

- Deep-sea trawling destroys seabed habitat at a faster rate than the aggregate loss of the world's tropical rain forests.

- European scientists have calculated that bottom-dragging trawlers in the North Sea destroy 16 pounds of marine animals for every pound of marketable sole that is caught.

TRAWLER DOORS
(Fig. B)

Heavy doors keep the mouth of the net open and on the sea-floor. Rubber and steel rockhoppers roll across the seafloor, while floats lift open the net above them.

Fig. A

Trawler

Trawler marks

Corals

Codend

Trawler

½ acre

Door

Floats

Rollers

Door

Belly

Fig. B

HOOK AND LINE

CAPTAIN CARLTON "JACK" YOUNG SR.

Mr. Jack, as he is fondly known, has been fishing in Belize for more than 40 years and is a widely recognized leader in Belize's fishing and conservation communities. He has been the chairman of the Placencia Fishermen Co-Operative and a member of the Fisheries Advisory Board, the Friends of Nature, and the Glover's Reef Advisory Committee; and he has advised the Minister of Fisheries on fisheries policy. Most important, Mr. Jack has played a key role in bringing about measures that protect Belize's precious Nassau grouper and parrotfish, the reef, and the rights of Belize's fishermen.

JACK: Well, my family are fishermen. I've been fishing since I was a kid. Over 40 years. I fished with my grandfather and my relatives during the summer holidays until I came of age and started to fish commercially. In those days, we just used hook and line so we mostly fished for yellowtail and snappers. I'm still using the hook and line.

There were a lot more fish back then, compared to now. Even in the '90s, we had a lot of fish. Today, the fish are depleted for some reason. Some people feel like it's overfishing and maybe it is. I'm very skeptical about overfishing. I know it plays a big part but there are a couple of other factors: change of temperature, change of climate. I wouldn't blame everything on overfishing. It is also habitat; in some areas, the corals are gone. The snappers like the coral and so they don't come back to spawn. And the hurricane we had a while back really damaged the habitat. Sometimes it seems like the fish are there but they don't want to bite the line.

Here in Placencia, we have an alternative to fishing because of tourism. The majority of the fishermen are tour guides, and they can make some kind of money doing that. They still fish when they can.

We have good ocean in Belize but nobody is taking care of it. The government needs to give the fisheries department more money to protect the reserves. If we don't do that, we may be in serious trouble five years from now.

CONSIDER THESE FACTS:

- Small scale fisheries employ 25 times more people than larger, industrial fisheries (about 12 million compared to ½ million), and use only one-quarter the fuel. Artisanal fisherman discard less sea life, too.

- Ten species of fish account for more than one-quarter of all commercial fishery production.

- Nine of those ten species are on the verge of collapse (meaning that catches have dropped below 10 percent of the highest catch on record).

- Since 1988, the commercial fishing industry's overall catch has declined by more than ½ million tons per year, even though its equipment has become better, faster, and more efficient at finding and catching fish.

- Catches in nearly one-third of the world's fisheries have collapsed to less than 10 percent of their peak levels.

- If we don't change our fishing habits, seafood populations could be wiped out by the second half of this century.

As for the rest of us, if this carnage continues, says the world's leading expert on the topic of overfishing, Daniel Pauly, of the University of British Columbia, we'll eventually see the seafood selections on restaurants' menus dominated by one durable species.

"We are heading to a world," says Pauly, "where there will be lots of jellyfish soup."

10 SPECIES
OF FISH ACCOUNT FOR
MORE THAN

25%

OF ALL COMMERICIAL
FISHERY PRODUCTION

JELLYFISH BLOOMS

Jellyfish are 95 percent water, but these prehistoric creatures may be the hardiest living beings in the oceans. They are among the small number of species that benefit from overfishing and climate change, and we're already seeing the effects.

Anecdotal stories of jellyfish blooms suddenly overwhelming a seaside beach or gumming up fishermen's nets have been growing in recent years, and scientists have confirmed these tales aren't exaggerations. In fact, in 2006, the African country of Namibia became the first place in the world where scientists proved that a species of five-inch-wide jellies had successfully displaced the country's fish species. The country's once-diverse marine life had been overwhelmed by jellies, which outnumbered seafood species such as sardine and anchovy by a shocking four to one.

Why do jellyfish thrive in the modern era? It's simple: Overfishing takes away their competition. An area of the Bering Sea—known as America's "fish basket" as it provides more than half of the country's domestic seafood—has become so clogged with jellies that fishermen now call it "Slime Bank." And in an unfortunate twist, jellies feast on fish larvae, making it even more difficult for fish to recover from intense fishing pressure.

Thanks to climate change, warming waters also allow jellies to expand their range into areas previously off-limits. That's why you are more likely than ever to encounter a collection or "smack" of jellies on your snorkeling vacation—some, but not all, of which can sting painfully or even fatally.

There is one easy way to combat jellyfish overpopulation: Eating them. Jellies are a delicacy in Asia; imagine if we turned our massive, industrial fishing power to scooping up rather than avoiding jellies. Anyone in the mood for stew?

I don't think I exaggerate when I say Daniel Pauly is the world's foremost expert on fish and fisheries. This book would not be possible without his research, which, simply put, has defined the way we talk about fish—or at least the way we *should* talk about them.

I've gotten to know Pauly over the years as a fellow board member at Oceana. A speaker of many languages, he has lived and worked all over the world, everywhere from Germany and Indonesia to the United States and West Africa. In other words, Pauly is a true citizen of the world. What better person to study the world's most international creatures?

For many years, he was the director of the University of British Columbia's Fisheries Centre, where he is still a professor. His work has truly been transformative. Probably best known for uncovering China's misreporting of its fish catch in the early 2000s, Pauly's revelatory analysis led to the discovery that the global fish catch had actually been dropping since the late 1980s, at a time when everyone still thought we were catching more and more fish every year. For ocean conservationists—and yes, even the fishing companies that refused to accept the findings publicly—this changed everything. No one could continue to argue that the oceans' bounty was inexhaustible.

Already the author of more than five hundred scientific papers, he and his team are still churning out critical data on fish populations. He's also intent on making the real-world changes that we need to protect marine ecosystems and the world's seafood supply. With a combination of intelligence, leadership, and vision, he's a formidable match for those who would decimate our oceans with their shortsighted approaches to fisheries management.

MOON JELLYFISH, Indonesia

EXPERTS SAY WE'RE within a CENTURY—POSSIBLY EVEN LESS— OF INHABITING A WORLD WHERE THE ONLY VIABLE SEAFOOD LEFT in the OCEANS will be JELLYFISH.

AS DESTRUCTIVE AS THE SEARCH FOR AND USE OF FOSSIL fuels is to the oceans, public enemy number one when it comes to the destruction of life in the high seas is, far and away, overfishing. In scale and seriousness, it can be compared to the razing of the rain forests in South America and the mass extermination of the buffalo in the American West. The oceans are, in fact, our planet's last frontier, and it's no exaggeration to say that we are fishing them to death.

I'm not being overly dramatic here. Every statistic churned out by the men and women who study the seas tells us the cycle of life that has kept Earth's seas filled with life for hundreds of millions of years is at a tipping point. In much the same way that scenarios of destruction by a nuclear war tell us that virtually the only survivors would be single-celled organisms, experts in marine science say we're within a century—possibly even less—of inhabiting a world where the only viable seafood left in the oceans will indeed be jellyfish.

That's if nothing changes in the ways that we catch and consume the bounty of the seas. We still have time to turn things around, but before we can take effective action, we need to understand how we reached such a state of distress. Overfishing is a global problem, one that requires, as we'll shortly see, global solutions. But the first step every nation needs to take before widening its lens to a worldwide view is to examine its own issues.

Looking at the depleted waters that run the length of America's eastern seaboard today, it's hard to believe how abundant the life in those waters was when the first

Cod fishing on the Grand Banks, Newfoundland

European settlers arrived at the turn of the seventeenth century. Journals, diaries, and logbooks from that time describe a fish-filled Garden of Eden in the rivers, bays, and coastal ocean shallows.

Here's an excerpt from the book *The Unnatural History of the Sea*, by Callum Roberts, PhD. It shares what a scouting party led by John Smith encountered in 1608 when they sailed from their compound in Jamestown to explore the tributaries near the mouth of the nearby Chesapeake Bay.

> We spied many fishes lurking amongst the weeds on the sands, our captaine sporting himself to catch them by nailing them to the ground with his sword, set us all a fishing in that manner, by this devise, we tooke more in an houre then we all could eat.

Another Jamestown colonist described the shores of the bay flush with oysters and "many great crabbs rather better in tast then ours, one able to suffice 4 men."

Among the more exotic of these settlers' first exports back to England was pickled sturgeon, many as tall as a man when they were pulled from the water. The way one colonist described it, sturgeon were so plentiful in the Chesapeake Bay watershed that fishing for them was more like gathering vegetables from a garden.

Meanwhile, farther north, in New England's coastal colonies, marine life was just as abundant.

Striped bass, for instance. "Of these fishes," one New Englander wrote, "some be three and some four foot long, some bigger, some lesser. At some tides a man may catch a dozen or twenty of these in three hours."

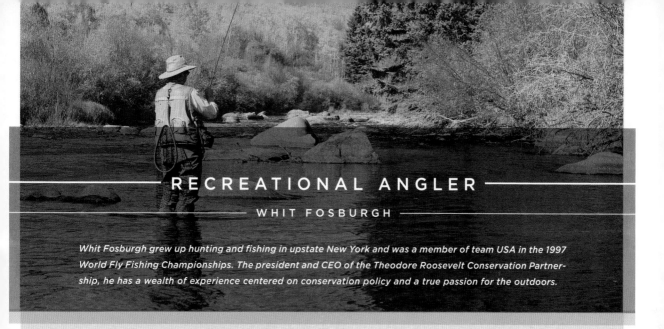

RECREATIONAL ANGLER

WHIT FOSBURGH

Whit Fosburgh grew up hunting and fishing in upstate New York and was a member of team USA in the 1997 World Fly Fishing Championships. The president and CEO of the Theodore Roosevelt Conservation Partnership, he has a wealth of experience centered on conservation policy and a true passion for the outdoors.

It all started with a six-inch brook trout. Every summer, my brother and I would explore every pocket and pool in the trout stream that ran though our property in upstate New York, looking for the elusive "keeper" that we could bring home to eat.

From these fish we learned about the fish's habits and requirements and how watersheds work. We also learned about conservation, as those keepers got harder and harder to find. We expanded to largemouth bass in lakes, and then to rivers, including the Upper Delaware system, where we first encountered fish from the ocean, American shad and other species running hundreds of miles up the East's last major undammed river to spawn. When we finally fished in the Long Island Sound for striped bass from the ocean—it was an epiphany.

For millions of Americans, the mystery and anticipation associated with fishing in the ocean provides a very real and tangible connection with the natural world around us. Hunters and anglers were the original conservationists, fighting for public lands, environmental laws, and game regulations to protect and restore the species they loved to pursue. They even voted to tax themselves, with excise taxes on outdoor equipment used to fund conservation. Today, saltwater recreational angli-ng is a multibillion-dollar business, employing almost 400,000 people.

Recreational anglers (and all Americans) lose when stocks are decimated by overfishing, when ocean habitats are destroyed by bottom trawls, or when agricultural runoff poisons our estuaries. When the regulators fail to manage commercial fisheries properly, recreational anglers pay the price, either through fewer fish in the sea or through outright closures of vast areas.

Recreational anglers and environmentalists need to work together to restore and protect our fisheries. Anglers have a fundamental responsibility to support science-based conservation measures aimed at rebuilding fisheries—but we must also make sure to encourage people to use and enjoy our oceans. If we lose the connection between people and the oceans that angling provides, we lose a very strong voice for conservation.

Worlds record. Tuna weighing 680lbs.

Opposite, top: A 400-pound sturgeon being carried into a fishmonger's shop in London, 1947; *middle left:* a right whale, nineteenth century; *bottom left:* white shark, hammerhead shark, and swordfish, engraving by Gotthilf Heinrich von Schubert, nineteenth century; *bottom right:* a 750-pound sturgeon at New York's Fulton Fish Market, 1928. *Above:* A 680-pound tuna caught off Cape Breton, Canada, 1920.

Then there were salmon. On the eve of the Revolutionary War, an English merchant wrote in his diary of the rivers of Newfoundland and Labrador, "It was so full of salmon, that a ball could not have been fired into the water without striking some of them."

Atlantic salmon in those days averaged about twenty-five pounds each. Many were twice that size, measuring as much as five feet from head to tail. New England's coastal rivers were so choked with salmon that a popular local legend—later proven untrue—asserted that servants on some of the area's estates got sick of it and refused to work if they were fed it more than twice a week.

The servants, so the legends went, felt the same way about lobster. Far from being the delicacy this seafood is today, lobsters were indeed so plentiful along the New England coastline in the seventeenth and eighteenth centuries that their meat was said to be fit only for convicts and slaves. Their primary use was as fertilizer for farmers' fields.

WE STILL HAVE TIME to TURN THINGS AROUND. OVERFISHING is a GLOBAL PROBLEM that REQUIRES GLOBAL SOLUTIONS.

Hard to believe. Just as hard to believe is that the coastal waters in seventeenth-century New England were so thick with whales that the colonists didn't have to leave shore to target them. Masses of surging, blowing whales pushed so close to the rocky coastline that the townsmen set up on-shore whaling stations, and as soon as a whale was spotted, they'd hurriedly launch their boats, kill the whale in no time, and haul it ashore. "Shore whaling," as they called it, was the norm throughout the latter half of the 1600s, but by the end of that century, the coastal whale populations had been fished out and the colonists finally had to start taking to the sea to pursue them.

But the king of the waters, as far as New England fishermen of the 1600s all the way up to the early 1990s were concerned, was the cod. And it's cod, as Mark Kurlansky details in his wonderful book *Cod*, that are a textbook case of how a species is overfished to the point of collapse.

Kurlansky describes how, more than a century before those first permanent settlers landed in Jamestown and up in New England at Plymouth, the explorer John Cabot sailed through the waters of what he called the

Unloading salmon in Canada, circa 1896

Fishing for sturgeon in the Volga River, Russia

"New Isle" and sent back to his English sponsors reports of coastal waters so thick with cod that they could simply be scooped up with baskets.

Nearly four centuries after that, in 1873, the French author Alexandre Dumas, whose *The Three Musketeers* had been published almost thirty years earlier, visited New England during an American tour and wrote that the fish there were so abundant that it was calculated that if their eggs were allowed to reach maturity, within three years, "you could walk across the Atlantic dryshod on the backs of cod."

The prevailing wisdom at that time was articulated by the biologist Thomas Huxley, best known for bravely defending Charles Darwin when Darwin first went public with his controversial theory of evolution. Speaking at an international fisheries convention in London in 1883, Huxley delivered his now-famous remarks on the question of whether overfishing the oceans might ever become a problem: "Probably all the great sea fisheries are inexhaustible; that is to say, that nothing we do seriously affects the number of the fish."

Inexhaustible. That's how almost everyone at that time viewed the oceans' supply of fish. That's the way many people still view it today. It's hard to imagine bodies

A TALE OF TWO FISHERIES

There is no better illustration of how not to manage a resource than the collapse of the Northwest Atlantic cod fishery. And there is no better example of how to do it right than Alaska's management of its salmon.

Salmon's importance to the Alaskan economy predates the very concept of an "economy." For centuries before the first white men arrived on their shores, many of Alaska's native tribes relied on salmon as a mainstay of their diet, as well as primary feed for the dogs that pulled their sleds through the winter. That tradition continues today, thanks to the Alaskan government's inclusion of natives among the membership of its natural resource management boards, along with the state's reliance on science-based decisions.

Alaska is the only state whose constitution includes an article devoted to the management of natural resources, recognizing the importance of both private and commercial fishing and hunting to the state's economy and to its culture. Salmon runs are closely monitored by biologists, whose data dictates yearly adjustments in catch limits. As a result, Alaska's salmon catches have, in many cases, climbed, and most populations have remained stable or even increased—results that have earned the state's fisheries management a reputation as being among the best in the nation.

The flip side is seen in the Northwest Atlantic, where political priorities pushed science aside as Canada and New England faced a cod crisis that began in the 1970s. The first response by both nations was to extend the region's territorial borders, pushing the hundreds of foreign ships that had been trawling their waters for decades far out to sea.

Rather, however, than use the opportunity to restrict fishing and allow the cod to recover, both the Canadian and New England fleets geared up and replaced the foreign ships with their own. "The idea," remarked one biologist, "was that the streets were paved with fish and now that the Europeans were gone, it would come to the Canadians."

What came instead was what many consider the greatest resource management disaster in history. The numbers of cod plunged to near-extinction levels. Fishing moratoriums were declared by both nations that remain in place to this day. Tens of thousands of Canadians lost their jobs. And the region's cod population has still not recovered.

NEW FISHING GROUNDS

Historically, the answer to depleted fish stocks was moving on to other countries. West Africa, for example, has long attracted distant fishing fleets from other continents. The practice has increased substantially in recent years, finally reaching the present, staggering levels. For many West African countries, the armada of foreign fleets has meant a sharp decline in marine diversity and new difficulties for local artisanal fisheries.

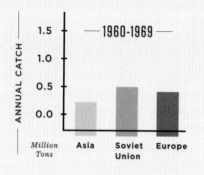

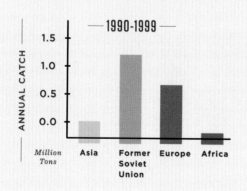

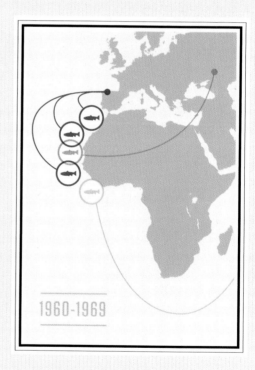

Source: The Sea Around Us Project

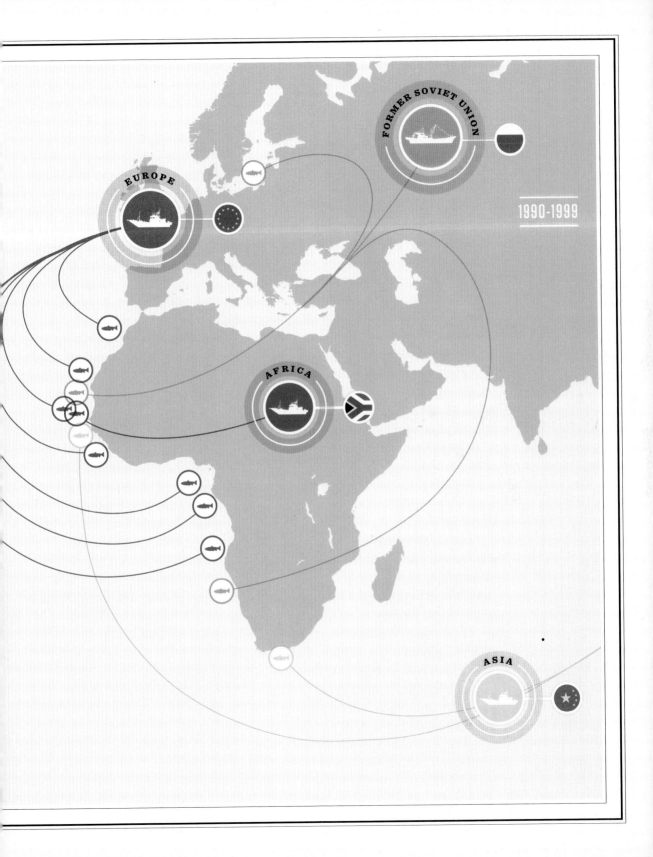

FORMER SOVIET UNION

EUROPE

1990-1999

AFRICA

ASIA

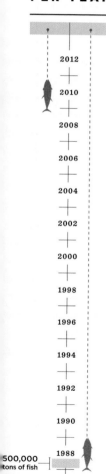

SINCE 1988
COMMERCIAL
FISHING'S CATCH
HAS DECLINED BY

500

THOUSAND TONS
PER YEAR

2012
2010
2008
2006
2004
2002
2000
1998
1996
1994
1992
1990
1988

500,000
tons of fish

of water that are so inconceivably vast being "fished out" by men in boats, no matter how big or sophisticated those boats might be.

Certainly, no one conceived that it could happen to a fish as plentiful as the cod. But it did.

At the turn of the 1980s—just over a century after Dumas made that visit to New England—the nearshore fishermen in that region, most of them the small-scale artisans described earlier, noticed a drastic drop in the yields of their catches. And they knew exactly why: Those huge commercial trawlers outfitted with onboard fish-processing facilities were netting so many cod miles out, toward the edge of the continental shelf, that the fish had no chance to migrate inshore to spawn, as they'd done for eons.

The smaller fishermen tried suing, but they had no chance against the legal and political might of the industrial fisheries, who counted McDonald's restaurants and Gorton's, which was using cod to make its fish sticks, among their customers. When the local fishermen warned that their dwindling catches were evidence of the onset of overfishing, the industrial fisheries pointed out that *their* catches were continuing to increase. So what could the problem be? No one suggested that those rising numbers might reflect the power and efficiency of the industrial fisheries' machinery rather than fewer cod in the water.

And then, sure enough, in 1992, the bottom fell out. The numbers of cod caught by all fisheries, large and small, in the waters off Nova Scotia and Newfoundland dropped off a cliff. There's nothing gradual about an event called a "collapse." This disaster was so sudden and so sweeping that the Canadian government immediately issued a moratorium, shutting down every cod fishing operation in the region.

Literally overnight, nearly forty thousand fishermen and processing plant workers in Newfoundland found themselves out of jobs. The government held out a small thread of hope that "in a couple of years" things would get back to normal. But two years later, in January of 1994, the government announced an extension of the moratorium. And this time, no hope of recovery was offered.

The same circumstances shattered New England's cod industry, which had shared fishing rights to the Georges Banks, some sixty miles off the coast, with the Canadians since the 1970s. Those Gorton fish sticks sold in supermarket frozen food aisles and those Filet-O-Fish sandwiches handed out the windows of McDonald's drive-thrus, which for years had been made with the flaky white meat of cod, were now, as one expert drily stated in a *Nature* magazine cover story, being made with haddock, redfish, or, as Mark Kurlansky put it in his book, "whatever is left" in the water.

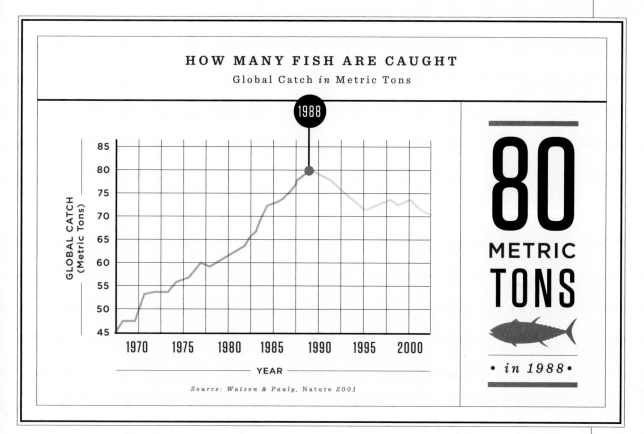

HOW MANY FISH ARE CAUGHT

Global Catch *in* Metric Tons

1988

80

METRIC

TONS

• in 1988 •

Source: Watson & Pauly, Nature 2001

SO THAT'S WHAT HAPPENED TO COD. BUT IT DIDN'T happen *just* to cod.

In 1988—at almost exactly the same time that the cod population was collapsing in the North Atlantic—the annual worldwide fishing catch declined significantly for the first time in history. The decline was masked for twelve years by exaggerated yields reported by China until, in 2001, Daniel Pauly and Reg Watson, of the Fisheries Centre at the University of British Columbia, uncovered the distortions and reported them in *Nature*. In fact, since 1988, the global fishing industry's catch has dropped by an average of more than ½ million tons a year—a truly worrying trend that the industry has mostly ignored or outright denied. But the Food and Agriculture organization of the United Nations refers, since this article was published, to the world catch with and without reported Chinese catches.

Yet another shock was the 2003 release of study results from a highly respected marine conservationist, the late Ransom Myers, that revealed a tremendous decline in the populations of the oceans' "big predators"—the large species at the pinnacle of the marine food web. Myers found that since 1950, there had been a 90 percent drop in the numbers of twenty-five of the ocean's largest predators.

We're talking about the majestic giants of the sea: marlin, swordfish, bluefin tuna, king mackerel, sharks, and other species. Apparently, as far as the commercial fishing industry is concerned, size *does* matter. The biggest fish have historically been among the fishermen's biggest targets. But how to explain such a steep, sudden drop in the numbers of these twenty-five species in the relatively short space of fifty years?

Swordfish, for instance, has been a sought-after delicacy since long before 1950. A nicely seared swordfish steak has been an expensive highlight on restaurant menus for decades. A century ago, the average weight of a swordfish was about three hundred pounds. By 1960, it had slightly dropped, to 266. Today, the average is ninety pounds. Something happened to cause such a huge change in just the past sixty years. But what?

Something happened to bluefin tuna as well. Unlike swordfish, bluefin is a relative newcomer to the high-priced big-fish market. It's a gorgeous creature, as long as fourteen feet and as large as fifteen hundred pounds. It flashes neon blue, pink, and silver as it slices through the water at breathtaking speeds, an oceanic missile that can accelerate faster than a Maserati, from zero to forty-five miles an hour in a matter of seconds. The bluefin is such a tremendously refined species that it's been said to represent "the peak of evolution in fish."

Bluefin tuna

SINCE 1950, THERE HAS BEEN A 90 PERCENT DROP in the NUMBERS of TWENTY-FIVE of the OCEAN'S LARGEST PREDATORS.

As recently as the late 1960s, bluefin tuna sold in the United States for no more than a couple of pennies a pound, and most was ground up for cat food. But fast-forward to 2010, when a single 513-pound Pacific bluefin sold at a Tokyo fish auction for a record $177,000, and it's easy to see that the situation is now quite different.

How did bluefin go from cat food to solid gold in a matter of decades?

This one's not hard to figure out. The answer is the sushi boom that hit America in the late 1970s and early '80s. In Japan, where lean meat is generally preferred, bluefin had been shunned for centuries because of its fattiness and bloodiness. But a slice of rich, creamy *toro*—the prime, ruby red meat of the bluefin's belly—suited Americans' tastes, and when sushi bars began proliferating in the trendiest sections of US cities, bluefin quickly became one of the most popular and priciest items on the menus. Meanwhile, a taste for bluefin had taken root in Japan during the postwar American occupation, and it became a rage there at the turn of the 1990s, when a new

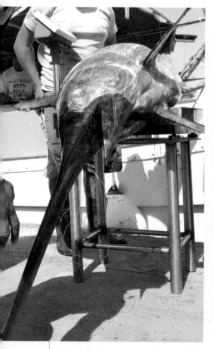

Swordfish

Shark

generation of young Japanese embraced it along with so many other "hip" American styles—and yet another high-seas gold rush was on.

That explains the market for bluefin and the subsequent drop in its numbers. But what about, say, sharks? Beyond occasionally being offered as a novelty, shark meat doesn't show up on the menus of too many restaurants in America. So where did nine out of every ten sharks that inhabited the world's oceans in 1950 go?

The answer is the relatively recent explosion in yet another seafood market, this one feeding one of the most controversial, wasteful, and certainly brutal fisheries in existence—shark fins.

On the face of it, there seems to be no reason for shark fins to have become, on a price-per-pound basis, the most valuable thing you can take from a living creature in the ocean. (They currently sell for as much as $300 a pound.) They are virtually

WHERE DID 9 out of EVERY 10 SHARKS THAT INHABITED the WORLD'S OCEANS in 1950 GO?

$300 per pound

flavorless. A shark fin is almost pure cartilage, which is so tough that it must be boiled for hours until it breaks down into spaghetti-like strands. These strands, still almost unchewable, are used to make a soup whose only taste comes from its other ingredients. Yet this soup sells for $60 a bowl in China, and in the most expensive restaurants in the Chinatowns of London and San Francisco, it goes for as much as $400 a bowl.

Why?

Here's the quick answer: For ages, shark fin soup was an Asian delicacy, a status symbol reserved for the wealthy, most prominently in China. There's a Chinese proverb that partly explains the appeal of such soup: "A thing is valued if it is rare."

So the market for shark fins has existed for a long time, mostly in China. But why the recent surge in shark kills, as noted in Myers's study?

This one is largely explained by the economic boom that has taken place in China over the past generation. As the ruling Communist Party has loosened its restrictions on capitalist trade, a large, upwardly mobile Chinese middle class has been growing. It is no longer just the rich in China who can afford the pleasures and prestige of shark fin soup. In China today, almost any significant social affair, from a wedding reception to a birthday celebration, is likely to feature shark fin soup on the menu.

The story of how shark fins find their way from the sea into soup isn't a happy one. As many as 70 million sharks netted or hooked worldwide each year have their

fins hacked off and their still-living carcasses tossed back overboard as soon as they're caught.

Nor is it likely that the guests slicing into their grilled swordfish steaks at a backyard barbecue have any idea about the armadas of longline fishing boats that ply the high seas day and night, each boat pulling as many as twenty-five hundred large baited hooks, each one strong enough to snag a full-grown, ninety-pound swordfish on a line that can be as much as forty miles long. The point here is that, while a growing market for each of the "big fish" on Myers's list partly explains the 90 percent drop in their populations over the past fifty years, something else is at work, too. And that "something else" is destroying not just the giants that sit atop the oceans' food web. It's threatening virtually every living thing in the ocean— everything but jellyfish. But the jellyfish could be next.

SHARK FINS have **BECOME,** on a **PRICE-PER-POUND BASIS,** the **MOST VALUABLE THING YOU CAN TAKE** from a **LIVING CREATURE** in the **OCEAN.**

That "something else" is the tremendously powerful global fishing industry that has developed over the past half century— the same half century that Myers studied. The size and sophistication of the world's commercial fishing fleets, thanks to vast leaps in techniques and technology, have grown to a point where they are on the verge of destroying Earth's entire oceanic ecosystem.

That's not an overstatement. This worldwide fleet of warships—and that's what they are, based on the scale of the assault they've unleashed upon their defenseless prey—has the power to undo within the next century what nature has taken millions of years to create.

In the next chapter, we'll look at the weaponry that makes such unthinkable destruction possible, as well as the global system of government subsidies that supports that destruction.

And finally, we'll look at what can be done to prevent it.

THIS WORLDWIDE FLEET of WARSHIPS has the POWER to UNDO WITHIN t

EXT CENTURY WHAT NATURE HAS TAKEN MILLIONS of YEARS to CREATE.

WHAT YOU CAN DO

- **TAKE ACTION TO PROTECT THREATENED AND ENDANGERED SEA TURTLES.** Visit: http://act.oceana.org/cms/letter/l-turtles-comprehensiveprotections/

- **HELP END SHARK FINNING: DON'T EAT SHARK FIN SOUP.**

- **LEARN ABOUT FISH AND THEIR BIOLOGY.** Visit: http://fishbase.org/

- **EAT SUSTAINABLY CAUGHT FISH AND TEACH YOUR FRIENDS AND FAMILY ABOUT SUSTAINABLE SEAFOOD, TOO.** Visit: www.montereybayaquarium.org/cr/seafoodwatch.aspx

- **SUPPORT MARINE-PROTECTED AREAS AND OTHER EFFORTS TO PROTECT OCEAN HABITATS.**

- **SUPPORT MARINE CONSERVATION ORGANIZATIONS.**

- **CONTACT YOUR US SENATORS AND REPRESENTATIVES** and urge them to support ending overfishing and ensure that the deadlines to rebuild overfished stocks are met.

- **ORGANIZE A SCREENING** of *The End of the Line* and collect donations for your favorite ocean conservation nonprofit.

- **CONTACT LOCAL RESTAURANTS AND TELL THEM NOT TO SERVE "RED-LIST" SEAFOOD.**

- **DON'T EAT BLUEFIN TUNA, AND CONTACT SUSHI RESTAURANTS TO ENCOURAGE THEM TO STOP SERVING IT.**

- **LEARN ABOUT THE MASSIVE PROBLEM** of fishing subsidies and support Oceana's efforts to curb global fishing subsidies.

CHAPTER FOUR

AN ILLUSION OF
ABUNDANCE

AUGUST 2004: YOU CAN SEE, OUT THERE

on the horizon, the largest fishing boat in the world—the *Atlantic Dawn*—plowing through the dark green Atlantic as the morning sun rises over the coast of West Africa.

Imagine standing on a beach where the sands of the Sahara meet the surf of the sea. Up and down the length of that beach sit the boats of the local Mauritanians' fishing fleet—long, slender wooden canoes, each one painted the color of a bright ripe fruit. Some have outboard motors, some do not. They call their boats pirogues. As for that massive trawler outlined against the western sky, they call it The Sea Monster and The Ship from Hell.

To call the *Atlantic Dawn* a boat is like calling King Kong a monkey. It's a floating fish factory, roughly the size of a US Navy destroyer, stretching nearly five hundred feet long—the length of more than one and a half football fields. It carries three thousand tons of fuel to power its twin diesel engines, which have a combined horsepower of 28,730. It can stay at sea for months at a time. Its crew of one hundred uses forklifts to move each day's haul, which can total as much as three hundred tons. It takes ten of those local pirogues a year to catch that much.

The *Dawn* weighs more than fourteen thousand tons when its holds are empty. Those icy refrigerated holds have the capacity to store more than seven thousand tons of fish frozen in twenty-kilogram blocks—enough to feed 18 million people a good, healthy supper.

The nets the *Dawn* drops to trawl for those fish have openings forty feet high and two hundred feet wide—large enough for a 747 jet to fit through. Each net could hold twelve of those same jets.

The *Dawn* can drop those nets as deep as a mile, beyond the edge of the continental shelf, and drag a half-acre swath of seabed with one pass. A net's rollers or even larger rockhoppers—long metal bars attached to the base of the net's mouth, each bar as much as three feet thick and weighing up to several hundred pounds—have the power to move a twenty-five-ton boulder, and they easily grind their way through forests of deepwater coral and ranges of subterranean seamounts as if they were made of papier-mâché. Metal "tickler chains" attached to those rollers stir up the sea bottom, creating noise and clouds of silt that flush the fish out of their hiding spots. The undersea silt clouds the *Atlantic Dawn* stirs up are so large that some by similar ships have

12×

EACH TRAWLING NET ON
THE ATLANTIC DAWN
—— CAN HOLD ——
TWELVE
—— **747's** ——

—— **THE NETS** the *DAWN* **DROPS** to **TRAWL** ——
FOR THOSE FISH HAVE OPENINGS FORTY FEET
HIGH and **TWO HUNDRED FEET WIDE—LARGE**
—— **ENOUGH** for a **747 JET** to **FIT THROUGH.** ——

The supertrawler *Atlantic Dawn*

shown up in images shot by satellites orbiting Earth. Go to Google Earth on the Web and see for yourself.

While the Mauritanian men back on the beach use the age-old methods their fathers and grandfathers used to lead them to fish—reading the water, its color, its currents; feeling the wind, its speed and direction; scanning the sky for circling seabirds; studying the waves, their heights and sets—and work the water by hand, the skipper of the *Atlantic Dawn*, with its bright green hull (a nod to the ship's Irish roots, as well as its owner's), directs his crew from the glass-enclosed bridge, a control center perched high above the ship's deck where he sits before a bank of computer screens and control panels as sophisticated as those in the cockpit of an F-22 fighter jet.

Those panels and screens feed the captain a steady stream of data from a dizzying array of cutting-edge devices, all only an arm's length and a mouse click away. The array of devices a top-of-the-line supertrawler like the *Atlantic Dawn* can choose from include:

- Satellite-connected fish-tracking buoys, which are called "fish aggregating devices" (FADs). Dozens of them are bobbing on the surface in thousands of square miles of ocean in various regions of the globe, some equipped with echo sounders to monitor fish movement, others with thermosensors to indicate sea temperature contours.

- Seabed-mapping software that provides 3-D images of the tangled reefs and rocky seamounts a mile beneath the waves—images that help the supertrawler's skipper precisely set his nets.

- Split-beam "fish finder" sonar, every bit as precise as a nuclear submarine's, that allows ships like the *Dawn* to home in on bunched schools of, say, hake, which show up as clusters of green dots on the bridge's flat-panel screens.

- Bird radar—from the antennae mounted on the ship's masts—that, from miles away, picks up flocks of seabirds, which tend to gather above schools of fish.

- Doppler radar water-temperature monitors that detect and precisely chart the outlines of fronts—the oceanic sweet spots where warm water meets cold and plankton collect and are fed upon by prey fish like anchovies and sardines, which in turn draw larger predators, the big guns of the sea, such as tuna and swordfish and sharks.

- Daily e-mails sent out by the National Oceanic and Atmospheric Administration that show satellite images of current sea temperatures all over the planet.

- GPS plotters that can guide the ship to the precise spot where it should drop its nets.

- Acoustic monitors (known as "suitcases") that are attached to the nets and beam up signals that show their precise location as they drag the ocean bottom.

- Electronic catch indicators (known as "eggs") that let the captain know how full a net is.

A host of other types of equipment is also available to the big-spending owners of supertrawlers like the *Dawn*, ranging from speedboats ready to be dropped for quick-strike scouting missions to onboard helicopters used for the same purpose.

With this range of weaponry, the *Atlantic Dawn* sounds more like a warship than a fishing vessel. And that's essentially what it is. Its approach to fishing is nothing less than an all-out assault with no regard for collateral damage, which includes the seafloor habitat its nets crush and destroy and the bycatch, the untargeted fish and other marine life that get trapped in those nets, most of them maimed or dead by the time they're separated from the catch and tossed back overboard.

TOWARD SUSTAINABLE FISHERIES

GLEN BROOKS

Commercial Fisherman

Glen Brooks is the president of the Gulf Fishermen's Association, a group of commercial fishermen with members around the Gulf of Mexico who organized to represent the interests of fishermen and seafood consumers. By advocating for changes in fisheries management to ensure a year-round sustainable fishery, they aim to keep Americans working and to bring fresh domestic seafood to the American public.

GLEN: I've been fishing about twenty-eight years. I grew up in a little fishing village called Cortez, one of the last historical working waterfronts in the state of Florida. I mainly fish for grouper (and some snapper). We traditionally long-line grouper.

Over the last twenty-eight years, the fishery has become overcapitalized. It's just way over-exploited. We've got too many fishermen chasing too few fish. That's not just in the commercial sector; that's in the recreational sector, too.

So we've been faced with new stringent quotas and regulations, most of them to the good for the fishery. That affects everybody—the commercial sector, the recreational sector, the infrastructure, the fish houses, the restaurants, etc. The number of boats going out has been reduced over the years due to these new regulations. One good new development is the IFQs (individual fishing quotas)—they control our overcapitalization problem in the commercial sector and help reduce our bycatch. If I'm down here in the Southern Gulf catching fish and I catch something I don't have shares for, like snapper, I can purchase them from another fisherman in the Northern Gulf who has extra and is not going to use them for one reason or another. Then I don't have to throw those fish back over-board dead, like in the old snapper management system. And vice versa, if someone needs grouper shares to land grouper bycatch in their fishery, I can sell or trade with them so they don't waste fish. When you throw a fish overboard and you're 90 percent sure that fish is dead, dying, or gonna die, it just literally makes a fishermen sick.

We have a problem with seafood fraud for grouper. People out there are buying cheaper stuff in place of grouper and selling it under the same name—this hurts our business by holding down the cost on our fish. We want to be in the forefront of exposing the people doing the fraud. But being associated with seafood fraud also hurts us. People go into our restaurants and say, "Well, I don't really believe it's grouper, so I'm not buying it." It's a double-edged sword.

Our organization, the Gulf Fishermen's Association, is working on all of these issues. Our motto is "Ensuring the Commercial Fishing Future for the Next Generation." We want a sustainable fishery and no one wants to waste a valuable, limited resource.

OCEAN HERO

BARBARA BOXER

US Senator

During my twenty-five years of work on behalf of the oceans, a core group of people has been there from the beginning. One of those people is Senator Barbara Boxer. When Bob Sulnick and I formed the American Oceans Campaign back in 1987, then-Congresswoman Boxer stood with us to help our voices be heard.

She still stands there today, as one of the staunchest and most powerful advocates of ocean protection and preservation on Capitol Hill. Since joining the Senate in 1993 and becoming the first female chair of the Senate's Environment and Public Works Committee when she was elected to that position in 2007, she has cosponsored eleven ocean-related bills and has individually sponsored four, including the National Oceans Protection Act of 2009, a comprehensive approach to ocean management that includes placing a priority on oceans in national policy decisions by creating a cabinet-level National Ocean Advisor to the president.

In a 2010 speech to the Ocean Leadership Public Policy Forum, Senator Boxer emphasized the economic importance of preserving the oceans.

"In these troubled times," she said, "we must make creating and preserving jobs our number one priority. The ocean economy generates $230 billion in economic activity and 3.6 million jobs nationwide, with about half of those revenues and two-thirds of those jobs coming from ocean tourism and recreation—industries that depend on a clean ocean. Clearly, if we are going to get our nation's economy back on track, ocean jobs have to be a part of that."

While making a case for the bottom line, Barbara reminded her audience at the end of that same speech that the oceans are about more than just dollars.

Pointing to a map showing the border of California's Sonoma and Mendocino Counties, she said, "In all of North America, this area has the strongest upwelling of the deep, nutrient-rich water that fuels marine life. It provides habitat for more than one-third of the world's whale and dolphin species, at least 163 species of birds, and more than 300 species of fish.

"Whenever I return to California," she said, "I remember why I am working so hard in DC to protect places like this."

Frozen tuna, Tsukiji Market, Tokyo

THE WORLD'S ENTIRE FISHING FLEET, FROM SUPERSHIPS LIKE

the *Dawn*—which was subsequently banned from African waters but still fishes off the coastlines of other continents under a new owner and a new name—all the way down to the tiniest one-man dinghy sitting on that West African sand, numbers roughly 4 million vessels. Just over 1 percent of those

> SUPERTRAWLERS REPRESENT JUST 1 PERCENT of the GLOBAL INDUSTRIAL FLEET and EMPLOY JUST 2 PERCENT of the WORLD'S TOTAL CREW.

boats—about forty-five thousand—weigh more than one hundred tons, qualifying them as "industrial" ships. These include longliners setting ribbons of death, mile-long lines with thousands of hooks, as well as various other forms of industrial fishing vessels.

But far and away, it's the trawlers that dominate what Daniel Pauly—the University of British Columbia professor and expert on overfishing whose work I mentioned in the previous chapter—calls "the industrial fishing complex," a $240 billion-a-year business. And it's giants like the *Atlantic Dawn* that dominate the trawlers. These supertrawlers represent just 1 percent of the global industrial fleet and employ just 2 percent of the world's total crew, but each year they harvest up to half the world's total catch. Nearly 50 percent. Keep that in mind for when we get to the discussion of ways to solve the world's overfishing crisis.

And have no doubt that we're facing a crisis. It's easy for people in well-to-do nations like ours to look at the well-stocked seafood sections of grocery stores, scan the plentiful choices on the menus of our finest seafood restaurants, and behold the mountains of fresh, gleaming salmon for sale at an outdoor emporium like Seattle's Pike Place Market and assume that all's well with the world's oceans.

But this is what Paul Greenberg, author of *Four Fish: The Future of the Last Wild Food,* calls "an illusion of abundance." If you check out the other end of the spectrum—say, the coastal villages of dozens of developing nations like Mauritania, where the fish stalls sit virtually empty, merely sprinkled with the undersize leftovers of the world's supertrawlers—you'd realize that all's not as well as it seems.

The men, women, and children in those villages certainly realize it. For nearly 3 billion people in the world, a major source of animal protein and minerals is the sea. For many of the 800 million people in the poorest regions of Africa and South Asia—places like Mauritania—not only is seafood the basis of their diet, but fishing is also the primary livelihood. With the invasion of industrial ships like the *Dawn* into their waters, hundreds of thousands—even millions—of these coastal poor will soon join the more than 1.4 billion people in the world who currently live below the starvation level. (We'll explain how these factory ships finagle their way into developing nations' two-hundred-mile Exclusive Economic Zones when we get to the subject of subsidies.)

Last year the world's total catch of fish and shellfish was roughly 92 million tons. We've already discussed the fact that this number has decreased in the past twenty-some years. While the size of the world's fishing fleet has also decreased during that time—to approximately 4 million boats today—the number and sizes of the boats heading out to the deep waters of the high seas (which we'll look at in the next chapter) have increased, adding much more fishing power. With that many boats going out farther and fewer fish coming in, there are all kinds of ramifications. Most obvious is the fact that the size of the catch per boat is shrinking. This increases the intensity of the competition to find and catch the fish that are still out there, whose numbers are also steadily decreasing. The fleets are constantly pushed to fish harder, fish farther, and fish deeper—all at enormous costs. Then, factor in the exponential growth of our planet's population—the current total of 7 billion is projected to increase to nearly 9.3 billion by the year 2050, and the number of people who depend on the oceans as their primary source of food is expected to more than double during that time. Consider the increase in the global consumption of fish, which has doubled since a generation ago, and the enormous increase in seafood consumption in developed nations—most notably Japan, China, and the United States—and we come face-to-face with the global crisis of overfishing.

That consumption reflects how, when it comes to the limited bounty of our oceans, the scales are tipped toward the wealthier nations of the world—at a tragic cost to the poor. Try these statistics on for size: The annual seafood consumption of

A VISIT TO CHILE

It was like every other fish market I've seen—stalls with beds of ice and signs listing prices of fish. Except . . . there weren't any fish. And instead of vendors selling the day's catch, the market was full of angry local fishermen. I was in San Antonio, Chile, the home port for one of Chile's main artisanal fishing unions. We were meeting with the fishermen to discuss Oceana's efforts to stop bottom trawling.

The local fishermen had, for generations, plied the waters off Chile in search of hake and other fish. They used wooden boats, just a little bigger than a rowboat. For years, those small boats had allowed them to make a living and feed their families. No more. Bottom trawlers and other big commercial boats were catching most of the fish now—largely to make fish meal for Chile's booming salmon farming industry—and leaving little to no fish for the artisanal fishermen to catch. That's why in Chile, bottom trawling is such a hot button issue that fishermen have blocked off major highways in protest. It is a life-or-death issue for them, as well as for millions of small-scale fishermen around the world.

Looking at the empty fish stalls and boats with *Se Vende* signs made it all very clear. It was impossible to ignore where all their fish was going (ultimately to make sure our markets are full of farmed salmon and other fish) and what our abundant fish markets hide (an ever-declining supply of fish in San Antonio and other ports). The market in San Antonio could be our future in the United States—someday we, too, will be facing these empty fish stalls unless we change how we manage our fisheries.

industrial nations is nearly three times that of the developing world, and yet 70 percent of the fish caught in the wild (and *90* percent of fish raised on farms, a topic we'll get to shortly) come from the waters of those developing countries. In other words, we're robbing the poor to feed the rich, either by catching "our" fish in their waters or by buying our fish from other industrial nations that catch them that way and telling ourselves that our hands are clean.

Daniel Pauly calls this imbalance a "Ponzi scheme"—feeding one end of the chain with continuous input from the other. And indeed, like a Ponzi scheme, this system is bound to collapse once the input finally—and inevitably—dries up.

Which is exactly what is now happening—not just in the fisheries of the developing world, but also in fisheries everywhere on the planet. According to a recent report by the United Nations' Food and Agriculture Organization (FAO), there are nowhere near enough fish left in the seas to support the armadas of boats going after them. In fact, the report states that if the fishing power of the current global fleet of 4 million boats were cut in *half*, we would still be catching more fish than the oceans can afford to give up. The World Wildlife Fund (WWF) agrees, stating that the global fishing fleet is currently two and a half times bigger than "what the oceans can sustainably support." Another FAO study reports that on most of the world's fishing grounds, fish populations are in rapid decline or already depleted.

THERE are **NOWHERE NEAR ENOUGH FISH LEFT** in the **SEAS TO** **SUPPORT** the **ARMADAS** of **BOATS GOING AFTER THEM.**

And still the industry pushes on. Rather than responding to these warnings and restricting catches in order to allow threatened species to reproduce and recover their numbers, the commercial fleets simply drag, dredge, and hook one part of the ocean until nothing is left, then move on to new fishing grounds and do the same thing all over again. They've done it this way since fishing first became a commercial enterprise, but the curtain is finally closing. There are precious few new grounds left.

With the relatively shallow waters of the planet's continental shelves essentially fished out, the industry has turned to its last resort, steering its boats farther out to sea and into the last frontier left on the planet—those same ocean depths beyond the continental shelves where the oil industry has lately been sinking its wells. The high costs, risks, and unknowns that we've already seen arising with "tough oil" are mirrored in the challenges the fishing industry faces as it begins dropping its nets into the dark, frigid depths of the high seas in search of "tough fish."

WEAPONRY

Fishing technology has advanced in leaps and bounds in recent years, as declining fish populations have forced the industry to look farther and deeper in order to catch fish.

- **TRAPS** are used to catch lobsters, crabs, and sometimes fish. Individual traps can be sustainable if they're fitted with trap doors that allow juvenile lobsters to escape. Long lines of traps, however, can even entangle whales with their floating lines.

- **DREDGES** catch scallops and fish by dragging across the seafloor. They can crush corals, catch sea turtles, and disturb all kinds of seafloor life.

- **PURSE SEINE NETS** catch schooling fish like tuna by encircling the school with a wall of netting. They can capture dolphins and other natural predators feeding on the school, though it is possible to release dolphins by backing down the net if the operator takes the time.

- **TRAWL NETS** catch shrimp, cod, haddock, and other fish. Bottom trawls drag weighted nets across the seafloor, crushing corals or any other marine life in their path. Bottom trawls also discard more unwanted fish than almost any other form of fishing and are extremely destructive. Midwater trawls drag large nets through the water to catch pollock and other schooling fish, and when their nets are full, they may also drag on the bottom.

- **GILLNETS**, one of the most widely used methods in the world, are sometimes employed for catching salmon and sharks. When not closely tended, gillnets can entangle and drown sea turtles, seabirds, and marine mammals. Some gillnets also snag large numbers of juvenile fish, which contributes to overfishing.

- **LONGLINES** catch tuna and swordfish with miles of baited hooks that also capture sea turtles, sharks, and endangered sawfish. One longline can have thousands of hooks.

- **HARPOONS** are used to catch tuna and swordfish in one of the most responsible fishing techniques; They have little to no bycatch, which leaves the surrounding marine habitat intact. Harpoon fishermen target fish from the front of a boat and sometimes work with spotter planes to find fish.

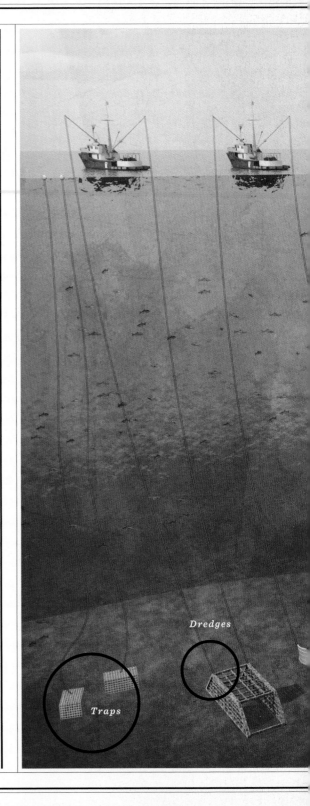

Dredges

Traps

Purse
seine nets

Gillnets

Longlines

Trawl nets

Harpoons

We'll take a close look at this last frontier in the next chapter. But in order to understand and assess the costs and concerns that come with the risky business of deepwater fishing, we need to take stock of the damage and destruction the industry has already wrought in the fished-out waters it's leaving behind.

———

WE'VE ALREADY TALKED ABOUT THE DAMAGE ACIDIFICATION inflicts upon reefs. Also of consequence is the destruction inflicted by the weaponry of the industrial fisheries, particularly the bottom trawlers. Some people refer to those heavily weighted nets with their rollers and rockhoppers as "ocean bulldozers."

The image is apt. I mentioned earlier that those rollers have the power to push aside twenty-five-ton boulders. They pulverize everything in their path, crushing deep coral, grinding boulders to rubble, wiping out populations of old fish and other creatures, which will take generations to recover, and leave behind a flat, lifeless moonscape of gravel and sand.

ROLLERS PULVERIZE EVERYTHING in their **PATH, CRUSHING** the **CORAL, GRINDING** the **BOULDERS** to **RUBBLE, WIPING OUT POPULATIONS** of **JUVENILE FISH** and **OTHER CREATURES** for **GENERATIONS.**

This destruction is often com-pared to clear-cutting a forest. But it's actually far worse. Calculations show that the total area of seabed trawled by the world's fishing fleet each year is 150 times the area of the forests cut. Studies have estimated that each year, trawl nets disturb a seabed area twice the size of the contiguous United States.

And it's not just the sea bottom that suffers. Those silt clouds I mentioned earlier—the blooms of fine-grained sand churned up by the trawl nets, some as much as seventeen miles in diameter—are incredibly destructive as well. They can change the chemistry of the water itself, releasing pollutants trapped in the seafloor mud. And those suspended near-microscopic grains of silt can enter and clog the breathing and feeding systems of all kinds of marine life, from coral polyps to sea turtles.

It can take decades, even centuries for a seabed to recover from a single pass of a bottom-trawl net. The before-and-after images of a bottom-trawled reef forest are heartbreaking. But to the fishing industry, this kind of destruction is nothing more than collateral damage, as are the millions of tons of unwanted fish and other forms of marine life that are accidentally caught in their nets or snagged by the hooks of longliners every year. No one knows the true amount of the dead and dying sea life that is

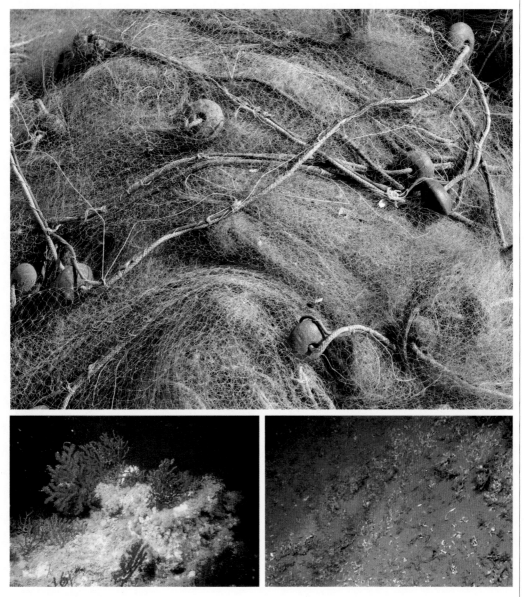

HEALTHY untrawled coral   Seafloor AFTER bottom trawling

BYCATCH: A GLOBAL PROBLEM

In the Gulf of Mexico, for every 1 pound of shrimp caught by a trawler, 4 to 10 pounds of marine life is thrown away.

FOR EVERY
1 POUND
of Shrimp
CAUGHT

· 1 *pound of* ·
SHRIMP

UP TO
10 POUNDS
of Marine Life
IS THROWN AWAY

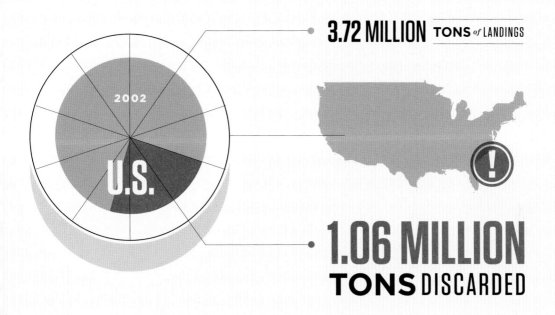

3.72 MILLION TONS *of* LANDINGS

1.06 MILLION
TONS DISCARDED

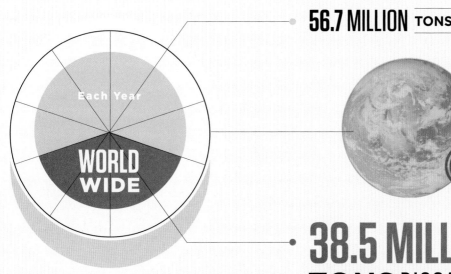

56.7 MILLION TONS *of* LANDINGS

38.5 MILLION*
TONS DISCARDED

*Believed to be too low by many scientists.

Marine biologist John Halas is an inventive and tireless defender of coral reefs. His groundbreaking development of an environmentally friendly anchor and buoy system has prevented damage to vital coral colonies around the world.

Halas was working at the Key Largo National Marine Sanctuary in 1981 when he observed that careless anchoring was causing coral damage on the ocean floor. He took action and initiated an experimental mooring, or fastening, system to provide boaters with an alternative means of securing their vessels. The system works by drilling into the ancient limestone substrate in the seafloor, then cementing a stainless steel eyebolt into the bottom. A floating line shackles to the eyebolt and extends through a plastic buoy, which boaters attach to and secure their boats.

This early experiment was exactly the fix needed to protect the reefs, and what's now known as the Halas Mooring Buoy System went on to revolutionize coral reef management and protect countless acres of reef. Halas has traveled the world to personally assist sanctuaries with implementing the system, and there are now more than 400 buoys in the Florida Keys Sanctuary and more than 50 countries using the system.

Halas's ingenuity and take-charge approach to ocean conservation has been applauded by many conservation groups. In 2003 the National Oceanic and Atmospheric Administration (NOAA), an agency of the US Department of Commerce, awarded him their Bronze Medal (the highest honorary award NOAA has) for the mooring device development.

70% OF THE REMAINING **COD POPULATION** | HAS BEEN LOST TO **BYCATCH**

discarded by fishermen—after all, on the vast majority of fishing boats, there's no one there to watch. Some scientists believe bycatch worldwide could be as much as a third of the landed catch—with the most destructive fisheries discarding 80 to 90 percent of their catch. Some 20 million tons per year counts only the creatures that are actually hauled up from the sea and thrown back. There's no telling how many creatures are maimed or killed by those nets and hooks but never get hauled up. One thing we do know for sure—the reported totals of discarded fish are grossly inaccurate.

We also know that sharks make up huge numbers of bycatch victims—some 50 million a year are accidentally snagged by trawlers, longlines, and gill nets. That's half of the world's total shark catch.

And those cod that are trying to make a comeback in the Georges Bank region off New England? As much as 70 percent of the remaining cod population in those waters in recent years has been lost to bycatch.

Along with fish, millions of other marine animals, ranging from dolphins to rays, skates, turtles, and whales, are unintentionally captured or killed each year in commercial fishing operations. Even birds become victims—albatrosses, in particular. Albatrosses habitually follow fishing boats, feeding on the bycatch and scraps that are tossed overboard. They are also attracted to the baited hooks of longliners, particularly in the oceans of the Southern Hemisphere, where an estimated one hundred thousand of them perish each year on those hooks.

GUITARFISH, RAYS, and OTHER BYCATCH
are tossed from a shrimp boat, Mexico.

Probably the most publicized bycatch victims are sea turtles. Six species of sea turtles inhabit US waters, and all six are currently classified as either threatened or endangered by extinction. A study found that worldwide in 2000, longliners unintentionally hooked two hundred thousand loggerhead turtles and fifty thousand leatherbacks. Even more disturbing than those numbers is the gruesomeness of the fate of turtles hauled up by deep-sea nets—particularly shrimpers' nets. Turtles (and other creatures) rapidly swept to the surface in those nets can suffer extreme cases of the bends, with their eyeballs actually popping out and their organs exploding.

Another grim, haunting image is what the industry calls "ghost nets"—drift nets, gill nets, and purse seine nets that accidentally get detached from the boats. Written off as lost, these floating death traps drift eerily beneath the surface of the high seas, entangling and killing whatever creatures are unlucky enough to cross their paths. Again, there is no way of knowing exactly how many fish and other animals die in these nets, or, indeed, how many such nets are out there, but guesses are that the number is in the millions.

IN THE YEAR 2000, **200,000 LOGGERHEAD TURTLES** and **50,000 LEATHERBACK TURTLES** were **UNINTENTIONALLY HOOKED WORLDWIDE**

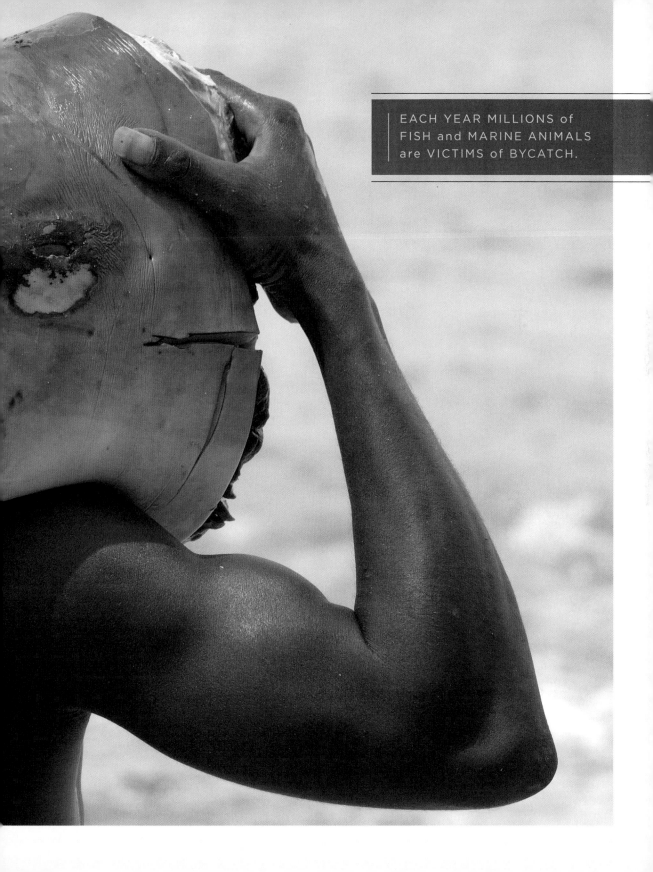

EACH YEAR MILLIONS of
FISH and MARINE ANIMALS
are VICTIMS of BYCATCH.

MILLIONS.

MILLIONS OF TONS. MILLIONS OF BOATS. MILLIONS OF FISH.
Millions of people.

What does it all add up to? What do these numbers mean in the end? What can we learn from them? How can we apply them in order to deal with the oceanic crises we now face?

The men and women who spend their lives studying the seas, and who have been sounding the alarm in recent years about the deadly ramifications of overfishing, ask themselves these questions every day.

They've understood for some time now how the oceanic food web operates, how for eons a natural balance existed among the predators and prey of the sea, with the apex predators—those big guns at the top, the tuna, sharks, swordfish, and such—maintaining order by regulating the number of the fish they prey on in the food chain levels below them, and with those prey fish acting as predators of the prey at the levels below *them*.

It was a wonderful, self-correcting system. When the numbers of a particular prey species decreased for some reason or other—disease, starvation, whatever—their predators would move to different, more abundant prey, allowing the suffering species to recover its health and its numbers. The predators also helped preserve the richness and strength of prey species by the Darwinian process of removing sick and weak fish from their populations. A fundamental principle of marine biology emerged from studying this process: More predators lead to greater diversity in the food web.

It was a beautiful, if cruel, system and all was in balance—until a new apex predator arrived, one more powerful than all the others.

Us.

Humans.

And in a biological blink of an eye, we began to wreak havoc upon this sublime system. Ransom Myers's study—the one revealing that 90 percent of the largest fish in the sea, the apex predators, had vanished since the 1950s—reflects the historic tendency of the fishing industry to go for the biggest fish first. The result has been a dramatic drop not only in the numbers of these fish, but also in their *sizes*. Check out these examples.

- In the 1950s, the average blue shark weighed 114 pounds; by the 1990s, that average was down to 48 pounds.

- The average weight of a bluefin tuna caught today in the Sea of Japan is half of what it was twenty-five years ago.

- In the 1950s, it was routine for New Englanders to haul in lobsters weighing twenty pounds (the world record is a forty-four-pounder); today, it's hard to find a five-pounder.

90%
OF THE LARGEST
FISH IN THE SEA,
**THE APEX
PREDATORS,**
— HAVE —
VANISHED
SINCE THE **1950s**

It's this kind of downsizing that Daniel Pauly is talking about when he says, "We're eating today what our grandparents used as bait."

Besides the effects on the sizes and quantities of the prime fish populations, the industry's onslaught upon the ocean's apex predators has caused a ripple of disruption throughout the food web, with smaller prey species, freed from the presence of predators, becoming the new top predators and wreaking havoc in what was previously a stable environment.

> **"WE'RE EATING TODAY** what **OUR GRANDPARENTS USED** as **BAIT."**

Think of what can happen when you take all the wolves out of a forest. The deer can multiply at an incredible rate and devour the shrubs and trees until they've effectively denuded the landscape—until there's no forest left.

It's the same way with the oceans.

A prime example of this is what happened along the United States' Mid-Atlantic coast during the past three decades when the populations of the eleven largest species of sharks in that region declined to levels of functional elimination. The result was an explosion in the abundance of one of those sharks' favorite foods—the cownose ray. Within a couple of years, more than 40 million cownoses were cruising the coastal waters from Long Island to Miami, with that number rising at a remarkable rate of 8 percent a year.

FISHING DOWN
the
FOOD CHAIN

Overfishing alters ocean ecosystems, leading to fewer and smaller fish over time. Historically people have often targeted the largest fish for food, like tuna, cod, and salmon. Once overfishing begins, fishermen must spend more time and resources searching for the same fish as they become scarcer, using increasingly powerful technology to find the last hidden fish. If overfishing isn't stopped, these fish eventually run out and overfishing expands to previously untargeted, usually smaller species, some of which were considered undesirable. As a result, the world catch is now primarily made up of small fish like pollock rather than large predators like grouper, and this shift to smaller and smaller species over time is called "fishing down the food chain."

(Fig. A)
SHARKS, KILLER WHALES are apex predators that feed on large fish in the food chain.

(Fig. B)
TUNA, SALMON are large fish that feed on schooling fish, squid, and shellfish.

(Fig. C)
SARDINES, POLLOCK, SQUID are small prey species that form large schools and feed on microscopic animals, plants, and leftovers.

(Fig. D)
ZOOPLANKTON are microscopic animals that eat tiny plants.

(Fig. E)
PHYTOPLANKTON make sugar using solar energy, just like plants on land, and form the base of the food web.

Fig. A

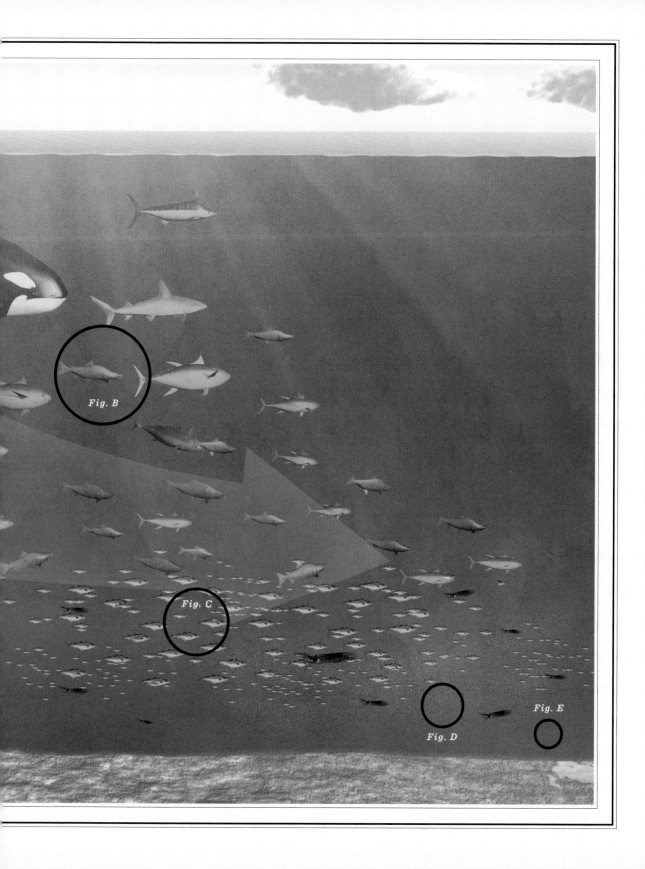

Fig. B

Fig. C

Fig. D

Fig. E

Why should we care about cownose rays? Well, the cownose's favorite foods are scallops, clams, and oysters. It didn't take long for those tens of millions of rays to completely ravage the century-old scallop fishery off the North Carolina coast. Once they were done with the scallops, the rays moved on to clams. If you've noticed clam chowder missing from the menu of your favorite eatery, this quite likely is the reason why. In the same way that the predator-prey relationship has been downsized as a result of overfishing, so too have the primary targets of the fishing industry. As one stock becomes fished out, a different—typically tinier, less desirable—species takes its place. After Canada's cod fishery collapsed in the 1990s, for example, blue whiting, which until then had been a second-rate species, suddenly became *the* fish to catch. In the Pacific Northwest, overfishing of Japanese sardines prompted a shift to the previously largely ignored Japanese anchovy.

At this RATE WE'LL EVENTUALLY BE HARVESTING NOTHING but BAITFISH and JELLYFISH.

A glaring aspect of this industry-wide shift toward catching smaller, lower-level species of fish is that the target market is no longer human consumption—instead, the vast majority of these fish will wind up being used as feed for farmed fish (again, we'll look at fish farming shortly). You can see this trend by just glancing at the current list of the global industry's ten most fished species—the anchoveta, a small anchovy primarily caught off the coast of Peru, almost all of which is ground into fish meal, tops the list by a wide margin.

This is what marine scientists mean when they talk about "fishing down the food web." They're not joking when they tell us that at this rate we'll eventually be harvesting nothing but baitfish and jellyfish. There is, in fact, already a huge market for jellyfish in China and Japan. *Los Angeles Times* reporter Kenneth Weiss, in an award-winning series called "Altered Oceans," describes an industrious Georgia fisherman who nailed down his own corner of the jellyfish market, sending fifty thousand pounds of the gelatinous blobs to buyers in Japan every week. One side effect—among many—of fishing down the food web is the depletion of food stocks for the wild fish themselves. When we begin netting the ocean's prey fish by the millions of tons, the predators left have nothing to eat. And so we wind up with the specter of dolphins starving to death because the sardines and anchovies they've eaten for ages are now being caught to feed caged farmed salmon and tuna.

You would think, at this point, that the fishing industry might step back, examine the landscape of destruction wrought by overfishing, and realize it's killing the very goose that lays its golden eggs.

Jellyfish being prepared for transport in Georgia (center) and China

You would think it would take a good hard look at its catch-all-you-can-and-move-on method and consider a different approach, one that might control the size and the composition of catches, as well as where and when nets are dropped and hooks are baited, to allow the fish and shellfish it targets to replenish their populations at sustainable levels—in other words, to *survive*.

That's what you would think, right?

But instead, like the oil industry, the industrial fisheries keep pushing on in the same fashion, driving their boats farther out into the oceans, into the deepest waters on Earth—those of the high seas themselves.

Let's turn now to the business of finding and fishing the last unharvested swaths of ocean left on Earth, and the exorbitant costs that come with that business—environmental costs, financial costs, and the highest cost of all: the price of human dignity and life.

WHAT YOU CAN DO

- **ASK FOR POLICIES THAT STOP BOTTOM TRAWLING AND DESTRUCTIVE FISHING.** Visit: www.environmentamerica.org/ action/ocean-conservation/stop-overfishing

- **DON'T BUY CORAL JEWELRY.** Visit: www.toopprecioustowear.org/

- **EAT AT RESTAURANTS THAT SERVE SUSTAINABLE FISH.** Visit: www.Fish2fork.com. Ask how your fish was caught and don't buy trawl-caught fish.

- **LEARN ABOUT THE WORLD'S OCEANS AND THE GOVERN-MENT OF THE SEAS.** Visit: www.mcbi.org/shining_sea/s2ss_ globe.htm

- **VISIT/VOLUNTEER AT A SEA TURTLE HOSPITAL, SUCH AS THE KAREN BEASLEY CENTER IN TOPSAIL ISLAND, NORTH CAROLINA, TO SEE IN PERSON THE EFFECTS OF DESTRUC-TIVE FISHING GEAR ON WILDLIFE.**

- **VISIT/VOLUNTEER AT A MARINE MAMMAL REHABILITATION CENTER, WHERE THE PATIENTS ARE OFTEN INJURED BY FISHING GEAR.**

- **WORK A STINT AS A BYCATCH OBSERVER ABOARD A FISHING VESSEL.** Visit: http://www.st.nmfs.noaa.gov/st4/nop/ observer_providers.html

CHAPTER FIVE

THE LAST
FRONTIER

IT'S A WELL-KNOWN FACT AMONG MARINE

scientists that we have better maps of the surfaces of Mars and the Moon than we do of the deepest reaches of our oceans. Most of us know that the oceans occupy some 71 percent of our planet's surface, as I stated early in this book. But few realize that the *volume* of the oceans makes up 99 percent of Earth's living space.

French illustration from 1445 of Alexander the Great in a diving bell

Or that the average depth of the high seas is roughly two and a half miles.

Or that the ocean's deepest point, a spot called the Challenger Deep in the western Pacific's Mariana Trench, is more than thirty-six thousand feet down—more than six miles, well over a mile deeper than Mount Everest is tall.

Or, to return to this chapter's opening sentence, that less than 5 percent of the world's ocean floor has been explored. This is why deep-sea explorers, scientists, and, yes, fishermen use epithets like "The Last Frontier" and "The Last Great Wilderness" when referring to the deepest, darkest, bone-chillingly frigid depths of the planet's oceans, where the pressure is high enough to crush an automobile.

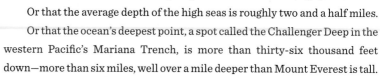

FOR CENTURIES EVEN THE most **LEARNED SCIENTISTS ASSUMED** that **NO LIFE-FORM COULD SURVIVE** at the **GREATEST DEPTHS** of the **OCEANS.**

For centuries even the most learned scientists assumed that no life-form could survive at the greatest depths of the oceans. That notion prevailed until a four-year, around-the-world expedition took place in the mid-1880s. A British steam-assisted sailing ship called the HMS *Challenger* (a two-hundred-foot warship converted for scientific purposes) sounded the oceans' floors to depths beyond twenty-six thousand feet and, using miles of hemp rope and piano wire attached to primitive, refrigerator-size "sampling trawls" made of cloth and wood, hauled up hundreds of muddy loads from the bottom of every ocean on the planet and wound up with more than 4,700 new species of life, ranging from dozens of varieties of deep-sea sponges, sea urchins, tube worms, and plankton to otherworldly species of lobsters, clams, shrimp, sea spiders, and even fish. With that, the theories of a lifeless sea bottom were put to rest.

But no human had seen these species alive, in their native habitats. Most of the specimens pulled up by the *Challenger*'s crew were dead upon arrival, killed by the pressure changes they underwent as

Specimen jar from HMS *Challenger*

Scientific staff, crew, and visitors aboard HMS *Challenger*, late nineteenth century

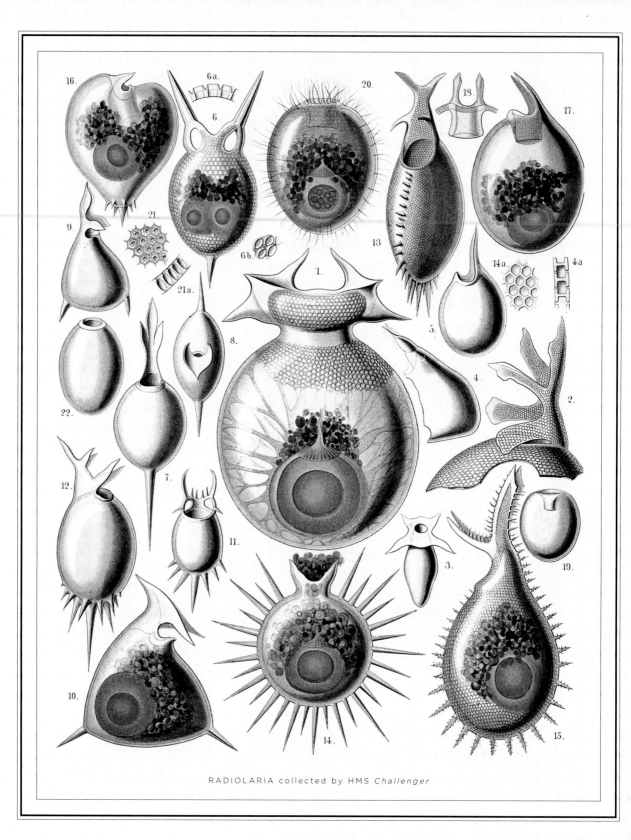

RADIOLARIA collected by HMS *Challenger*

Top left: OTIS BARTON in his bathysphere, 1930; *top right:* DR. WILLIAM BEEBE and OTIS BARTON being lowered in a bathysphere, 1943 *bottom left:* exterior of the bathyscaphe TRIESTE; *center:* NAVY LT. DON WALSH; *right:* explorer AUGUSTE PICCARD and his son JACQUES with the bathyscaphe TRIESTE, Italy

they were hauled to the surface. By the 1930s explorers had penetrated the depths in primitive, ball-shaped "bathyspheres," hoping to see some of this deep-sea life for themselves.

First they were dropped down a quarter mile, then a half, and so on, until finally, in 1960, a pair of deep-sea scientists—a Swiss oceanographer named Jacques Piccard and a US Navy lieutenant named Don Walsh—were lowered more than six miles down, in a bathyscaphe called the *Trieste*, to the bottom of the Challenger Deep. There, through two six-inch-thick portholes and with the illumination of pressure-proof quartz lightbulbs mounted on the outside of the vehicle, Piccard and Walsh actually saw a small fish flit by, as well as a shrimp and, on the sandy sea bottom, the fresh tracks of crawling sea cucumbers.

THE
MARIANA TRENCH

The deepest part of the world's oceans, the Mariana Trench is located in the western Pacific Ocean, to the east of the Mariana Islands, near Japan. It was created by ocean-to-ocean subduction, a phenomenon in which a tectonic plate topped by oceanic crust is pushed beneath another plate topped by oceanic crust.

The Mariana Trench is 36,201 feet (11,033 meters) deep, 1,580 miles (2,542 kilometers) long, and 43 miles (69 kilometers) wide.

MOUNT EVEREST
(Fig. A)

The Mariana Trench is so deep that Mount Everest, at 29,029 feet (8,848 meters), would fit inside the deepest part of the trench with 7,172 feet (2,186 meters) of water above it.

DEEP-SEA CREATURES

DUMBO OCTOPUS *(Fig. B)*
HUMPBACK ANGLERFISH *(Fig. C)*

THE CHALLENGER DEEP
(Fig. D)

THE DEEPEST POINT of the Mariana Trench is called the Challenger Deep, named after the British exploration vessel HMS *Challenger II*, and it is located 210 miles southwest of Guam. This depth was reached in 1960 by the *Trieste*, a manned submersible owned by the US Navy.

(Fig. E)

THE PRESSURE at the deepest part of the Mariana Trench is more than eight tons per square inch.

Source: www.marianatrench.com

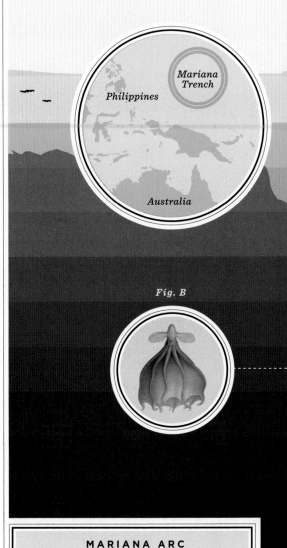

Philippines

Mariana Trench

Australia

Fig. B

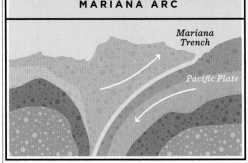

MARIANA ARC

Mariana Trench

Pacific Plate

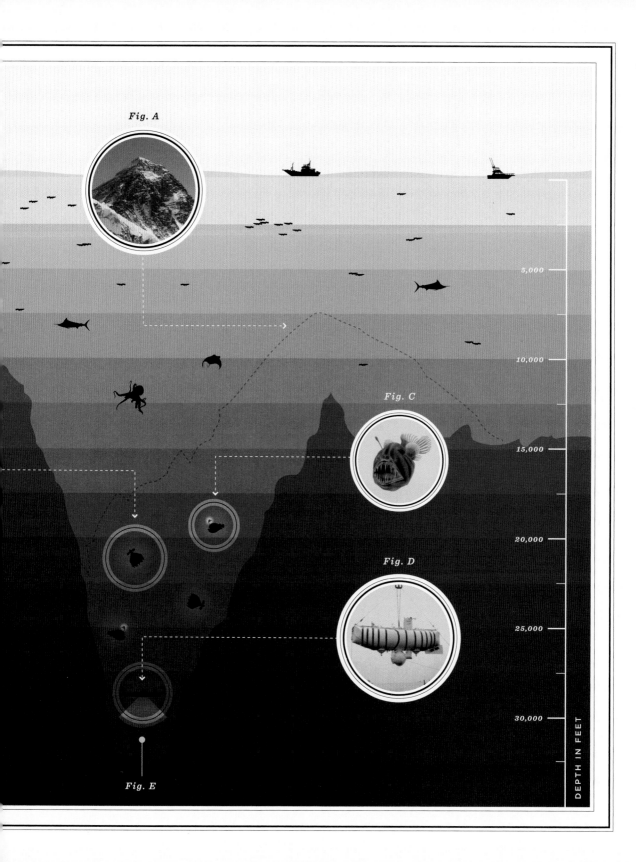

Fig. A

Fig. C

Fig. D

Fig. E

5,000

10,000

15,000

20,000

25,000

30,000

DEPTH IN FEET

**"THE DEEP"
BEGINS AT
1,300
FEET (¼ MILE)**

So much excitement was aroused by the *Trieste*'s discovery that it was as if someone had found little green men on the Moon. Yes, there *was* life down there in the abyss, and plenty of it.

Around the time of the *Trieste*'s historic descent, some of the world's fleet of industrial trawlers were already leaving the relatively shallow and increasingly crowded waters of the inner continental shelves and pushing out toward their far edges, where the fairly flat seafloor began sloping downward to create the vast, lightless abyss of the high seas.

Scientists generally concur that what's called "the deep" begins at 1,300 feet—a quarter mile. The first fishermen to drop their nets that far were the Soviets. At about the same time that the Beatles were invading America in the mid-'60s, deepwater Soviet trawlers, along with refitted research vessels from other Eastern bloc nations—primarily Poland and East Germany—were already probing the slopes that fell away from the outer continental flanks in the Atlantic and the Pacific.

The Soviets quickly found that dragging their nets over the rough ground of those rocky slopes shredded them to pieces. This prompted them to build the first crude rollers and rockhoppers, as described earlier. As they dropped their nets deeper, they came upon odd, exotic species of fish—roundnose grenadier, black scabbardfish, Baird's smooth-head, rabbitfish, scorpion fish, Greenland halibut—some of which were commercially feasible (that is, edible),

THE LOWER the NETS WERE DROPPED, THE SPARSER the CATCHES BECAME.

but most of which were not. The halibut was a keeper because it tasted like, well, halibut. And the grenadier, which tasted like cod, was marketable as well.

But the lower the nets were dropped, the sparser the catches became. Yes, there was life down there in the deep, but most of that life was of more interest to scientists than to commercial fisheries. Those Soviet ships were seeking practical places to drop their nets—undersea habitats dense enough with sea life to warrant dragging the bottom, and not so deep that trawling the bottom was unfeasible.

They finally found what they were looking for in the form of seamounts.

SEAMOUNTS ARE JUST WHAT THEY SOUND LIKE—SUBMERGED mountains thrusting upward from the seafloor. When they break the sea's surface, these mounts are islands, like those of Hawaii or the Galápagos or the Azores. Only the ones that are completely submerged are considered seamounts.

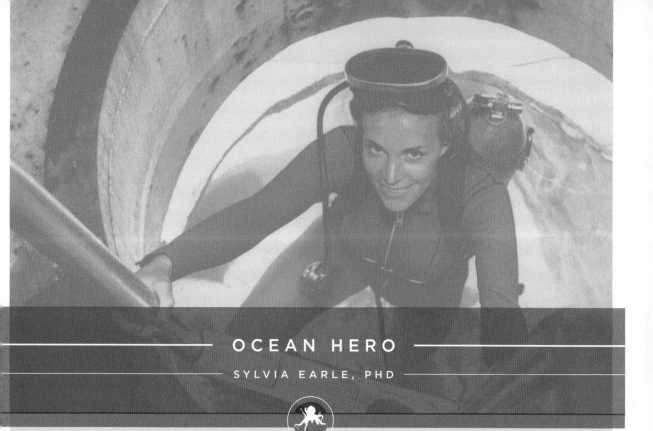

OCEAN HERO

SYLVIA EARLE, PHD

They don't call Sylvia Earle "Her Deepness" for nothing. She is an intrepid explorer who has led sixty expeditions, logging more than six thousand hours underwater. She holds the women's world record for solo diving, descending to an astonishing depth of 1,000 meters (3,300 feet).

And as founder of the Mission Blue Foundation and chair of the Advisory Council for the Harte Research Institute for Gulf of Mexico Studies, Dr. Earle is a leading voice for ocean conservation. She was named *Time* magazine's first "Hero for the Planet" in 1998.

As the first female chief scientist of the US National Oceanic and Atmospheric Administration, Dr. Earle played a crucial role in establishing marine protected areas, including more than 140,000 square miles of ocean in the Papahānaumokuākea Marine National Monument in Hawaii—an area larger than all of America's national parks combined. Her Mission Blue Foundation combines the forces of the National Geographic Society, where Dr. Earle is an Explorer in Residence, with governments and businesses such as Google to restore the health and productivity of the oceans.

Dr. Earle likes to call marine protected areas "hope spots"—because she knows firsthand that underwater ecosystems that are released from the intense pressures of fishing and other human activities will thrive. She travels the world to tell stories about the oceans and inspires people to help protect our blue planet. I highly recommend her books, including *Sea Change: A Message of the Oceans* and, most recently, *Ocean: An Illustrated Atlas*, with Linda K. Glover.

SEAMOUNTS

Far beneath the ocean waves, whole submerged mountain chains, called seamounts, have yet to be explored. Seamounts were mostly ignored by scientists until the 1980s, when fisherman began pulling up huge catches of orange roughy from some in the southern Pacific. Until then, seamounts were thought to be barren and scientifically uninteresting. We have only just begun to understand their ecological significance.

As marine scientist Tony Koslow details in his meticulous book, *The Silent Deep: The Discovery, Ecology and Conservation of the Deep Sea*, seamounts are now considered equivalent to the Galápagos Islands—isolated ecosystems that are home to many species found nowhere else.

These underwater mountains can rise as high as about 13,000 feet (4,000 meters) above the seafloor, nearly as tall as the highest peaks in the Rocky Mountains in the western United States. They are home to an incredible variety of marine life that scientists have just started to quantify. Only a thousand of the estimated thirty to fifty thousand seamounts in the Pacific have even been named.

But like terrestrial mountains that are cut apart by strip mining or have their tops removed, seamounts can be destroyed by industrial activity. Trawling for seafood species such as orange roughy can destroy the unique ecology of the seamount before it's even been discovered.

- *(Fig. A)* Only a small percentage of seamounts have been mapped, but scientists estimate that the Pacific Ocean alone contains thirty to fifty thousand seamounts above 3,280 feet (1,000 meters) tall. If you add smaller seamounts, the number jumps to 600,000 to 1.5 million seamounts. The Pacific's volcanic Ring of Fire is the most likely place to find large seamounts.

- Seamounts are extinct volcanoes rising abruptly from the ocean floor. If they break the water's surface, they become volcanic islands like Hawaii. The tallest seamounts can top 13,000 feet (4,000 meters) and still be 3,280 feet (1,000 meters) or more underwater.

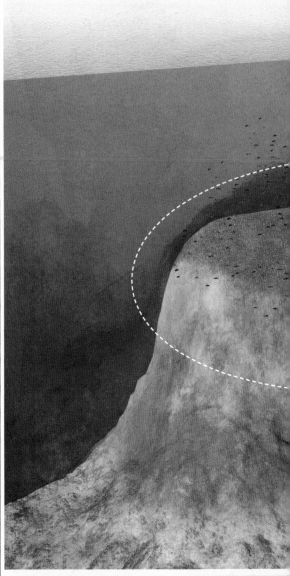

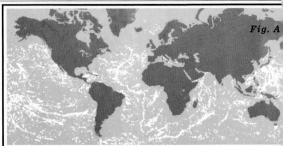

Fig. A

Ocean currents

Up to
3,280 feet

13,000 feet

EXTRAORDINARY BIODIVERSITY is found around seamounts.

Because of the volatility of the still volcanically active ocean floor regions, it's hard to get a firm count of the number of seamounts on the planet. Scientists posit that there are about nine thousand large, well-defined seamounts in the Pacific, with another three thousand in the Atlantic. These are only a small fraction of all seamounts worldwide, which some estimates suggest may exceed six hundred thousand. Relatively few have been explored, and only about a thousand have been named.

To marine scientists, seamounts are rich, fascinating objects for research and study. To the global fishing industry, they were a godsend once the Soviets discovered how abundant fish were on these undersea mountains, particularly in their upper reaches.

While most of the deep-sea floor is blanketed with mud, seamounts, because they rise into the paths of strong ocean currents, are swept clean of mud and sediment, allowing rich gardens of corals, sea fans, and sponges to grow, especially near the summits. These gardens, which filter and feed on the organic matter in those currents, attract fish and other sea life by providing both refuge and food.

Even more important, as far as the fishing industry is concerned, is that upwelling (the rising of cold, nutrient-rich currents from the deep) tends to occur around seamount summits, attracting great swarms of plankton, which attract great swarms of small fish, which attract great swarms of larger fish—which is what those industrial trawlers are after.

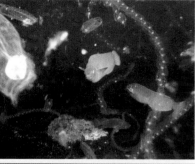

The oceans' predators have long known the seamounts are there. Schools of tuna use them as refueling stops during their transoceanic migrations. Albatrosses will fly hundreds, even thousands of miles to gorge themselves on the fish and squid circling the peaks of these undersea mountains. If the high seas can be likened to vast deserts, then seamounts are the oceans' oases.

The first big breakthrough for the high-seas fishing industry came in 1969, when a Soviet trawler discovered massive concentrations of fish called armorheads around a seamount formation northwest of Hawaii. The next year, the Japanese had joined the deepwater hunt in the Pacific, and in a matter of months, both Soviet and Japanese trawlers were dropping their nets a mile down, onto the slopes of those undersea ridges, and hauling up more than thirty-four thousand tons of armorheads (which look like snapper) in one year. That particular boom lasted less than a decade before crashing as suddenly as it started, with the annual take plummeting to a paltry three thousand tons in 1977.

While they might have been curious about why that boom so rapidly became a bust, the Soviet and Japanese fishermen didn't waste time pondering such questions. They were eager to move on to the next seamount—as were trawlers from Australia, New Zealand, China, the United States, Great Britain, Spain, Norway, and the rest of the world's industrial fishing powers, which were all now leaving behind their own thinned-out coastal waters to fill their nets in the deep waters of the high seas.

TRAWLERS
DROPPING THEIR
NETS A MILE DOWN
HAUL UP
— MORE THAN —
34,000
• TONS •
OF ARMORHEADS
IN ONE YEAR

FREEDIVING

MARTIN ŠTĚPÁNEK

Martin Štěpánek is one of the world's stars in the emerging sport of freediving. Unaided by scuba tanks, he has broken several world records for depth and length of time underwater, including the record for holding one's breath: eight minutes and six seconds. With a view of the underwater world unencumbered by diving equipment, Štěpánek has a unique perspective on our changing oceans. He spoke to Oceana's Suzannah Evans.

SE: What makes you want to do free-diving versus scuba diving?

MS: I enjoy scuba diving as well; don't get me wrong. I just find a lot more freedom in freediving. To me, it's the purest way of connecting with the ocean because you don't wear any extra equipment that separates you from the environment. Therefore the experience you're having out of it is much more pure and more intense. Also, the animals you encounter on a freedive allow you to get much closer to them because they are not afraid of you—they're thinking you're one of them; they respect you much more.

SE: While you've been diving, have you noticed any changes in what you're seeing over the years? What is it that you see under the water that you really want to preserve for the future?

MS: The changes are incredible. It's heartbreaking and really sad. The locations that I was diving ten years ago are not the same when I am diving them now. There are so many fewer fish, and the coral reef looks totally different. It's heartbreaking, really. Unfortunately, this applies everywhere I go. I dive all around the world, and it's not just one spot. I live in south Florida, but I travel quite a bit. This is something that I've observed pretty much everywhere.

In my backyard, there's a local beach. That's where we used to go freedive quite often, and we saw a beautiful reef with a lot of fish in it. What you see now is just the reef. If there're any fish on it, they're very skittish, very small. You don't see groupers anymore. There used to be a lot of groupers. You don't see snappers there either, and there used to be a lot of snappers. It's all gone.

The **LAST GREAT**

WILDERNESS

The next deepwater boom was the one that first triggered an alarm in terms of the environmental price tag attached to these high-seas fishing bonanzas.

This time it was a fish called a slimehead. Never heard of it? How about the more appetizing name the industry gave this creature once it realized the tremendous market that was waiting for it?

Orange roughy.

Now, there's a catchy name, one that would stand out on fancy fish house menus. Which it did, beginning in the early 1980s, when the Soviets, along with the New Zealanders, began swarming a range of underwater canyons and mountain peaks called the Chatham Rise, east of New Zealand. The Australians jumped in the game at about the same time by trawling the slopes of a seamount near Tasmania

called Saint Helen's Hill, all of them seeking this suddenly prized fish that could be found roughly a half mile below sea level.

There was nothing particularly extraordinary about this species they called orange roughy. Like so many deep-sea fish, it's a pretty ugly creature—roundish, typically about a foot long, with large owl eyes, a perpetual frown, and a big, bony head. Its most striking characteristic—and the inspiration for its market name—is the bright orange shade of its scales.

Its bland white flesh is essentially tasteless, but the highbrow restaurant industry had enormous success turning orange roughy into the "it" fish of the late 1980s and early '90s. Any chef with some skill and imagination could take the blank palette of an orange roughy fillet and turn it into a high-priced special of the day. Grilled lemon-lime herb orange roughy. Orange roughy Malienne. Pineapple-glazed orange roughy. Orange roughy amandine. The possibilities were endless.

Any of us over the age of, say, thirty-five remembers the orange roughy craze. It wasn't that long ago. The industrial fishing industry certainly remembers it. At its peak in the early 1990s, the global industry netted more than ninety-one thousand tons of roughy in a single year. The Australians' onshore freezing facilities were so overwhelmed that truckloads of the fish had to be driven to a landfill and unceremoniously dumped.

The **HIGHBROW RESTAURANT INDUSTRY** had **ENORMOUS SUCCESS TURNING ORANGE ROUGHY** into the **"IT" FISH** of the **LATE 1980S** and **EARLY '90S.**

ORANGE ROUGHY

Hoplostethus atlanticus

Also known as slimeheads, red roughy, or deep sea perch

| 1" | 2" | 3" | 4" | 5" | 6" | 7" |

NOMENCLATURE

(Fig. A)

Orange roughy were known as slimeheads and were considered trash fish until someone decided they were marketable and rebranded them.

REPRODUCTION

(Fig. B)

They spawn once a year in dense gatherings. The fish may travel as far as 125 miles (200 kilometers) to join the spawning party. Sexual maturity is reached between the ages of twenty-three and forty years. The biggest orange roughy are 2.5 feet long (about 75 centimeters).

TOTAL LIFE SPAN

More than one hundred years. Oldest orange roughy was verified to be 149 years old.

HABITAT

(Fig. C)

Orange roughy principally inhabit waters between 1,600 and 5,000 feet (500 and 1500 meters) at temperatures of 39°F to 45°F (4° to 7°C) over seamounts, steep continental slopes, and oceanic ridges.

SEAFOOD

Orange roughy is caught using weighted bottom trawl nets that often crush deep sea corals and other marine life. Orange roughy served in the United States is imported from New Zealand, Australia, China, Thailand, and other countries.

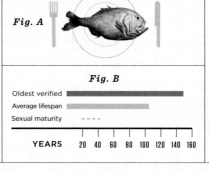

Fig. A

Fig. B

Oldest verified

Average lifespan

Sexual maturity   - - - -

YEARS   20 40 60 80 100 120 140 160

Fig. C

1,600 F

5,000 F

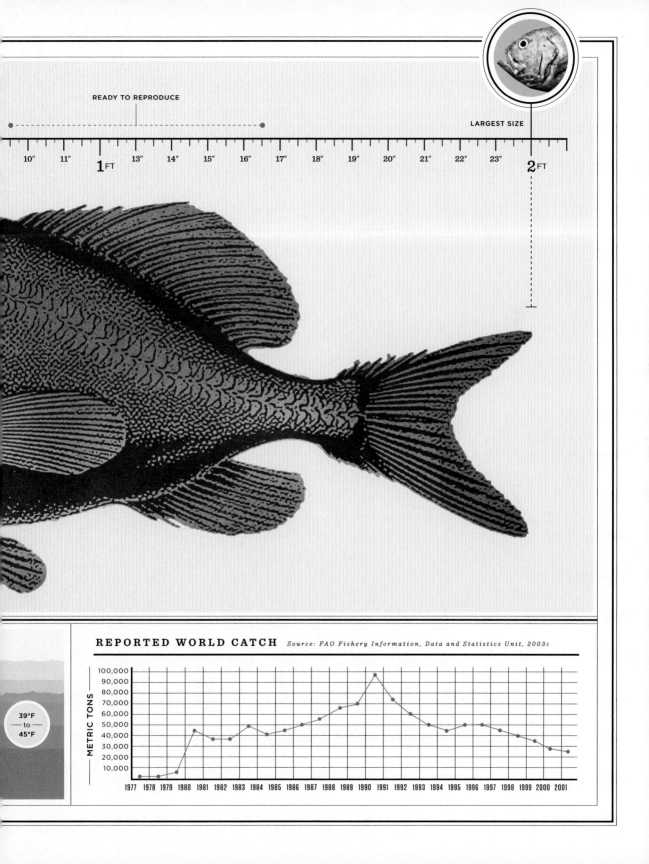

READY TO REPRODUCE

LARGEST SIZE

10" 11" 1FT 13" 14" 15" 16" 17" 18" 19" 20" 21" 22" 23" 2FT

39°F
— to —
45°F

REPORTED WORLD CATCH *Source: FAO Fishery Information, Data and Statistics Unit, 2003c*

METRIC TONS

100,000
90,000
80,000
70,000
60,000
50,000
40,000
30,000
20,000
10,000

1977 1978 1979 1980 1981 1982 1983 1984 1985 1986 1987 1988 1989 1990 1991 1992 1993 1994 1995 1996 1997 1998 1999 2000 2001

A decade later, by the early 2000s, the orange roughy boom, like the armorhead boom before it, went bust. The annual catch plummeted to less than fourteen thousand tons. Once again, the industry responded by shrugging its collective shoulders and moving on to probe the high seas for the next big thing.

But this time, in the trawlers' wake came the scientists, who were interested not only in the effects of the fishing industry on the deep-sea species of fish they were netting, but also in the effects of the trawling on the seamounts themselves. They wanted to know what it was doing to the cold-water corals and other deepwater fauna that provide the habitat for these delicate, slow-growing fish.

The scientists, after decades of study, already knew about the fragility of deepwater fish themselves, and of their habitat. They had learned that at the extremely cold temperatures and extremely high water pressures found in the great depths of the high seas, everything about the life-forms is slowed down. The greater the depth, the more otherworldly the life-forms become: humpbacked sharks with eyes that glow like headlights, tripod fish that stand on their fins like circus clowns walking on stilts, single-celled protozoans twice the size of a silver dollar. To the scientists, every one of these deep-sea creatures is worth a lifetime of study. But to the commercial fishing industry, the only feature that matters is the creatures' marketability. They couldn't care less that the average life span of an orange roughy is close to a century. That some roughy live as long as 130 years or more. That leafscale gulper sharks live to age seventy. That the average Baird's smooth-head's life span is thirty-eight years. Or that all of these slow-growing, long-lived fish reach sexual maturity (the age at which they become able to reproduce) later than humans do. Some orange roughy and grenadiers, for example, can't reproduce until age forty.

IN THE GREAT DEPTHS, EVERYTHING about the **LIFE-FORMS IS SLOWED DOWN. THE GREATER THE DEPTH,** the more **OTHERWORLDLY THE LIFE-FORMS BECOME.**

I know it may sound wonkish to cite this list of statistics, but think about what these numbers mean in terms of the impact overfishing has on species that take so long to replace themselves. Remember, truly sustainable fishing is based on not removing the target species' population at a faster rate than it can reproduce itself. When you pull out of the ocean a fish whose typical life span is longer than that of us humans and that, even when left alone, must wait decades before it is able to reproduce, it's easy to see the devastating impact that fishing it has not only on the current population, but also on the genetic characteristics of its future generations—if there are any.

Remotely operated underwater vehicle (ROV) Little Hercules during one of its first dives in Indonesia

To the SCIENTISTS, EVERY ONE of THESE DEEP-SEA CREATURES is WORTH a LIFETIME of STUDY....

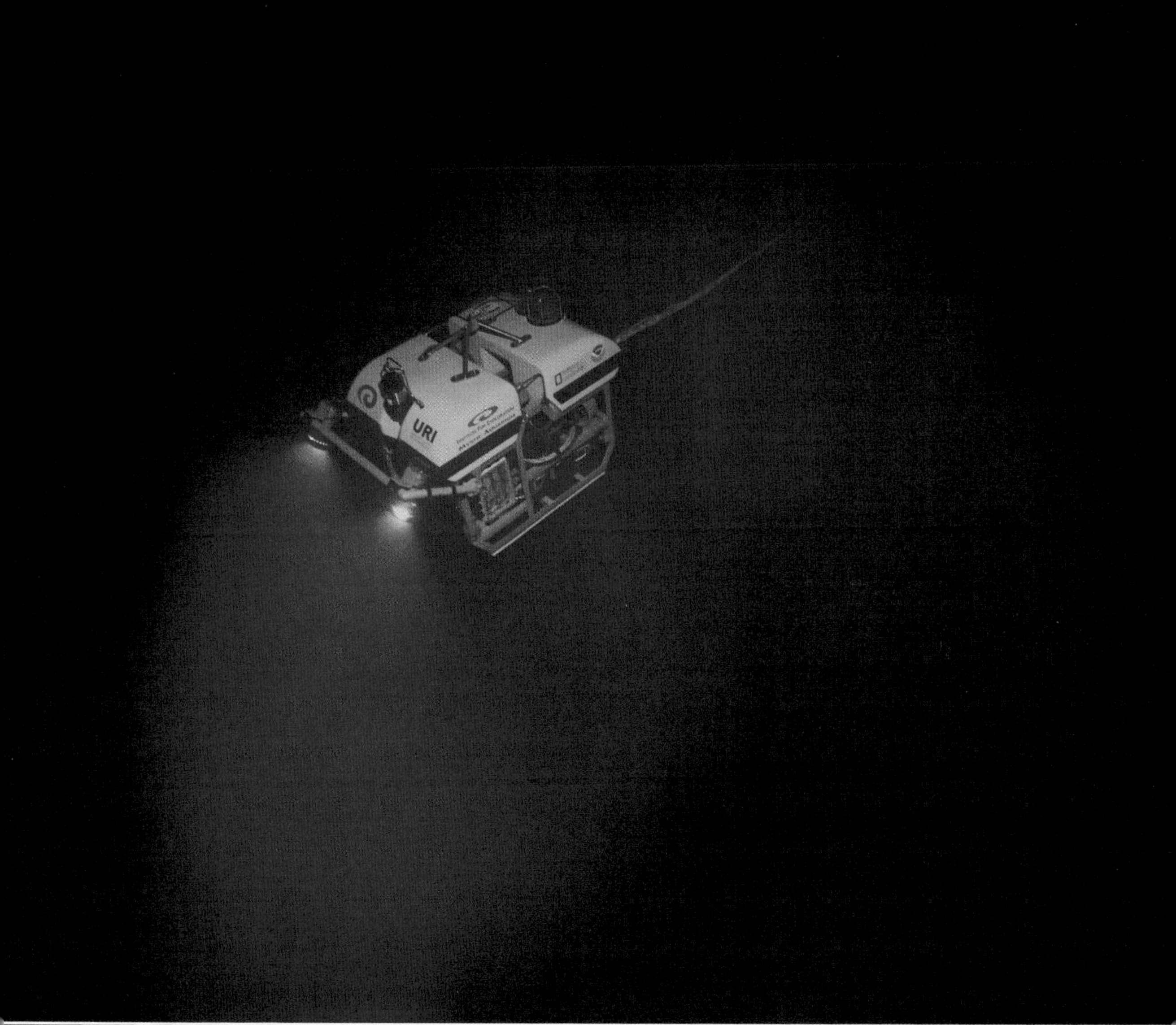

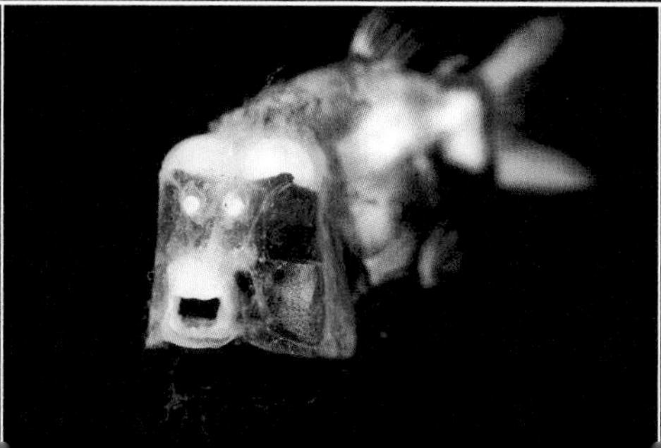

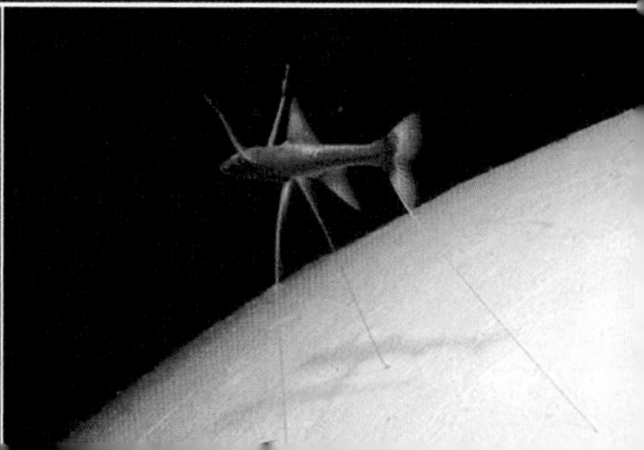

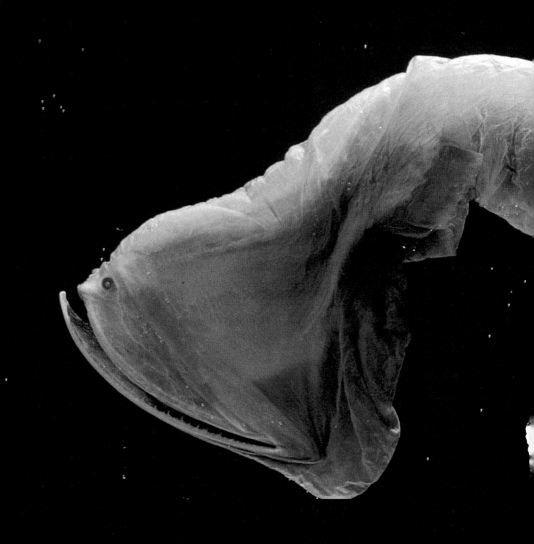

To the **FISHING INDUSTRY**, the **ONLY FEATURE** that **MATTER'S** is the **CREATURES'** MARKETABILITY.

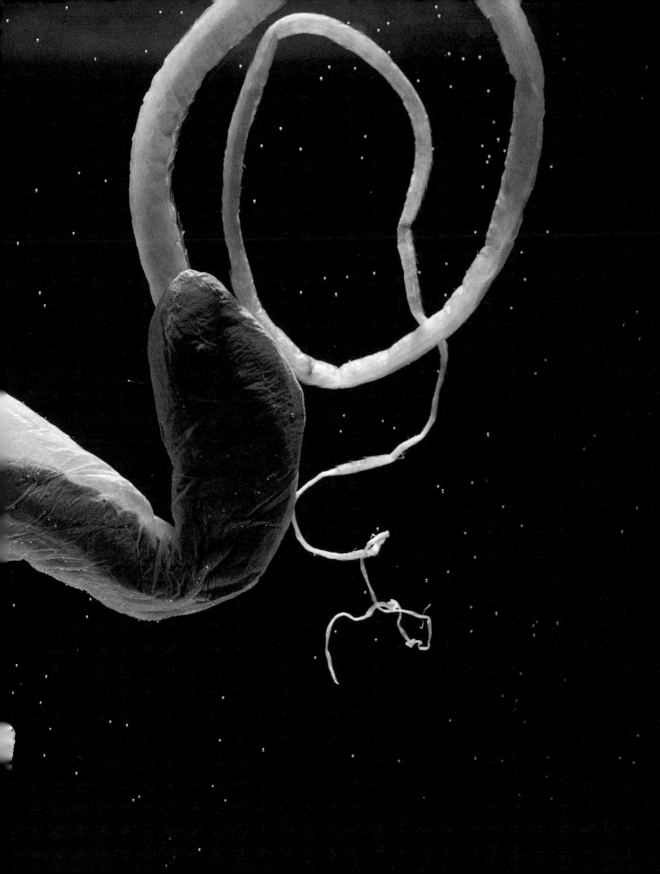

This is why sustainable fishing of deepwater species is almost impossible. It's why those first deepwater booms went bust so quickly and so dramatically. And why it will take decades before those populations of armorheads and orange roughy can begin to rebuild—if indeed they are able to.

═══════════

NONE OF WHICH SURPRISED THE SCIENTISTS WHO CAME IN to study those seamounts after the trawlers had left. What *did* surprise them—what shocked as well as sickened them—was the massive extent of the damage the trawlers' nets had done to the slopes and tops of those seamounts.

What had once been undersea gardens of Eden now resembled the ruins of a bombed city. Seamount slopes once blanketed with lush meadows of colorful corals and waving sea fans and with beds of glass sponges as delicate as their name implies were now as bare as a West Virginia mountainside strip mine.

Wide swaths of rubble sliced through forests of cold-water coral like roadways under construction, tracing the paths where the nets' heavy steel doors and rollers and rockhoppers had made their relentless passes.

COLD-WATER CORALS are among the **SLOWEST-GROWING LIFE-FORMS** on the **PLANET. THEY'RE OFTEN COMPARED** to **CALIFORNIA'S FABLED REDWOODS,** for **BOTH THEIR SIZE** and **THEIR AGE.**

This was heartbreaking stuff, especially the damage to the corals, which are so different from the more familiar shallow-water tropical corals enjoyed by vacationing snorkelers.

Like the slow-growing deepwater fish that feed and hide among them, cold-water corals, which abound in the mile-or-more depths where man once assumed nothing could live, are among the slowest-growing life-forms on the planet. They're often compared to California's fabled redwoods, for both their size and their age. Carbon dating has found samples of dead cold-water corals that grew as long as twenty thousand years ago.

Some living deepwater corals are as much as a few thousand years old. Most are at least hundreds of years old. The fact that they grow at a glacial rate as slow as one-seventh of

A FAMILY TRADITION
PHILIPPE COUSTEAU JR.

My grandfather, Jacques Cousteau, was a global icon . . . but to me he was Papa Grand, the nickname my sister, Alexandra, and I had given him.

For many years our routine was the same; we would head to dinner at a small Japanese restaurant in midtown Manhattan. It was his favorite and quickly became mine because I knew that each time we met, I would learn something new.

Dinner started off as usual—he would select a wine and we would get a very small taste, in order to "establish a palate." Then he would order food and launch into a nostalgic adventure exploring the various fascinating memories that came to his mind at the moment. While they all were fantastic and magical, they always proved to have a lesson, though not the lesson that many might think.

While people often assume that ocean issues dominated our discussion, that was rarely the direct topic of conversation. Instead, my grandfather spoke of many different things, such as the rights of women in developing countries and how critical they are to true sustainable development, climate change, deforestation, overpopulation, and more. He always spoke of the interconnectedness of these issues.

He believed that every child deserved to inherit a world where they could walk on green grass while drinking fresh water, standing under a blue sky, and breathing clean air. He spoke often of his conviction that no one should be able to take away that fundamental right for any reason. That conviction became my own, and his urgency became mine.

Today, in a society dominated by partisan social and political rhetoric, I remember his as a voice that inspired me and countless others to understand that each and every one of us, no matter who we are and no matter what we do, has a fundamental responsibility. And that responsibility is to give our children a world that is safer, healthier, cleaner, and more just than that which we inherited.

CORAL caught by a trawler in the Tasman Sea, 2005

FOR EVERY

2.25 TONS

OF ROUGHY CAUGHT

1 TON

—— OF ——

COLD-WATER CORAL
WAS PULLED FROM
THE TRAWLERS' NETS

an inch a year makes it all the more breathtaking to behold a specimen ten feet tall, of which there are more than a few.

It also makes it all the more horrific to realize that the net of a trawler can undo in one swipe what nature took all those hundreds or thousands of years to create. By moving into the high seas, the commercial fishing industry has now created a phenomenon that would have been unthinkable a generation ago and is a nightmare to any sea lover—coral bycatch.

One study of the Australian orange roughy fishery at the height of its "boom" period found that for every two and a quarter tons of roughy caught, one ton of cold-water coral was pulled from the trawlers' nets. A series of photographs obtained by Greenpeace in New Zealand showed crewmen on a deepwater trawler untangling a massive chunk of coral from a net—a chunk taller than a man and more than five hundred years old. They had to use a shipboard crane to lift it and drop it back into the sea.

We're not talking just about the loss of something spectacularly beautiful here, although the respected marine biologist Callum Roberts, in his book *The Unnatural History of the Sea*, points out that for several decades now, deepwater trawlers have been methodically destroying undersea wonderlands of nature that would be treasured as national parks if they were on land. We're "leveling unknown Yellowstone Parks," Roberts writes.

Besides the loss of sheer beauty and the loss of the slow-growing sea life and habitat destroyed on these fished-out seamounts—fish and habitat that will take generations to recover, if they can at all—scientists have determined that this

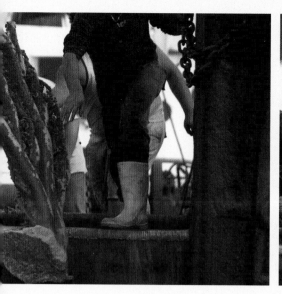

destruction is also robbing mankind of possible medical breakthroughs that might have been found in those undersea forests.

Studies done on undamaged deepwater seamounts have found among the cold-water corals and sponges and their associated ecosystems possible sources of medical treatments for diseases such as cancer, arthritis, and Alzheimer's. In much the same way that invaluable new medicines that might be developed from the flora and fauna of South America's thickest jungles are being wiped out by the clear-cutting, digging, and drilling the timber and extractive industries are doing in those Amazonian forests, we're also seeing that opportunities for finding medical miracles in the depths of the high seas are being lost to industrial trawlers and their nets.

I don't want to sound like a Cassandra here, seeing nothing but doom all around us. There's plenty of hope, plenty that can be done to change things for the better. We've already covered some of the things we can do about the issues we've looked at so far, and we'll cover much more in the pages to come. But before we can act to initiate change, we need to know just what the problems are, and how deep and far their tentacles reach.

The tentacles of this particular problem—the damage being done hundreds or thousands of miles out to sea, as well as within the territorial boundaries of developing nations—are long, twisted, and almost always beyond the reach of the law. (We'll talk about international law and the high seas shortly.) If we follow those tentacles back to their roots, we wind up onshore again, in the halls of the governments of the world's richest nations, which directly finance much of this destruction by giving money to the fishing industry in the form of grants called subsidies. Let's look next at exactly where those tentacles lead.

WHAT YOU CAN DO

- **SUPPORT THE END OF HIGH SEAS BOTTOM TRAWLING.**
  Visit: www.savethehighseas.org/action.cfm

- **AVOID EATING "DEEP SEA" FISH, SUCH AS ORANGE ROUGHY; GET A SEAFOOD GUIDE AT:**
  www.blueocean.org/fishphone

- **EXPLORE HIGH SEAS AREAS.**
  Visit: www.mcbi.org/what/hsbooklet.htm

- **FOLLOW THE EXPLORATIONS OF NOAA'S DEEP SEA EXPLORERS.** Visit: http://oceanexplorer.noaa.gov/

- **LEARN MORE ABOUT THE CREATURES THAT LIVE IN THE DEEP SEA BY READING CLAIRE NOUVIAN'S FASCINATING BOOK *THE DEEP*.**

- **CONTACT YOUR SENATORS AND REPRESENTATIVES AND TELL THEM TO SUPPORT MORE FUNDING FOR DEEP-SEA RESEARCH AND EXPLORATION.**

CHAPTER SIX

CONVENIENCE

ROBERT KENNEDY JR., WHO'S ONE OF MY

environmental heroes, made this wonderful remark several years ago: "You show me a polluter," he said, "and I'll show you a subsidy."

He could just as well have substituted "deepwater trawler" for "polluter."

If we backtrack for a moment to those Soviet boats that were virtually alone out there on the high seas back in the mid-1960s, a question arises: "Why them, and why *just* them?"

The answer lies in how prohibitively expensive it is to fish that far out to sea, and in the fact that, at the time, the Soviet fishing industry was owned and financed by the strongest communist government on Earth. While boats from capitalist nations had to either bankroll themselves or find investors for such a high-priced venture— neither of which was easy to do at that time—the Soviet fleet was financed by the leaders in Moscow, who were eager and able to send fishermen to explore what looked like a possible gold mine out there in the high seas.

When they turned out to be right and word of their success spread, among the first nations to join them was Japan, probably the most seafood-oriented culture on the planet, and one that was replete with private investors wealthy enough to cover the enormous expenses of long-distance deepwater fishing expeditions. New Zealand and Australia were also able to jump into the deep-sea game fairly early thanks to sheer geographic luck—they happened to have a couple of the world's most financially promising seamounts located virtually in their oceanic front yards, so their boats didn't have to go far to cash in.

By the turn of this century—the year 2000—the high seas had become much more crowded, with the "big boys" in the fishing industry controlling the game. Vessels flagged to eleven of the world's most-developed fishing nations—most notably Spain, Norway, Portugal, and Russia—accounted for more than 90 percent of the reported high-seas bottom-trawl catch at that time, virtually cornering a global seafood market that had experienced a huge surge during the previous decade.

> ## "YOU SHOW ME a POLLUTER and I'LL SHOW YOU A SUBSIDY."
> — ROBERT KENNEDY JR. —

Part of this surge was due to a steady rise in the world's population, which, as I noted earlier, still shows no sign of slowing down.

And part was due to increased attention to health by consumers in nations like the United States. People were turning to fish rather than beef or poultry for the protein in their diets.

This rising demand for seafood was a primary factor in an explosion in the size of the world's industrial fishing fleet between 1970 and 1990—precisely the same

time period during which the gold rush on the high seas developed. During those two decades, the number of fishing vessels with a hold for storing fish more than doubled, from 585,000 to 1.2 million, according to the FAO. That's an average of more than thirty thousand new ships joining the world's fleet each year. Because of the dwindling sizes of the fish catches in their own national waters, many of these vessels were outfitted for long-distance journeys into international waters far out on the high seas. Which meant they were that much more expensive to build and required enormous amounts of expensive fuel to get them to where they were going and to keep them going for long periods of time.

There's no way the world's fishing industry could have afforded to build, launch, and keep that many ships at sea during those two decades—not to mention the tens of thousands of ships that have been built since then—without some significant help.

Which they got, in the form of government subsidies.

GOVERNMENT SUBSIDIES HAVE PLAYED A SIGNIFICANT PART in the global fishing industry ever since the end of World War II.

Back at that time, people in Europe were recovering from the devastation of war, and people in newly independent nations in Africa and Asia were figuratively hungry for jobs and literally hungry for food. So government subsidization of European nations' fisheries and European and US aid to help those new developing nations modernize their dilapidated fisheries made a lot of sense.

Over the next couple of decades, however, Europe got back on its feet, while most of those emerging Asian and African nations, unfortunately, still struggled with economic and political instability that has continued to this day. And the global fishing

industry, aided by a gusher of government subsidies, had put so many vessels on the world's oceans that the issue of overfishing had become a serious concern. At this point—certainly by the 1980s—government subsidies were seen by most impartial observers as a bad thing that was feeding an already overfed industry and encouraging the kinds of oceanic destruction we've detailed in previous chapters.

But first, let's get a fix on just how large the subsidies industry has become.

There's no question that the size and scope of the fishing-industry subsidies today go far beyond anything imagined in the wake of World War II. Much of today's massive global fishing industry is built on a foundation of these government handouts.

Recent studies estimate that the world's commercial fishing industry receives $25 billion to $29 billion a year in government subsidies—an amount equal to roughly 25 percent of the dockside annual value of the world catch, which fluctuates between $80 billion and $100 billion. Some subsidies support beneficial programs, such as management and research. However, the vast majority of subsidies drive increased and intensified fishing even on depleted stocks, this preventing their rebuilding, and thus resulting in detrimental effects on the supply of fish.

To no surprise, some of the biggest fishing nations, like the members of the European Union and Japan, are among the world's top subsidizers. But the developing world is catching up. The ten largest developing fishing nations, including countries such as China and Brazil, are estimated to provide subsidies nearly equal to those of their industrialized counterparts.

Not surprisingly, a significant chunk of the global fishing industry's subsidy money goes to fuel. A 2005 *New York Times* story reported that if the fishing industry were a country, it would tie the Netherlands as the world's eighteenth-largest oil consumer.

• IN 2000 •
THE WORLD'S
FISHERIES
HAD BURNED
13 BILLION
GALLONS OF FUEL
TO CATCH
80 MILLION
TONS OF FISH

That same story cited a study that found that, in 2000, the world's fisheries had burned 13 billion gallons of fuel to catch 80 million tons of fish. The fish-per-gallon ratio has only gotten worse since then, as boats have ventured farther and farther out to sea to catch fewer and fewer fish, and oil prices have continued to rise.

"This is the only major industry in the world," Daniel Pauly, a coauthor of that study, told the *Times*, "that is getting more and more energy-inefficient." In another interview, he boiled the whole thing down to its essence.

"There is surely a better way for governments to spend money," he said, "than by paying subsidies to a fleet that burns 1.1 billion liters [290 million gallons] of fuel annually to maintain paltry catches of old growth fish from highly vulnerable stocks, while destroying their habitat in the process."

More than a few experts have pointed out the irony that the same taxpayers whose tax dollars fund subsidies that pay poorly managed fishing fleets to keep doing things the wrong way are also paying at the other end of the line, when they buy seafood at the supermarket or eat out at a restaurant. Factor in the destruction caused by that deep-sea fishing and you've got a triple whammy: The public is paying to help catch those fish, we're paying to eat them, and we're paying to help destroy our oceans in the process. I don't think many of us would support fishing subsidies if we were fully aware of these facts.

Nor would most of us support subsidies if we realized how bloated the world's fishing fleet has become. As I mentioned in Chapter 4, the global fishing fleet is currently up to 250 percent larger than it needs to be to catch what the oceans can sustainably produce.

Subsidies are, arguably, the biggest global challenge facing the oceans. So only a truly international body can make a difference when it comes to ending harmful subsidies. Fortunately, the World Trade Organization (WTO) is perfectly positioned to stop the subsidies that are driving unsustainable fishing everywhere and causing our oceans to be literally fished to death.

The WTO seems like an unlikely savior for the oceans. It certainly is not an organization known for its environmental savvy. But I can't overemphasize how much a WTO agreement that ends bad subsidies could protect and preserve the oceans and all the fish and wildlife that live in them. In one fell swoop, the WTO could wipe out those subsidies.

The WTO is the 153-country organization responsible for setting and enforcing the rules of international trade. In 2001,

At WTO headquarters, Geneva, 2009

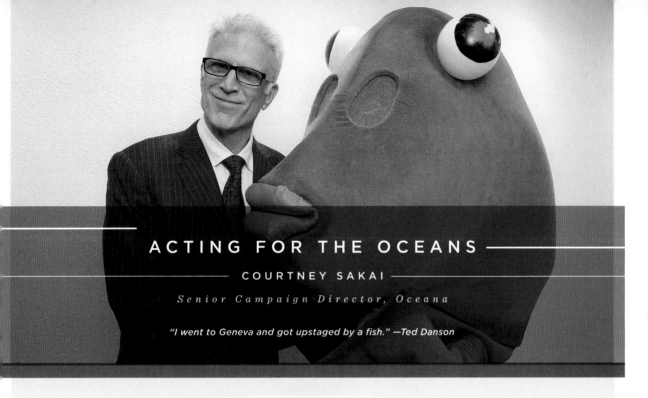

ACTING FOR THE OCEANS

COURTNEY SAKAI

Senior Campaign Director, Oceana

"I went to Geneva and got upstaged by a fish." —Ted Danson

So began a new adventure in Ted's life-long journey to save the oceans. We were in Geneva, Switzerland, with Ted and Oceana's mascot, Finley the Fish, to generate attention and support for the efforts of the World Trade Organization (WTO) on fisheries subsidies.

The WTO is not the first place you think of when you think about the environment. But years ago, it recognized the importance of healthy fishery resources to trade and development and the connection of subsidies to overcapacity and over-fishing. Simply put, governments and their respective taxpayers are financing a world with too many boats chasing too few fish. Before many others had even acknowledged this massive problem, the WTO had already launched a negotiation on fisheries subsidies.

The WTO and its 153 member countries set and enforce the rules of international trade. So it is hard to imagine a more appropriate forum to address fisheries subsidies. But it is even harder to imagine what Ted Danson, a giant red fish, and trade negotiators would have in common.

But it worked. Ted, Oceana, and our quirky tactics (in addition to serious work) were not only appreciated but also embraced by the WTO—and soon we were immersed in this new strange world of international trade. We were able to make this obscure and nearly unheard of issue into a global environmental priority that is now solidly on the international trade agenda.

In hindsight, it really isn't difficult to understand. The world relies on the oceans for food, livelihood, and commerce—important issues that international diplomats think about every day. And some things are simply universal, like humor and Sam Malone from *Cheers*.

The world's fisheries are in critical condition. Many fisheries are on the brink of irreversible collapse, so the clock is ticking on what could well become an environmental and human catastrophe. The scope and magnitude of "overfishing subsidies" is so great that eliminating them is likely the single greatest action that can be taken to protect the world's oceans. Will the WTO be a savior of the oceans? We hope so.

trade ministers recognized the contribution of subsidies to the decline in world fish populations and initiated a dedicated negotiation on fisheries subsidies as part of the WTO Doha trade "round." This was the first time in history that conservation objectives, in addition to commerce priorities, led to the launch of a specific trade negotiation.

Of course, nothing with an organization like the WTO happens in an instant. It's a long process of negotiation. I'll spare you the details, but I've been involved for several years, along with Oceana, traveling to Geneva to meet with diplomats from dozens of countries and WTO officials, including Director-General Pascal Lamy.

THE WTO is **PERFECTLY POSITIONED** to **STOP** the **SUBSIDIES THAT ARE DRIVING UNSUSTAINABLE FISHING EVERYWHERE AND CAUSING OUR OCEANS** to be **LITERALLY FISHED TO DEATH.**

Incredibly, we have found a lot of support for ending harmful subsidies. Everywhere I went, people from countries around the world told me their stories. They graciously thanked us for our work and gave us their commitment. But it also made me realize what an important and difficult task they have. The more I listened, the more I realized that there are a wide range of positions, and that none of them are wrong—they are different but still legitimate perspectives and views.

In the past few years, the WTO fisheries subsidies negotiations have made steady progress. In 2007, the WTO produced a draft agreement on fisheries subsidies that incorporated and in some cases even exceeded our suggestions. But as in the story of every trade negotiation, there are starts and stops, so my colleagues at Oceana and I are still working to ensure that the WTO follows through on ending harmful subsidies.

Imagine that—a legally binding international agreement that could change single-handedly the way we fish, putting us on the track to sustainable fishing. This is one of those issues in which economic sense makes good ecological sense. Charles Clover, author of a valuable work on overfishing called *The End of the Line: How Overfishing Is Changing the World and What We Eat*, is right when he calls subsidies nothing but "a racket." They are not, however, the only racket in the high-stakes business of global fishing.

Another is something called flags of convenience.

Spanish fishermen

MORE THAN 60 PERCENT OF OUR PLANET'S OCEANS ARE BEYOND
national jurisdiction. That is, they lie not only beyond nations' twelve-nautical-mile
territorial seas but also beyond their two-hundred-mile exclusive economic zones
(EEZs). The combined surface area of those remote waters—the high seas—constitutes fully half of the surface area of the entire Earth.

An area that vast, that distant, and that difficult to traverse is a frontier in more
ways than one. Besides the biological frontier of the high seas' largely unexplored
depths, which we've already looked at, there is also the *legal* frontier that makes the high
seas so similar to the largely ungoverned Wild West of nineteenth-century America.

The fact that these waters belong not to just one nation, as the American frontier
did (well, most of it anyway), but to the international community as a whole has made
both the creation and the enforcement of an effective set of rules and regulations
governing fishing on the "global commons" a terrific struggle.

In 1982 the United Nations was finally able to replace the moldy seventeenth-
century "freedom of the seas" rules that had governed international waters with the
UN Convention on the Law of the Sea (UNCLOS), which is designed to guide the sig-
natory nations in their use of the high seas, for everything from shipping to fishing to
pleasure sailing and cruising. When it comes to fishing, those provisions include:

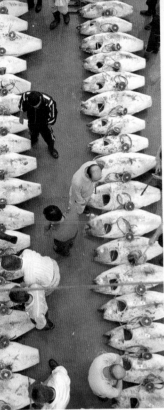

- Safety and pollution standards for the inspection and licensing of vessels
- Certification of a ship's equipment and crew
- Specifications ensuring the rights and humane treatment of crew members
- Quotas on the number of vessels a nation can permit to operate
- Restrictions on the size of catches
- Protection of endangered species of sea life
- Protection of particular regions of sensitive ocean and ocean-floor habitat
- Dozens of other arcane rules and regulations that combine to constitute the body of seagoing statutes known as international maritime law

Of course it's one thing to create laws and another to enforce them. It's an enormously daunting challenge to police an oceanic domain that covers literally half of Earth. And it's made even more difficult by the massive amounts of time, effort, and money spent by some of the most powerful players in today's global fishing industry to *avoid* those rules and regulations.

Among the most effective tools used by the industry to game the system are flags of convenience.

No one has even pretended that flags of convenience were created for any purpose other than one: to give the owners of commercial ships a way to avoid the taxes, laws, and other inconvenient restrictions placed on them by their own countries.

International maritime law requires that every commercial vessel be registered by a state. That state is responsible for licensing the ship as well as for taking legal responsibility for the ship's actions. The law requires that the ship fly the flag of that state for purposes of identification; this is called the ship's "flag state," and under UNCLOS, a ship sailing the high seas is subject only to the jurisdiction of its flag state.

You would think a ship's flag would be the same as the nationality of its owner, as well as the location of the ship's home port. More often than you might think, you would be wrong.

You might also think that the flag state—the state responsible for enforcing all the international laws the ships flying its flag are subject to—would take that responsibility seriously and be diligent in its duties. Again, more often than you might assume, you would be wrong.

RUSSIAN TRAWLERS docked in Kirkenes, Norway, 2009

HERE'S HOW THE GAME HAS BEEN PLAYED OVER THE YEARS.

Beginning around the 1920s, two sources of pressure were squeezing American shipowners and merchant marine companies: the growing strength of US merchant marine labor unions that were demanding fair pay and decent working conditions for their members, and the rising costs of building ships in the United States compared to other countries where wages were much lower and taxes were almost nonexistent.

So those owners and companies began registering their vessels in other nations that required nothing more than a nominal fee to allow foreign ships to fly their flags.

It's an **ENORMOUSLY DAUNTING CHALLENGE** —— to **POLICE** an **OCEANIC DOMAIN** —— **THAT COVERS LITERALLY HALF** of **EARTH.**

For the most part, these nations had little or no interest in enforcing the laws and regulations governing these ships. Furthermore, their ignoring those laws allowed the shipowners to man their ships with crews from . . . anywhere. This allowed the owners to hunt for sailors—typically those from downtrodden, developing nations—who were willing, and often desperate, to work for wages that were far lower and under conditions far worse than those demanded by union-backed workers from developed countries. This added up to a very good deal for the shipowners. Very convenient.

And these were, and still are, unabashedly called flags of convenience.

The practice itself was, and still is, called flagging out, and it is a form of the "outsourcing" that is the cause of such anguish in the United States.

Early on, the US shipowners' nation of choice for flagging out—the most convenient host—was Panama. In the wake of World War II, Liberia, the African nation created as a colony for former US slaves, became another favorite for US shipowners seeking a flag of convenience. So did the Pacific's Marshall Islands, where so many US nuclear bomb tests were carried out in the 1950s that in 1956 the Atomic Energy Commission called this tiny cluster of atolls and five islands, with a population today of just over sixty thousand, "by far the most contaminated place in the world." As one can imagine, the fees paid for flags of convenience provide a welcome stream of revenue.

YOU WOULD THINK a SHIP'S FLAG —— would be THE SAME AS —— THE NATIONALITY of its OWNER, as well as the LOCATION of the SHIP'S HOME PORT. MORE OFTEN ———— than you MIGHT ———— THINK, YOU WOULD BE WRONG.

Naturally, American fisheries' early lead both in the practice of using flags of convenience and in where they chose to flag out their boats soon prompted the rest of the fishing world to follow suit. A 2005 study by the World Wildlife Fund, the International Transport Workers' Federation, and the Australian government tellingly titled *The Changing Nature of High Seas Fishing: How Flags of Convenience Provide Cover for Illegal, Unreported and Unregulated Fishing* found that more than one thousand large-scale fishing vessels were sailing under flags of convenience. "The countries which issue [flags of convenience]," the study stated, "turn a blind eye and exercise little or no control over the vessels concerned."

Of those countries, none issue more flags today than Panama, Liberia, and Malta. In fact, those three tiny nations account for the flags of almost 40 percent of the world's entire merchant fleet measured by deadweight tonnage.

Other popular targets for flagging out are the Bahamas, Bermuda, and a little country whose name often seems to crop up when discussing free-flowing, relatively unpoliced international finance: the Cayman Islands. There are even some entirely landlocked nations that provide flags of convenience, such as Bolivia, Slovakia, and Mongolia. It's so simple to flag out a ship that some nations, including Panama, allow the application process to be initiated online and completed by fax, making it easy to forge documents. The sweep of this practice is so broad it's almost dizzying. That BP drilling rig, the Deepwater Horizon? It flew a Marshall Islands flag of convenience.

And that supertrawler the Mauritanians call the Ship from Hell, the *Atlantic Dawn*? Now, there's a case study in gaming the system from several ends. Bear with me here, because this one is a wild—and revealing—little ride.

Center:
A Ukrainian
CUSTOMS
INSPECTOR
in the Sea
of Azov,
2006

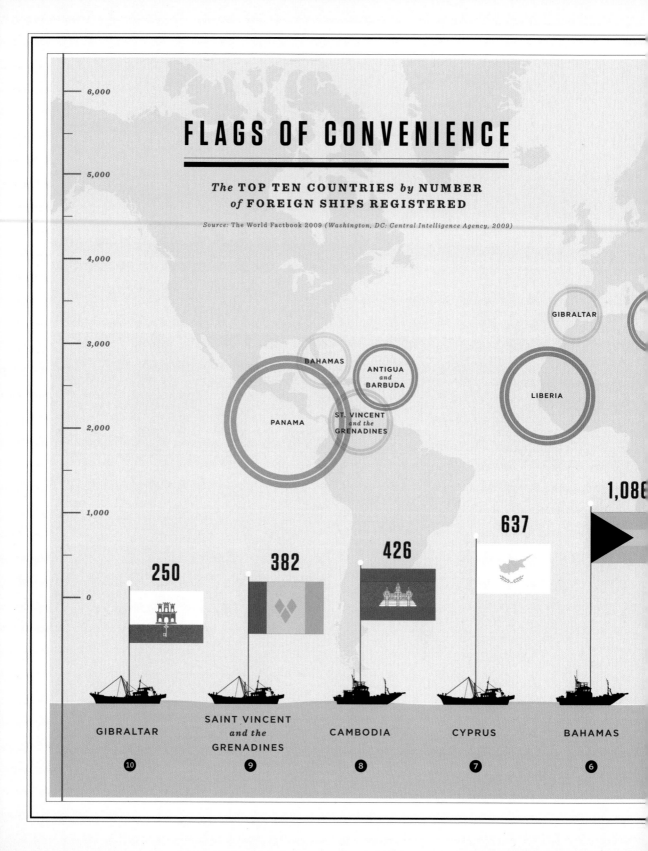

FLAGS OF CONVENIENCE

The TOP TEN COUNTRIES by NUMBER of FOREIGN SHIPS REGISTERED

Source: The World Factbook 2009 *(Washington, DC: Central Intelligence Agency, 2009)*

6,000

5,000

4,000

3,000

GIBRALTAR

BAHAMAS

ANTIGUA
and
BARBUDA

LIBERIA

ST. VINCENT
and the
GRENADINES

PANAMA

2,000

1,086

1,000

637

426

382

250

0

GIBRALTAR

SAINT VINCENT
and the
GRENADINES

CAMBODIA

CYPRUS

BAHAMAS

10

9

8

7

6

5,244

2,356

1,401

1,284

1,186

CAMBODIA

MARSHALL
ISLANDS

ANTIGUA
and
BARBUDA

MARSHALL
ISLANDS

MALTA

LIBERIA

PANAMA

5

4

3

2

1

Gutting tuna aboard Belize-flagged longline fishing vessel

The *Dawn* was built in the late 1990s by an Irish fishing magnate named Kevin McHugh. McHugh intended the ship to have its home port on the west coast of Ireland, in the quaint little village of Killybegs (population three thousand), on the Bay of Donegal. McHugh lived in Killybegs, which is one of Ireland's leading fishing ports.

But before the *Dawn* could drop anchor anywhere, it had to be built, and McHugh, savvy in the ways of subsidies, went for the best deal he could get. That wound up coming from Norway, whose government pitched in more than $6 million to help defray the Irishman's construction costs—subsidies that were certainly welcomed by the Norwegian shipbuilding industry, although it's hard to say how the rest of Norway's taxpayers felt about it.

The *Dawn* was formally commissioned in Dublin on the last day of August 2000, but only after McHugh and the Irish government had arranged a convoluted behind-the-scenes deal that included skirting Ireland's laws restricting the size of its domestic merchant fleet by having those laws rewritten to allow for exactly the amount of tonnage by which the *Atlantic Dawn* exceeded the nation's legal limit on weight. As the *Dubliner* magazine put it, "Lo and behold, the Irish tonnage allocation was magically increased by precisely 14,055 tonnes."

Among McHugh's other tactics was arranging a flag of convenience for the *Dawn*'s sister ship, a supertrawler called the *Veronica* (after McHugh's wife), in order to make room for the *Dawn*. Perhaps he consulted a Web site called International Ship and Aircraft Registries (www.flagsofconvenience.com) to choose the winning flag. After hunting around for the best deal he could find, McHugh had the *Veronica* removed from Ireland's fishing registry and unceremoniously flagged out to—where else?—Panama.

SHIPOWNERS CAN MAKE THEMSELVES LEGALLY ANONYMOUS, and **ALMOST COMPLETELY UNTRACEABLE,** by **HIDING BEHIND LAYERS** of **SHELL CORPORATIONS** that make them **ALMOST IMPOSSIBLE** to **PROSECUTE** for **CIVIL** or **CRIMINAL VIOLATIONS.**

It was only after all these maneuverings that the *Atlantic Dawn* finally, triumphantly, sailed into Killybegs, where traffic was backed up for fifteen miles as tens of thousands of Irish men, women, and children bursting with pride jockeyed for position to catch a glimpse of what they called the Celtic Tiger, which you have to admit has a nicer ring to it than the Ship from Hell.

═════════

THIS IS JUST ONE EXAMPLE OF WHAT FLAGS OF CONVENIENCE can do when combined with a boost from subsidies. There are others. The obvious issues include:

- The intention of the UNCLOS agreement that a "genuine link" (to quote the agreement) between the owner of a ship and its flag state can be violated.

- Nations that have no resources or interest in enforcing international maritime law can become flag states for no reason other than money.

- Shipowners can make themselves legally anonymous, and almost completely untraceable, by hiding behind layers of shell corporations that make them almost impossible to prosecute for civil or criminal violations.

But critics of the practice of flagging out also point to a broad range of criminal activities—arms smuggling, money laundering, drug smuggling, trafficking in illegal goods like liquor and cigarettes, and human trafficking and prostitution—that are all made easier by using ships flying flags of convenience. They even point out how relatively easy it would be for terrorists to use an unpoliced, uninspected, flagged-out ship as a floating bomb by loading it with explosives, sailing it into a crowded harbor, and detonating it.

These are all gravely serious matters, but our focus here is on the oceans. What we're concerned with is the ways in which the exploitation and outright defiance of international law by commercial fisheries affect the oceans and the sea life within them, as well as the crew members who fish for that sea life.

Organizations that monitor illegal fishing around the world often use the term "pirate" to refer to both illegitimate fishing itself and the vessels used to perpetrate it. When you boil it down, flying those flags of convenience comes about as close to hoisting the skull and crossbones of a Jolly Roger as a twenty-first-century trawler can get. And in fact, as a number of startling cases illustrate, sometimes these vessels do in fact become outright pirate ships, blatantly breaking laws and defiantly answering to no one.

FAR FROM HAVING a CHILLING EFFECT, THESE FINES ARE —— SIMPLY CONSIDERED —— by the INDUSTRY to be PART of the COST of DOING BUSINESS.

Many of them operate in remote waters far out to sea, staying there for months, sometimes even years at a time, and being met by companion ships that unload their catch, refuel their tanks, replenish their supplies, perhaps replace some of their crew, and then send them back on their way, often without keeping records of any of these activities.

It's not rare for a vessel to reflag, or "flag hop," several times a year, and to change its name as well, adding even more layers to the obscuring web of shell companies that the owners of the vessels use to hide from the law.

In the relatively rare cases in which a ship happens to be caught breaking one or more of the international laws, the maximum fine is $100,000—less than two weeks' take for most of these ships. Far from having a chilling effect, these fines are simply considered by the industry to be part of the cost of doing business. Now, here's where government assistance, when subverted by people who know how to exploit the system, can have unintended results, including helping to increase the size of the pirate fleet that's currently roaming the world's oceans.

This game, according to Daniel Pauly, involves something called a decommissioning subsidy, which is intended to help cover the cost of retiring a boat (whose original construction, it should be noted, was most likely subsidized as well). Decommissioning subsidies are big in Europe, where they actually drive fleet modernization and the growth of effective fishing efforts.

The process is simple: Take the decommissioning subsidy and use it as collateral for a boat construction loan, and sell the decommissioned boat. Typically it will be bought by someone in a developing nation in Asia or Africa, where the aging, decrepit, leaky vessel will wind up, as often as not, avoiding inspections in order to sail and continuing to break the law (and pollute the waters it travels through) by the very fact that it's fishing at all. Once again, the original owner laughs all the way to the bank, pocketing the profit he's made by double-dipping the system.

It's impossible for governmental authorities to police so much illicit activity going on in so many places all over the world, so independent organizations like the London-based Environmental Justice Foundation (EJF), Greenpeace, and Oceana have taken it upon themselves to help out, staging their own sting operations in order to show the public—and the government officials who vote on such things as subsidies—how the dark side of the fishing industry routinely uses aspects of the system to subvert the system itself.

Of course it's hard to say just how large the global pirate fishing industry is, but London's *Guardian* newspaper reported last year that illegal fishing accounts for between 13 and 31 percent of the worldwide annual total catch. Those figures are close to estimates made by the Environmental Justice Foundation.

Whatever the exact amount, no guessing needs to be done about where most of the world's pirated fish are sold. It's Europe, which, according to the *New York Times*, imports 60 percent of the seafood it consumes, with a significant portion of that total being what the *Times* called "contraband"—fish caught or shipped in violation of international quotas, treaties, and laws. The European Commission estimates that $1.6 billion worth of illegal seafood enters Europe each year.

Charles Clover, the *End of the Line* author, calls pirated fish—often poetically referred to as black fish—"Europe's dirty little secret." But it's not much of a secret anymore.

What *is* secret quite often is where the fish on your dinner plate came from, and how it got there. Seafood fraud has become rampant, not just in Europe but all over the world. It's not unusual for catches to be intentionally mislabeled—caught by an illegal boat, then packed in boxes bearing the stamp of a legitimate, legally licensed vessel. The catch then enters a nation's market, typically through a port where inspections are known to be lax.

For example, a favorite port of entry for illicit catches entering European markets is Spain's Canary Islands, which are notorious for their virtually nonexistent

ILLEGAL FISHING
ACCOUNTS FOR
13-31%
— OF THE —
**WORLDWIDE
ANNUAL CATCH**

inspection standards. This is how, say, a load of dorado (also known as mahimahi) caught off the coast of West Africa by a French longliner might wind up in an outdoor market in Berlin, packed in a box stamped with the distinctive bright red logo of the Chinese fishing industry.

Retailers of questionable seafood typically have a "don't ask, don't tell" policy when it comes to the sources of their products. In hard times, they're simply happy to have it, and the past several years have been hard times. The combination of surging demand and scarce supply has driven up prices—doubling or tripling them, or even more—which encourages even more pirate fishing and even more illegality throughout the system, starting where the boats drop their nets and proceeding all the way to the supermarket seafood counter where that fresh tuna fillet is wrapped for you.

Not long ago in London, a kilo (2.2 pounds) of cod—the main ingredient in traditional fish-and-chips—cost $60, a whopping five times what it had cost just four years earlier. What was once a quick, cheap snack now bears the price tag of a gourmet entrée.

And if it does happen to still bear that familiar low price, you can bet that the "fish" in that fish-and-chips you're eating isn't cod. More likely, it's something like dogfish shark.

Seafood fraud is remarkably easy to pull off. And unfortunately, it happens all the time. You'd hate to think they would do this, but there are restaurants that knowingly substitute a cheap fish for the expensive one on the menu and pocket the difference. A 2009 investigation by the Scripps Television Station Group found that twenty-three out of thirty-eight restaurants in Kansas City, Phoenix, Baltimore, and Tampa were "charging patrons for top-notch seafood while actually peddling inferior fillets."

A favorite cheap substitute is tilapia, which I'll talk about more when we get into fish farming. That tilapia is an essentially tasteless fish makes it easy to camouflage

Above and right: PIRATE FISHING EXPEDITION, West Africa, 2001

it as something else, and it was going for about $2.20 a pound at the time of the Scripps investigation. Red snapper, a high-cost fish on any restaurant's menu, cost more than twice that at the time, about $5.20 a pound. So it was no surprise that, more than once, the reporters found tilapia substituted for red snapper. Also high on their list of mislabeled fish was cheap Asian catfish substituted for grouper.

Grouper seems to be a favorite target for seafood fraud. After a restaurant owner in Florida found that his supplier was shipping him boxes of frozen Asian catfish, which were going for as little as $1.52 a pound at the time, that were labeled as grouper, which cost four times that amount, he fired the supplier and alerted the *St. Petersburg Times* newspaper. The *Times* commissioned DNA tests that showed that six out of eleven Tampa Bay–area restaurants advertising grouper were actually serving Asian catfish "or other cheaper substitutes." One upscale restaurant was charging $23 for "champagne braised black grouper" that was actually tilapia.

Another avenue of fraud is substituting farmed fish—which we'll look at in the next chapter—for more expensive wild fish without letting the customer know. Several years ago, the *New York Times* tested salmon in eight city grocery stores and

---

SEAFOOD FRAUD is REMARKABLY EASY to PULL OFF. AND UNFORTUNATELY, IT HAPPENS —————— ALL the TIME. ——————

Above: FROZEN FISH being unloaded from a ship that was seized for fishing illegally
Left: US Coast Guard boarding a CHINESE VESSEL rigged for high-seas driftnet fishing

SUSTAINABLE EATING

JOSÉ ANDRÉS

James Beard Foundation Award–Winning Chef

José Andrés is recognized all over the world for his innovative food and critically acclaimed restaurants in Washington, DC, Los Angeles, and most recently, Las Vegas. The author of several cookbooks, including Tapas: A Taste of Spain in America, *and the host and executive producer of the PBS series* Made in Spain, *Andrés is also the founder of World Central Kitchen, a nonprofit focusing on providing food to people in humanitarian crises around the world. He spoke to Oceana's Suzannah Evans about cooking with sustainable seafood.*

SE: Spanish cuisine relies heavily on seafood. How have the issues of overfishing and sustainability affected you as a Spanish chef?

JA: We are very fortunate in Spain that we have a lot of coastline, and that means we have always been able to take advantage of the tremendous richness of the Atlantic and the Mediterranean to feed ourselves. On *Made in Spain*, I went to

Andalusia to show the ancient practice of *almadraba*, or tuna fishing, which is really more like driving cattle. The word is Arabic, but the practice is probably even older. Every year the tuna return to the Mediterranean and have to pass through the Straits of Gibraltar. The people would build a system of nets and drive the tuna. It was a way for the people to take advantage of what nature provided to feed

themselves. They used every part of the tuna. Sadly, the tuna population is not what it was, and it has become an expensive delicacy. The people who live along the coast of Andalusia who fed themselves for generations on the tuna can no longer afford it.

SE: What can a chef do to help promote sustainable seafood to his customers?

JA: Put it on the menu. We know there are fishes that make more sense to use than others, and we need to think about that when we make our menus. There is no need to sacrifice quality or taste. For example, sardines are one of the best fishes for eating and are sustainable. Anchovies, mussels, oysters—the ocean gives us so many good things that we can feel good about using.

AT THE ROOT OF SEAFOOD FRAUD is our old **NEMESIS, OVERFISHING.** YOU WOULDN'T SEE SOMEONE SUBSTITUTING DOGFISH SHARK for COD IF COD were still **PLENTIFUL.**

found that six of the eight stores were selling salmon that was said to be wild, but was actually farmed, for as much as $29 a pound. Farmed salmon, at the time, cost between $5 and $12 a pound.

Taras Grescoe, in his book *Bottomfeeder*, recites a litany of common substitutions: in Canada, haddock for cod; in South America, shark for tuna; in the American Midwest, cheap zander for pricier walleye; in Australia, Nile perch for more expensive barramundi. As far as grouper goes, says Grescoe, the customer might instead get hake, emperor fish, green weakfish (there's a name for you), or painted sweetlips (there's an even wilder name)—all of which are relatively inexpensive substitutes.

And then there's the fish scammer's pièce de résistance, passing off the bottom-dwelling, scum-sucking monkfish—also known as the frogfish, goosefish, and bellyfish—as lobster, as long as there's enough cream sauce to hide it in.

Enterprising newspaper and TV reporters continue to expose these frauds, which seem to be particularly prevalent in Florida, but as long as there's profit to be made, it seems there will always be someone willing to cut corners, or to outright lie, in order to make a few extra dollars.

At the root of seafood fraud is our old nemesis, overfishing. You wouldn't see someone substituting dogfish shark for cod if cod were still plentiful. And the fraud undermines any efforts to convince the restaurant-going public that overfishing is a real concern. How can you believe that grouper is at risk when you have a so-called grouper sandwich every day?

The best we can do is educate ourselves and ask the right questions—which we'll get to in the last chapter.

6 OUT OF 8 **STORES TESTED** WERE FOUND TO BE **SELLING SALMON** — THAT WAS — **SAID TO BE WILD,** — BUT WAS — **ACTUALLY FARMED**

NO DISCUSSION OF CHEATING BY THE FISHING INDUSTRY WOULD be complete without a look at the effects the lax and loopholed system has on the crews who wind up manning many of these ships. This is where the human rights violations mentioned earlier come into play.

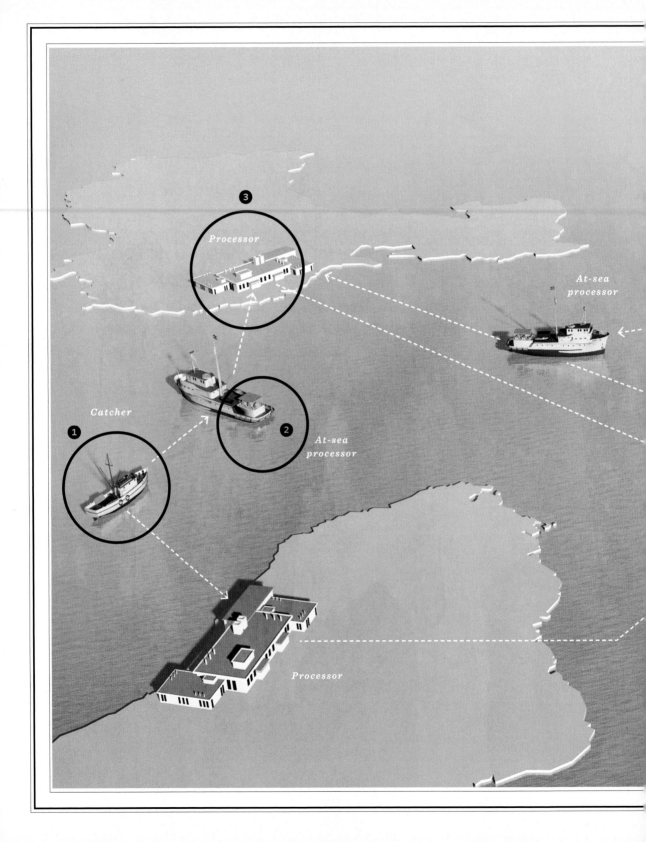

SEAFOOD
SUPPLY CHAIN

Seafood in the United States travels a long and complicated path to reach our plates, making it difficult to verify its origin, safety, and sustainability.

In general, fishing vessels catch fish that is processed at sea and/or on land before it is transferred to distributors that move seafood around the country to retail outlets where it is served or sold to consumers. Seafood is imported most of the time, often passing through China or other countries for packaging on its way to the United States.

With opportunities for fraud at every step along the way, the end product has often been transformed beyond recognition and substituted for an entirely different species of fish.

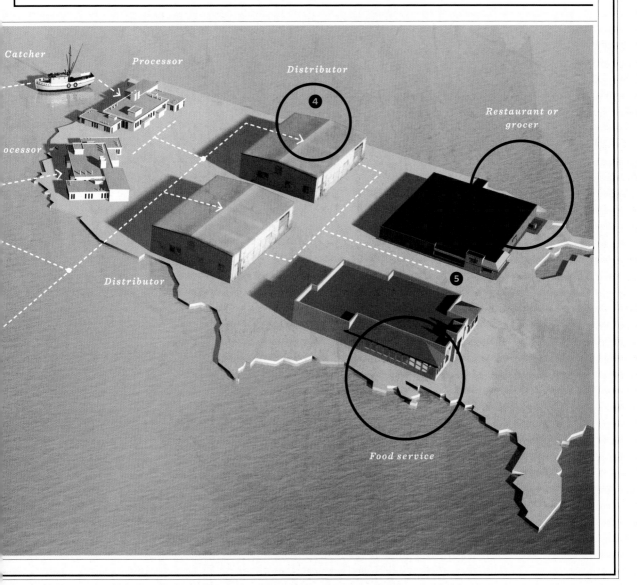

Catcher

Processor

Distributor

4

Restaurant or grocer

ocessor

Distributor

5

Food service

We've described how, once a ship is registered under a flag of convenience, the flag state often places no restriction on the nationality of the crew, leaving the ship-owner free to recruit the cheapest labor possible from countries that can do nothing to protect those laborers even if they want to, leaving the crews with only the flag state to protect them. And most flag states, as we've detailed, care little for anything other than collecting their registration fees.

This situation, not surprisingly, has led to widespread mistreatment of crews on flagged-out ships, with the members of some of those crews being turned into virtual prisoners at sea, according to the International Transport Workers' Federation (ITF). The worst of these ships, says the ITF in one report, are "floating sweatshops," forcing their crews to live in horrific conditions, go without sufficient food or water,

HOW CAN YOU BELIEVE THAT GROUPER is at **RISK WHEN YOU** —— **HAVE** a **SO-CALLED GROUPER SANDWICH EVERY DAY?** ——

work long periods of overtime without compensation, get little if any shore leave, and receive no medical attention to speak of.

Again not surprisingly, more of these ships can be found off the coast of West Africa than anywhere else in the world. That region is, as we've noted, one of the busiest industrial fishing hot spots on the planet, its waters once replete with more than a thousand species of fish ranging from sea bream, white grouper, pink African sole, firm-fleshed barracuda, jelly-fleshed eel, anchovy, sardine, and octopus to the ever-popular staples of tuna, sea bass, and the like. Six countries in West Africa—Mauritania, Senegal, the Gambia, Cape Verde, Guinea-Bissau, and Guinea—are particularly victimized by foreign fleets from Europe and Asia.

In 2006, the EJF and Greenpeace teamed up to survey those West African waters, and in the waters off the coast of Guinea they found that more than half of the 104 boats they tracked were fishing illegally. The investigators' cameras recorded vessels whose names were hidden to prevent reporting, boats whose names were changed from week to week (so several vessels could use the same permit), and boats that offloaded their catches to pickup ships far from shore in the dead of night so they could avoid quota limits and continue filling their nets.

But it was a subsequent investigation by the EJF that turned up a particularly shocking story. A pair of articles published in September 2010 by the *Guardian* detailed discoveries made by an EJF investigator who, along with naval forces from Sierra Leone, boarded a "hi-tech" South Korean trawler to check for fishing violations. What the investigator stumbled upon was far more horrifying.

OCEAN HERO

JULIE PACKARD

Executive Director of the Monterey Bay Aquarium

Julie Packard is the executive director of the Monterey Bay Aquarium and a board member of the David and Lucile Packard Foundation, a major marine funder. She also chairs the board of the aquarium's sister institution, the Monterey Bay Aquarium Research Institute, and has served on numerous other boards and committees related to conservation.

Born in Los Altos, California, Packard received her bachelor's and master's degrees in biology from the University of California at Santa Cruz. Her principal scientific interests were marine algal ecology and aquaculture. She is the daughter of the late Lucile and David Packard, the cofounder of Hewlett-Packard.

In the late 1970s, Packard helped, with her family, to found the Monterey Bay Aquarium, the nation's first major public aquarium dedicated to interpreting a single region—the Monterey Bay. Packard has served as the aquarium's executive director since its opening, and today the Monterey Bay Aquarium is widely acknowledged as a leader among aquariums worldwide. With a mission to "inspire conservation of the oceans," it has expanded the public's worldview by bringing new animals to light—from jellies to deep-sea animals. As Packard has said, "For too long the oceans have been out of sight, out of mind, even for people who care about the environment."

The aquarium's seafood guide has helped millions of people make choices that can help the oceans. "We can vote with our dollars for seafood that's caught or farmed in sustainable ways," says Packard. "It creates market demand that will get the attention of fishing enterprises and aquaculture producers. As we help change the way seafood is caught and farmed, we'll help ocean ecosystems stay healthy."

Under the headline "Modern-Day Slavery: Horrific Conditions on board Ships Catching Fish for Europe," the story described the "human degradation" experienced by the vessel's thirty-six crewmen, who were from China, Vietnam, Indonesia, and Sierra Leone. This crew and others who were interviewed reportedly were forced to work eighteen-hour shifts in a 104° to 113°F fish hold with no ventilation, were fed food pulled from "disgusting boxes" in galleys filled with cockroaches, had only salt

MORE FLAGGED-OUT SHIPS CAN BE FOUND off the **COAST** of **WEST AFRICA** than **ANYWHERE ELSE** in the **WORLD.**

water to use for washing, and slept on makeshift bunks fashioned from cardboard and wood planks in a windowless corner of the fish hold where the ceiling was too low for the men to stand upright.

Crew members from relatively nearby Sierra Leone were paid not with money, but with boxes of trash fish—a common term for bycatch—that they were expected to sell locally. "If anyone complained," the story reported, "the captain would abandon them on the nearest beach."

It's been bad enough that in recent years the local fishermen in these West African countries—and in other developing coastal countries in Asia and elsewhere—have had to cope with the repercussions of hundreds of factory ships from wealthy nations trawling the ocean depths and siphoning off large numbers of fish before local fishermen could catch them nearer to shore from their pirogues.

Crew on
rusting Chinese
fishing vessel,
West Africa,
2006

But seeing foreign trawlers that have made what's called access agreements fishing *inside* those borders, dropping their nets as close as six miles from shore, virtually vacuuming the shallow sea bottom clean and leaving next to nothing for the locals—no wonder the Mauritanians took to calling boats like the *Atlantic Dawn* ships from hell.

As angry as the native fishermen are at the foreign invaders, they should be just as furious with their own government officials, because they—the politicians who rule these West African nations—are the ones who have sold their own people's fishing grounds to foreign powers in exchange for money and, in some cases, even for weapons.

These deals are called access agreements, and, like government subsidies and flags of convenience, they are yet another benign-sounding instrument that has enabled the global fishing industry to extend its reach farther than it would otherwise be able to go, causing the destruction of even more fish, more ocean habitat, and, in this case, untold thousands of human lives as well.

LIKE GOVERNMENT SUBSIDIES AND FLAGS OF CONVENIENCE, the purported purpose of access agreements is positive and healthy. In theory, according to UNCLOS, these agreements were created to allow a nation with surplus stocks of fish and no means to efficiently harvest them—typically, a developing nation—to allow those that have those capabilities to pay a fee to the host nation so it can come in and harvest the surplus stocks. The fee is supposed to, at least in part, go toward developing and modernizing the host nation's fishing industry.

In reality, however, whatever surplus stocks there might have been in these host nations' waters, if any, are now long gone because of the fleets of foreign fisheries that swept in and decimated the waters off their shores, leaving the local fishermen with almost nothing to catch. The politicians, meanwhile, often redirect the fees for their own purposes, sending little—if any—of the money to the fishermen, or to improving the nations' fisheries infastructure, such as ports and markets.

WHATEVER SURPLUS STOCKS there MIGHT HAVE BEEN in these HOST NATIONS' WATERS, if any, ARE NOW LONG GONE because of the FLEETS of FOREIGN FISHERIES that SWEPT —— in and DECIMATED the WATERS OFF THEIR SHORES. ——

Not surprisingly, considering that their own fishing grounds have long been virtually barren, the developed nations buying most of these access rights are members of the European Union. Over the past decade, EU nations have bought access to waters located from the Arctic Circle down to the Falkland Islands.

Again not surprisingly, the vast bulk of the roughly $400 million a year the EU spends to buy foreign fishing rights goes to nations along the West African coast. Currently, more than eight hundred EU-company-owned industrial fishing boats ply the busy West African waters, with Spain alone licensing a fleet of two hundred trawlers in the region. China, Russia, and South Korea are also busy players in these waters.

With the violence of civil unrest and even civil war riddling the lives of many of the 8 million African people who live in this stretch of coastal nations, and with the political instability that plagues some of their governments, it's not surprising that many of these cash-for-access fishing deals are corrupt. The recent history of Mauritania provides a perfect case study.

As with any other issue in a region like this—whether you're looking at Africa or the Middle East or Southeast Asia—you have to have at least a basic understanding of the area's political and ethnic history in order to understand the issue itself, whether that issue is fishing rights or the right to build settlements on disputed territory.

In the case of Mauritania, although the nation's inland Arab population is in the minority in terms of numbers, they control the government. So it's not surprising that their priorities lie with inland businesses and industry, not with the fishing culture of the ethnically sub-Saharan coastal Mauritanians. When the nation went through a severe drought in the mid-1980s, as well as several coups d'état and a war with Senegal, the government eagerly began selling fishing rights in order to raise much-needed cash. They even struck a deal with China that included not just cash but also two fighter jets in exchange for allowing Chinese trawlers into their EEZ.

In the wake of that deal, ninety-nine Chinese fishing vessels began dropping their nets in Mauritanian waters. A 2006 agreement with the EU allowed forty-three EU industrial fishing boats six years of access to Mauritania's waters at a price of $146 million a year. Meanwhile, the Mauritanian fishermen, whose boats were returning each day filled with fewer fish than the day before, saw none of the money that was pouring into their government's coffers.

The government didn't deny it. The *New York Times* reported that, when asked in 2007 where the fishing rights money had gone, a Mauritanian government spokesman explained that funds earmarked for the needs of their fishing industry had been diverted to "more pressing needs." According to a *Wall Street Journal* report in that same year, at least 340 foreign boats were licensed to fish in Mauritanian waters. The effect on local fishermen was devastating. One local man pointed to his empty pirogue and said, "Now the only thing we catch here is water."

It's not as if no one's been paying attention. The following year, a *New York Times* story headlined "Europe Takes Africa's Fish, and Boatloads of Migrants Follow" reported that "a vast flotilla" of industrial trawlers from foreign nations "have so thoroughly scoured northwest Africa's ocean floor that major fish populations are collapsing.

"'What we've done,'" the EJF's executive director, Steve Trent, told the *Times*'s reporter, "'is to export the overfishing problem elsewhere, particularly to Africa.'"

"NOW THE ONLY THING WE CATCH HERE IS WATER."

A *Times* editorial published that same year explained to its readers that "mechanized fishing fleets from the European Union and nations like China and Russia—usually with the complicity of local governments—have nearly picked clean the oceans off Senegal and other northwest African countries."

The result, besides destroying the oceanic ecosystems throughout that vast region, has been the destruction of the lives of the local fishermen, who, prompted by desperation and an absence of options, have over the past several years been fleeing to Europe in a mass exodus undertaken in the same pirogues they had once filled with fish.

Newspapers that only a year or two earlier were describing Mauritanians near starvation in their coastal villages were now describing thousands of them risking their lives to make the six-hundred-mile oceanic journey to the Canary Islands,

where the regulations for processing immigrants are as lax as they are for processing fish. Recognizing a growing source of desperate, easily exploitable people, human traffickers have been stepping up their efforts to arrange these Canary Island trips.

SO WE COME FULL CIRCLE, FROM THE subsidies that allow the world's fishing fleets to sail out to the most distant waters, to the flags of convenience that encourage pirate fishing and give the owners of these rogue vessels a way to avoid the regulations meant to protect both the fish and the habitat in those deep international waters, to the access agreements that bring all these boats close to shore and allow them to pillage the last relatively unfished regions on Earth.

Above and left: AFRICAN IMMIGRANTS intercepted by Spanish authorities in the Canary Islands

I've had plenty of opportunities to speak on this subject, and my message is always essentially the same: If these fleets weren't subsidized, they wouldn't be able to go into these African coastal waters—and around the world—to ravage the marine life populations.

That's about as plain as you can put it. Just as plain is the fact that these aren't ignorant people who are running this business, making these deals, sending those boats out all over the world. They're very, very smart.

They *know* what they're doing, and what they're doing is saying, "We know these fish populations are declining. We know we're wiping them out, but we're going to get as much as we can before the whole thing collapses."

No matter the consequences to the oceans, to the fish, to the people whose lives are destroyed in the process. This is greed we're talking about, pure and simple. *Greed.*

Again, there is still hope. All kinds of organizations are enlisting all kinds of people, all of them committed to fighting the good fight. We've highlighted some of them in these pages, giving them a chance to speak for themselves.

As for the fishing industry, they say there is still one last good hope left as an alternative to destroying the fish that are still managing to survive in our oceans.

Aquaculture, they say, just might be the answer.

Fish farming.

With that in mind, let's take a look at just how viable this "last good hope" really is.

THE CLOCK

7637840

FAK
NAMA

ΟΛΥΜΠΙΚ ΤΣΑΜΠΙΟ
ΧΑΝΙΑ

www.anek.gr

is TICKING

WHAT YOU CAN DO

- WRITE A LETTER TO YOUR TRADE MINISTER OR TRADE REPRESENTATIVE.

- CALL OR WRITE YOUR CONGRESSMAN AND US SENATOR.

- WRITE A LETTER TO THE EDITOR OF YOUR LOCAL NEWSPAPER.

- SHARE THIS INFORMATION WITH FIVE OF YOUR FRIENDS OR COLLEAGUES.

- EAT LOCAL, SEASONAL SEAFOOD WHENEVER POSSIBLE.

- SUPPORT OCEANA'S EFFORTS TO END HARMFUL FISHING SUBSIDIES BY ENCOURAGING YOUR ELECTED OFFICIALS TO SUPPORT TRADE NEGOTIATIONS ON ELIMINATING SUBSIDIES. To learn more, visit www.oceana.org/act.

- BE AN INFORMED CONSUMER: KNOW WHAT KIND OF SEAFOOD YOU ARE EATING AND WHERE IT COMES FROM Educated seafood purveyors care about what they're feeding their clients and should be happy to tell you the provenance of your dinner. If no one can tell you where the fish came from, it's probably not a good thing to eat.

- ALSO, SOURCE YOUR FAVORITE SHELLFISH FROM LOCAL FISHERMEN. Avoid eating other shellfish until you have reassurances that they were not fished by industrial trawlers.

- SUPPORT LOCAL, ARTISANAL FISHERMEN WHO RELY ON THE HEALTH OF LOCAL FISHERIES FOR SUBSISTENCE AS WELL AS GROUPS THAT PROTECT THEIR INTERESTS.

CHAPTER SEVEN

BLUE REVOLUTION

IT'S INTRIGUING HOW OFTEN, WITH SO MANY

things we consider to be new, innovative, or modern, we find out that people were doing essentially the same things thousands of years ago.

Aquaculture—fish and shellfish farming—is certainly one of those things.

One of the cultures we most often turn to when looking for the ancient roots of almost any modern technology is China. And sure enough, archaeologists have discovered that the Chinese were using networks of ponds to cultivate carp as early as 2500 BC. At about the same time, a tribe of Aboriginal Australians devised grids of small channels and dams in order to raise eels, which were a staple of their diet.

Besides being fascinating in their own right, the variety of ingenious ways in which our predecessors farmed seafood has something to show us today about practicing aquaculture in eco-friendly, sustainable ways.

- Ancient Japanese collected seaweed they caught using oyster shells and cultivated it on bamboo poles.

- Early Egyptians and, after them, fish farmers in imperial Rome bred fish trapped in ponds and small lakes created by flooding.

- The Menehune people of Hawaii constructed networks of fishponds deep in the dark forests of the volcanic highlands after a Tahitian invasion in the twelfth century drove them into seclusion.

We may wind up looking back to some of these cultures for keys to help us work our way out of the environmental mess we've created with modern industrial aquaculture.

And make no mistake, if you take one glance at the current condition of the world's aquaculture industry, it's clear that we've created a mess. Perhaps with the best of intentions, but nevertheless, a mess—a mess that has become yet one more way in which we are affecting our oceans and the web of life those oceans are struggling to sustain.

It's been roughly two decades since the people who study the seas became seriously concerned about something they call the fish gap—the difference between the size of the world's demand for seafood and the size of the global fishing industry's annual catch. Over the course of that time, the gap has steadily widened, as the world's population has continued to grow while the size of the annual seafood catch has not. The FAO projects that by the year 2015, the gap will have widened by some 50 million tons, assuming that per capita seafood consumption stays steady. That's an unlikely assumption, considering that the planet is populated by more people every year, and that more of those people than ever are eating seafood.

"FISH GAP": THE DIFFERENCE BETWEEN THE SIZE —— OF —— THE WORLD'S **SEAFOOD DEMAND** AND THE SIZE OF **THE GLOBAL** FISHING INDUSTRY'S **ANNUAL CATCH**

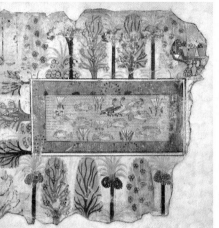

Depictions of early aquaculture and fishing from Egypt, France, and Tunisia

How to close a chasm like that? For many people, the answer has been aquaculture. Their hopes are pinned on supplementing the wild fish and shellfish catches with seafood raised on aquatic farms.

Those hopes were sky-high back at the turn of the 1980s, in the wake of the Green Revolution of the '60s and '70s. The Green Revolution had been engineered in response to concerns over how to feed the billions of starving people in the underdeveloped nations of the world. Organizations and individuals in the developed world coordinated a massive project of exporting newly developed high-yield hybrid seeds and modern agricultural techniques and equipment, along with teachers and advisors, to farmers in the Third World. This project resulted in a dramatic increase in grain production in those countries.

Excitement over the early success of that movement (which was tempered in subsequent years by concerns about its reliance on pesticides and chemical fertilizers) prompted a similar movement that turned to the sea—specifically, to aquaculture—to further address the issue of feeding the world's poor. The subsequent boom in the construction of fish farms all over the world was called—what else?—the Blue Revolution.

WE MAY WIND UP LOOKING BACK TO ANCIENT CULTURES for KEYS to HELP —— US WORK OUR WAY OUT of the —— ENVIRONMENTAL MESS we've CREATED.

FISH FARMING

Fish farming is an ancient industry that has become increasingly sophisticated in recent years. A huge global demand for seafood has made fish farming, or aquaculture, the world's fastest-growing food industry. Nearly half of all seafood is farmed, and that number is rising every year. But many forms of aquaculture are assailed by conservationists for being too hard on the marine environment. The quest for truly sustainable aquaculture has led to some interesting technological developments in recent years.

- **ONSHORE PONDS** *(Fig. A)*: Onshore fish farms can be among the most sustainable types of aquaculture, as the self-contained systems don't pollute a marine environment. Tilapia and catfish are among the species of seafood raised this way.

- **SALMON PENS** *(Fig. B)*: Open-water pens typically hold salmon, which are among the world's most popular farmed fish species. These pens can be up to ninety feet (about 27 meters) across and sixty feet (about 18 meters) deep and hold an average of fifty thousand salmon. Located in cold, coastal areas like Chile, Norway, and British Columbia, salmon pens can wreak havoc on native ecosystems with pollution and disease.

- **SEAWEED FLATS** *(Fig. C)*: Seaweed farming is a common practice in the Philippines and has grown in popularity around the world. These floating rafts are usually comprised of a 10-by-10-foot (3-by-3-meter) wooden frame with seaweed seedlings tied to a net of ropes. The establishment of seaweed farms can help protect marine ecosystems because seaweed thrives in healthy, clean waters. Carrageenan, a gelatinous extract made from the dried seaweed, is a component of an incredible array of goods from toothpaste to beer.

- **SPOTTER PLANES** *(Fig. D)*: Small aircraft are often used to spot large schools of fish or migrating big fish like bluefin tuna. In the case of bluefin tuna, the pilots radio the fish's location to boats on the water, which use purse seine nets to round up the tuna. The tuna are kept in offshore pens similar to the ones used to raise salmon in a process known as tuna ranching. The young tuna fatten up for a couple of months before they are sent to market. Spotter planes are illegal in many places, but they are often still used.

Fig. D

Fig. E

Fig. F

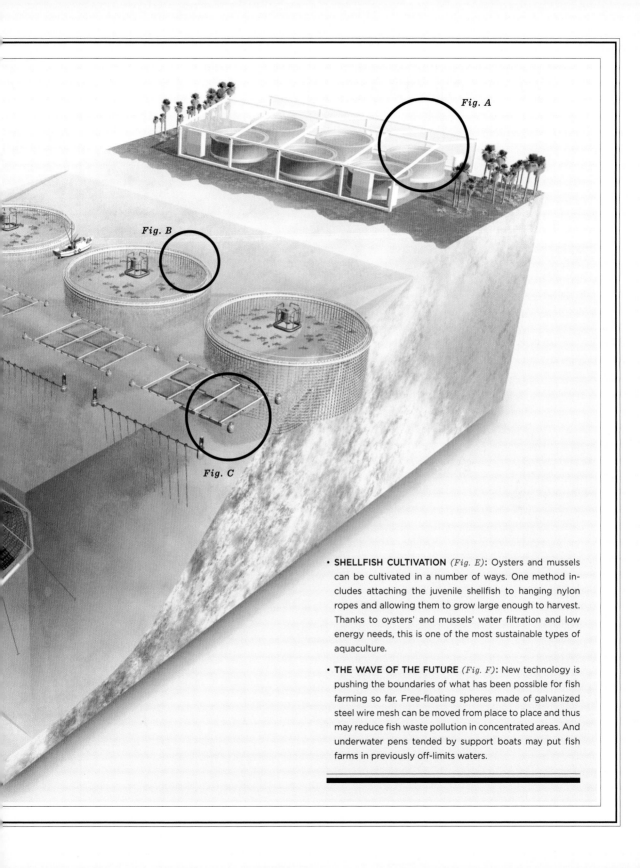

Fig. A

Fig. B

Fig. C

- **SHELLFISH CULTIVATION** *(Fig. E)*: Oysters and mussels can be cultivated in a number of ways. One method includes attaching the juvenile shellfish to hanging nylon ropes and allowing them to grow large enough to harvest. Thanks to oysters' and mussels' water filtration and low energy needs, this is one of the most sustainable types of aquaculture.

- **THE WAVE OF THE FUTURE** *(Fig. F)*: New technology is pushing the boundaries of what has been possible for fish farming so far. Free-floating spheres made of galvanized steel wire mesh can be moved from place to place and thus may reduce fish waste pollution in concentrated areas. And underwater pens tended by support boats may put fish farms in previously off-limits waters.

THAT BOOM HAS CONTINUED TO THIS DAY.

Aquaculture is currently the world's fastest-growing food production sector, with production increasing at an astounding rate of nearly 10 percent a year. In 2009, a reported 50 percent of all the seafood consumed worldwide was farmed. The FAO predicts that the figure could be as high as 60 percent by the year 2025, meaning that at that point the world would be eating more farm-raised fish than wild fish caught in the sea. The output of the world's fish farms is even on the verge of surpassing the global production of beef. Don't expect to see newspaper headlines marking that moment, but it's a milestone few people would have dreamed of twenty years ago.

And where are all these farms?

Again, no surprise here. The most fish farms, by far, are in China, which also produces more farmed fish than any other nation—in fact, more than twice as much as all of the other nations of the world *combined*. Recent figures show the Chinese churning out some 33 million tons of aquaculture products a year. That's 63 percent of the worldwide total of some 52 million tons.

India, which produces a relatively paltry 3.5 million tons a year, is the first runner-up to China. Vietnam, with 2.5 million, is third. The United States, with an annual total of nearly five hundred thousand tons, is edged out of the twelfth spot by Myanmar.

And what's everyone farming?

Here's where the numbers begin to really mean something, because now we're looking at which kinds of fish are being eaten, in what quantities, and by whom. When you realize that nearly half of that incredible Chinese total is carp—a freshwater fish deeply entrenched in Asia's history and food culture, but now almost completely absent from the Western world—the gap in tonnage between China and the rest of the world is not quite so stunning.

THE MOST FISH FARMS are in CHINA, which also PRODUCES MORE —— FARMED FISH than any OTHER NATION—MORE THAN TWICE—— AS MUCH AS ALL of the WORLD'S OTHER NATIONS COMBINED.

Setting carp aside, crustaceans and shellfish—primarily clams, oysters, and shrimp—lead the way as global aquaculture's most-produced species. Just for the record, most shrimp consumed in the United States is farmed. (Keep that in mind for when we get to the discussion of the farming process itself.)

Just behind crustaceans and shellfish on the list of most-farmed species is salmon. And it's salmon that dominates Americans' taste for farmed fish. As a nation,

FISH FARM

Guangdong, China

we eat a *lot* of salmon. We eat so much, in fact, that some marine science wags have taken to calling it "Spam of the Sea."

Yet very few of us know much about this particular fish beyond the fact that we love its rich texture and taste, and that each bite of that gleaming orange flesh is filled with those wonderful omega-3 fatty acids we've heard help prevent heart disease. How can you beat that? Something that tastes so good, and it's good *for* you as well (if you set aside concerns about its relatively high fat content). Raw in a sushi bar, seared on an outdoor grill, sliced on a bagel with cream cheese and onions—any way it's served, we Americans can't get enough of our salmon.

You might ask, *So what if we don't know where it came from? So what if it came from a farm? Why should we need—or want—to know all that stuff? If it's made its way to our supermarket shelves or the bins at our neighborhood outdoor seafood market, it must be okay. Right?*

Maybe, maybe not.

It depends on what you mean by "okay," and okay for whom or what.

Do we mean okay for ourselves, for our health and safety?

Or are we talking about whether it was okay for the fish itself? What did the fish you're eating go through before it got to your plate, and how did that affect the fish's health?

Are we talking about whether the conditions

As a nation, **WE EAT A LOT** of **SALMON.**

in that pen were okay for that fish and the tens of thousands of other fish that were crammed into the same pen?

Or if the surrounding seawater and ocean bottom are okay despite there being that many fish in that tight a space, despite the diseases and infections that often run rampant among them, and despite the chemicals and other contaminants used to combat those diseases?

Or are the wild fish that swim too close to those farms and are infected and sickened by the toxic stew seeping out of those cages okay?

Or is it okay that farmed fish escape from those cages and wind up fighting, infecting, and breeding with their wild counterparts? Or eating native fish at latitudes where salmon are farmed outside their native range? Is it okay that in cases where the farmed fish have been genetically altered, their breeding with wild fish creates freakish, deformed strains of fish?

Or is it okay that we feed farmed salmon with fish meal derived from smaller, perfectly edible fish, such as anchovies, which could be used to feed millions of poor people throughout the world?

These are just some of the issues and concerns that have arisen over the course of the past thirty years or so, as we've realized that the Blue Revolution of aquaculture, which began with such innocent hopes, has unleashed a Pandora's box of unforeseen horrors, turning those early dreams into a nightmare of industrial destruction and waste.

THE KEY WORD HERE IS "INDUSTRIAL."

We've already examined how the business of commercial fishing was disastrously altered once the armadas of massive factory ships, able and willing to exert their power far beyond sustainable limits, displaced the small-scale fleets of artisanal boats that had been, for the most part, fishing for generations in an environmentally friendly, sustainable fashion. We've seen that industrial fishing's pursuit of profit at the cost of preservation has wreaked havoc upon the world's oceans and upon the marine ecosystems those oceans sustain.

Well, essentially the same thing has happened with aquaculture.

Once the Blue Revolution kicked in, fish farming, which until then had been little more than a quaint anomaly compared to the big business

YET VERY FEW of **US KNOW MUCH** about **THIS FISH.**

of fishing the high seas, was suddenly seen to have potential as a big business itself. Large corporations—some of them multinationals—jumped in the game and turned fish farming into a global industry.

I've devoted a good portion of this book to describing how the global business of industrial fishing has caused so much destruction in the pursuit of profits. Unfortunately, the same thing has happened with the burgeoning business of fish farming. What began as a noble experiment to find a way to feed the world's starving people has become an industry that, too often, ultimately takes food away from many of the world's poorest and that also has damaging environmental consequences.

I made a quick reference to some of those consequences earlier in the chapter. One that I didn't mention is the one that's probably the most devastating: what results from how most of these farmed fish are *fed*.

1/3

OF ALL GLOBAL
CATCH

FISH MEAL AND FISH OIL

As much as a third of all global catch ends up as fish meal or fish oil. In aquaculture operations worldwide, carnivorous farmed salmon are the biggest consumers of fish oil, and a huge percentage of fish meal goes to them, too. More and more prey species are being over-fished, only to be milled into the meal and oil to feed aquaculture and to a lesser degree, to be used in agriculture and pet food.

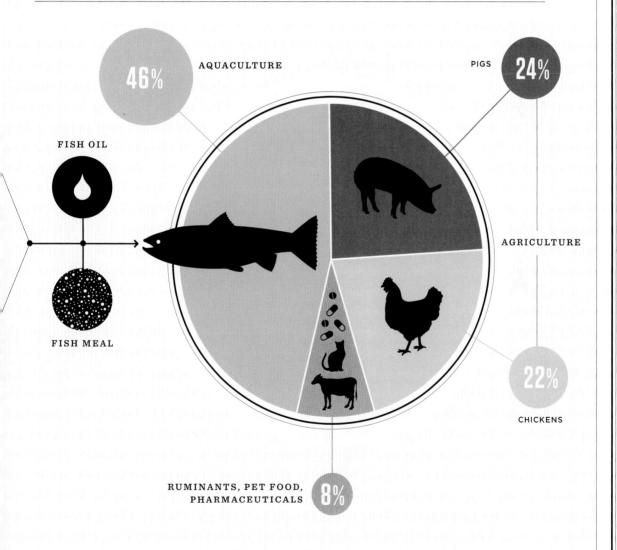

FISH OIL

FISH MEAL

AQUACULTURE
46%

PIGS
24%

AGRICULTURE

CHICKENS
22%

RUMINANTS, PET FOOD, PHARMACEUTICALS
8%

Source: Stiles et al. 2009. "Hungry Oceans: What happens when the prey is gone?" Oceana.

IT TAKES

3 TO 5 | TO PRODUCE 1 POUND OF

POUNDS OF FEED | SALMON

We've already talked about prey fish and the importance of the ocean's smaller species—species like anchovies, sardines, and menhaden—to the entire food web. It's these tiny so-called forage fish that form part of the foundation of the oceanic predator chain. Without them, the food fish—those larger species that people, especially Americans, love to eat—couldn't survive.

Well, these forage fish also form the foundation of the feed used by the aquaculture industry. In fact, that industry depends almost entirely on the fish meal and fish oil resulting from the processing of prey species to feed the salmon and tuna and other farmed fish crammed into those pens. The fish-farming industry's demand for "aquafeed" (their term for the meal and oil) has become so enormous that organizations like Oceana have singled it out as a significant driver of the global problem of overfishing. Those trawlers aren't just after the big fish. They've found that there's also enormous profit to be made by hoovering up those tiny anchovies and sardines, sand eels and sprats, menhaden and blue whiting. Krill—those tiny, shrimplike crustaceans blue whales completely depend on for their diet—are a target to sell to fish farms for feed.

Studies show that forage fish account for nearly 40 percent of all fish taken from the oceans today. A full 90 percent of those forage fish—many of which are perfectly edible and which, indeed, are staples of the diets of many people in developing nations (the people most in need of this kind of protein)—are processed into fish meal and fish oil. The aquaculture industry's purchasing share of that fish meal and oil has nearly doubled in the past decade, and it is used primarily to feed the two species of fish that are the most popular for Americans' consumption: salmon and tuna.

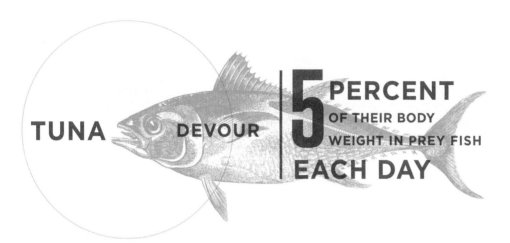

TUNA DEVOUR **5** PERCENT OF THEIR BODY WEIGHT IN PREY FISH EACH DAY

It just happens that these are two of the most voraciously carnivorous fish in the oceans. They are essentially eating machines. Farmed salmon consume more feed than all the other aquaculture species combined. It takes anywhere from three to five pounds of feed to produce one pound of salmon.

As for tuna, farmed bluefin tuna devour as much as 5 percent of their own body weight in prey fish each day. Think about that for a second. For a two-hundred-pound man, that means he'd be eating ten pounds of food a day. Ten pounds! At that rate, he wouldn't stay a two-hundred-pound man very long.

Which is precisely the goal in feeding that tuna. The intent is to *fatten* the bluefin for market, in much the same way cattle are fattened before they're finally slaughtered for beef.

Studies predict that if the aquaculture industry continues feeding its "product" at current rates, the demands of its fish will surpass the supply of wild-sourced fish meal in about 2020, and even sooner for fish oil.

But of far more concern to marine scientists and advocates of the oceans is the enormous *waste* involved in using the wild fish to feed these farmed fish. I hope you are as astounded, even as outraged, as I was to learn that as much as five pounds of fish taken from the ocean was used to create one pound of the farmed salmon you see sitting on ice in your grocery store's seafood section. It just doesn't make sense. And again, it's pulling the rug out from under the entire oceanic food web, which will collapse like a ton of bricks if this kind of fishing continues.

THERE IS SUCH A THING AS SUSTAINABLE AQUACULTURE

SCOTT CULLEN

Executive Director, GRACE Communications Foundation

Scott Cullen has spent most of his life in or near the water: surfing, sailing, paddling, fishing, ice boating, or swimming. He is the executive director of GRACE Communications Foundation (www. gracelinks.org), which works to promote and develop community-based production and consumption of food, water, and energy.

We know that ocean health is in decline and stocks of many popular food fish are largely depleted. As a result, aquaculture—the cultivation of aquatic animals—has expanded rapidly and is likely to continue in coming years. However, conventional aquaculture has been associated with water pollution, habitat damage, the release of captive fish into the wild (threatening wild populations), and negative impacts on local economies. Fortunately, another solution exists: land-based, recirculating aquaculture systems (RAS).

RAS: GREENER AND MORE JUST

These aquaculture systems have enormous potential to avoid the ecological and economic problems associated with ocean fish farming, providing safer, more sustainable domestic seafood for US consumers at all socioeconomic levels. And because RAS utilizes closed-loop facilities, it is highly unlikely that fish can escape the system; therefore RAS can be used to grow a wide range of fish (and plants) without threatening the environment or competing with local fisheries.

Perhaps best of all, the nutrient-rich wastewater produced by RAS can be used to grow aquaponic herbs and vegetables. Once the plants absorb the nutrients, the "cleaned" water circulates back into the fish tanks, closing the loop, at great benefit to the fish as well as the plants. RAS is a growing industry, and its proponents are working to increase the environmental sustainability of the process by developing ways to reduce energy use and by creating systems compact enough to be located on otherwise unusable urban properties.

As demonstrated in urban areas around the country, RAS can be located in underserved areas to provide a fresh source of protein and vegetables. This local scalability will result in a smaller carbon footprint due to reduced shipping distance, and operators will have, in addition to fish stocks, fresh vegetables to sell to local restaurants and markets, creating living-wage jobs as well as increasing access to healthful food.

The future of aquaculture will be charted in the next few years. A greener—and bluer—future is possible, but we must avoid the mistakes made by industrial livestock production ("factory farming"), which have led to environmental degradation, species loss, and public health risks, and pursue clean, locally based sustainable aquaculture.

AS IF ANY MORE EVIDENCE WERE NEEDED TO show that the aquaculture industry as it operates now is in need of reform, taking a quick look at the horrific conditions under which many of these fish are raised should close the case. I say "quick" because some of the details we're about to get into are pretty disgusting.

Here are some of the most prominent problems.

CROWDING

- A typical salmon farm is a network of submerged net pens located in relatively shallow seawater close to shore.

- A typical pen is composed of a metal or plastic frame and mesh netting that forms the sides and bottom (sometimes the top is covered with netting, as well). They range from thirty to ninety feet wide, and from thirty to sixty feet deep.

- An average pen holds about fifty thousand salmon, though it's not uncommon to see more squeezed in, sometimes upping the total to as many as eighty thousand.

- In a typical pen, each salmon (at an average length of two and a half feet) winds up with an area of water the size of a standard bathtub.

- These tightly packed pens have been described as "underwater chicken farms."

- A small farm might stock about two hundred thousand fish. Large farms stock well over 1 million.

- This many fish in such a small space produces a steady rain of feces that settles on the seafloor, sinks into the sediment, smothers bottom-dwelling organisms, and robs the water of oxygen, producing toxic algal blooms.

- A single fish farm with two hundred thousand fish can produce as much daily sewage as a city of sixty-five thousand people.

- Naturally programmed to migrate, to swim massive distances, to *move*, the frustrated salmon tend to thrash around against one another and the sides of the pen, opening wounds and sores that are prone to infection, disease, and parasitization.

INFECTION AND DISEASE

- Infections damage the health of the fish and lower their resistance to pathogens such as fungi, intestinal parasites, bacteria, and viruses including the one that causes infectious hematopoietic necrosis, which causes spinal deformities in some of the fish that survive it. Mortality rates in young fish are alarmingly high, too.

- Significant outbreaks of infectious salmon anemia (ISA) have recently been reported all over the world, from Scotland to Maine to Chile, the latter of which is the world's second-largest exporter of farmed salmon (behind Norway) and the biggest exporter to the United States. The virus, while not harmful to humans, is devastating to infected fish populations. The Chilean outbreak forced the closure of close to half of the nation's farms and the layoff of thousands of workers, while a 2002 outbreak in Maine led to the killing of 2.5 million sick fish and a federal insurance payout (from taxpayers' pockets) of $16 million. Two more outbreaks in Maine in 2003 resulted in the destruction of another 125,000 salmon.

- Cataracts and blindness are conditions commonly found among farmed salmon. But the most common—and destructive—condition, by far, is infestation by sea lice.

SEA LICE

- Sea lice are tiny parasites that attach to a fish and feed on its skin and flesh. There are many known species of sea lice, including the common salmon louse.

- A typical juvenile sea louse is the size of a grain of rice. A fully grown louse is the size of the head of a thumbtack and shaped like a tiny horseshoe crab. Females trail long white strands of eggs.

- One female sea louse can produce more than a thousand larvae in her lifetime. The larvae drift in the water, waiting to attach to a fish that's passing by. In the open sea, the vast majority of larvae die. In the closed area of a farmed salmon cage, an enormous number attach to the fish.

SIGNIFICANT OUTBREAKS of **INFECTIOUS SALMON ANEMIA (ISA)** have been **REPORTED ALL OVER** the **WORLD, INCLUDING CHILE,** the **WORLD'S SECOND-LARGEST EXPORTER** of **FARMED SALMON** and the **BIGGEST EXPORTER TO THE UNITED STATES.**

- In the wild, an adult salmon can survive an infestation of as many as several dozen sea lice. But in the confines of a pen, where *hundreds* attach to a single fish, the lice eat their way into the fish, causing bleeding from the fins and the eyes. Sometimes they eat all the way down to the bone. At the head, this can expose the salmon's skull in what's called a death crown.

 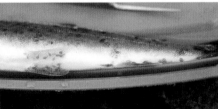

SEA LICE on a salmon and a sea trout

TREATMENTS

- The treatments for sea lice and other diseases that are common at fish farms can be as destructive as the diseases themselves.

- Pesticides and other industrial toxins are frequently used to kill sea lice. Hydrogen peroxide, chlorine, iodine, and a range of cancer-linked poisons are also often used. In *Bottomfeeder*, Taras Grescoe describes how a poison marketed under the trade name Slice is used at Canadian fish farms, even though it's banned in the United States and might be a marine toxin. The same chemical compound is also used on Chilean salmon farms. Even Agent Orange—the highly toxic defoliant used in Vietnam—has been found at some farms by inspectors. These poisonous chemicals not only contaminate the fish in the pens—as well as the humans who eat them—but also wind up being flushed into the surrounding waters, endangering wild fish in the vicinity. (We'll get to other ways those wild fish are endangered in just a moment.)

SALMON are fed pellets containing fish proteins and antibiotics.

- Antibiotics are commonly added to fish-farm water to prevent the spread of infectious diseases. But large doses of antibiotics can cultivate drug-resistant pathogens, and humans who ingest fish loaded with these antibiotics may become less responsive to them as well. In 2009, in response to an inquiry from Oceana, the Chilean government released data showing the abuse of antibiotics at Chilean salmon farms. The figures showed that Chile had used almost 600 times more antibiotics than its chief competitor in the salmon farming business, Norway, in 2007.

- Pesticides are sometimes sprayed on the surface water of the fish pens to keep insects away. Diesel fuel has even been used for this purpose.

- Grescoe describes in his book how even the eggs in a fish farm's hatchery are treated with chemicals to protect them from disease. Among the chemicals used is a formaldehyde-based fungicide called formalin, which is listed as a human carcinogen by the World Health Organization. Grescoe notes that another toxic fungicide called malachite green, which has been found to cause liver tumors in rats and carries the risk of birth defects in humans, is widely used on farmed fish in China.

- It's not uncommon to find highly toxic chemicals that are banned in one country being used in another. One example, reported in *Time* magazine, was one of a class of antimicrobial drugs called nitrofurans that are banned from use in food animals in Europe and the United States but that inspectors have found at high levels at shrimp farms in Thailand, Vietnam, and Myanmar. The *Time* report also noted that another chemical banned in food animals, an antibiotic called chloramphenicol that can cause fatal anemia in humans, has been used at Chinese shrimp farms.

TO PROTECT THEM FROM DISEASE, even **THE EGGS** in a **FISH FARM'S HATCHERY ARE TREATED** with a **FUNGICIDE CALLED FORMALIN, WHICH IS LISTED AS A HUMAN CARCINOGEN.**

- Even the nets in fish farms can be subjected to hazardous chemicals. To prevent deterioration, these nets are often treated with chemical antifoulants, many of which contain the heavy metals copper and zinc, both considered to be dangerous substances by the EPA.

COHO SALMON
hatching

ESCAPES

- Under normal conditions, farmed fish often escape through rips in the pen netting caused by, among other things, predators (like sea lions) anxious to get at the fish. Escapes are even more prevalent when the water is turbulent, such as when storms pass through. And some experts believe that escapes in some cases may be intentional releases by salmon operators who need to get rid of product (perhaps because the fish face some of the problems listed above). The farmers very often are insured against the escape of fish from their pens.

- Farmed Atlantic salmon (the only kind of Atlantic salmon we eat, since the wild Atlantic salmon population is extremely small and fishing for them commercially is prohibited) seem to escape more than any other fish. In one instance in July 1997, 350,000 of them escaped into Washington State's Puget Sound. Farmed Atlantic salmon have been found thousands of miles away from the nearest salmon farm.

- Chile, which as I said is second only to Norway in farmed salmon production, is infamous for the great number of escapes from its farms. As many as 10 million salmon disappear from farms in Chile each year! Last year, as a direct result of Oceana's campaign to reform the Chilean salmon aquaculture industry, the Chilean National Congress passed legislation that criminalized the escape of farmed salmon, with provisions for imposing significant fines as well as prison sentences on the farms' owners.

- Escaped fish can wreak havoc in the surrounding waters. If they carry sea lice or other parasites, they will pass them on to the wild fish they encounter. The same goes for any diseases they might have.

- Farmed fish will also compete with and even attack their wild counterparts, and in places like Chile, where there are no wild salmon, the escaped salmon—fierce top predators—disrupt the food web by eating large amounts of prey fish, insects, and crustaceans that other predators in the area normally would have eaten.

GENETIC POLLUTION

- Recently, genetic experimentation to speed up the growth process and boost production of farmed salmon has increased. Transgenic salmon—those whose DNA has been altered by inserting genes from other species—have been developed that reach market weight in half the time it takes a regular salmon—18 months, compared to 36. If these Frankenfish, as they have been dubbed, escape their pens, they could not only outcompete their wild, natural cousins, but also interbreed with them, damaging the gene pool and causing physical deformities in the wild population.

So there it is. When we wind up looking seriously at something straight out of some science fiction horror film—*Frankenfish*—you know something's terribly wrong. I'll say it again: I don't think anyone can claim that the aquaculture industry as it exists right now isn't in need of drastic reform. That's the bad news.

The good news is that **REFORM IS ALREADY HAPPENING.** In fact, even as I write these words, serious changes for the better are being made concerning every issue we've addressed in this book.

In the next, final chapter, we'll take a look at what is being done across the board to save our oceans and, in the end, ourselves. And we'll tell you how *you* can pitch in and do your part.

RESPECTING THE OCEAN

LAIRD HAMILTON

Laird Hamilton is known as the guiding genius of crossover board sports. The elder son of '60s surfing legend Bill Hamilton, Laird is a throwback to the time when surfers prided themselves on being all-around watermen. He learned to surf between the ages of two and three on the front half of a surfboard; and at age eight, when his father took him to the sixty-foot cliff at Waimea Falls, Laird looked down, looked back at his dad, and jumped. "He's been bold since day one," says Bill, "and hell-bent on living life to the extreme." Laird is the author of Force of Nature: Mind, Body, Soul, and, of Course, Surfing.

LAIRD: As humans, we have dominion over so much; it's easy to forget that in the scheme of things, we're really not in control. There's something humbling about knowing that you are at the mercy of a force so much larger than yourself. There's no better example of this than the ocean. The oceans cover three-quarters of the Earth's surface. Countless life forms make their home there. We're made of water. The water is where I make my living and where I find my inspiration. It's who I am. Many times, I feel like I belong there more than I do on land. And I consider anyone else who feels that way, who loves the ocean, a friend.

When I'm in California, I go paddling early in the morning, and it never takes long before I come upon a floating plastic bag. I'll pick it up and fill it with other garbage I find along the way. I only cover the tiniest fraction of the ocean's vast territories. It's scary to imagine what's out there. And there's stuff that's worse than what you see—disintegrating plastics and a whole toxic stew of chemicals with names you can't pronounce.

Everybody thinks the most important part of surfing is some technical move you make on the board. Wrong. The most important part of surfing is knowing the ocean, respecting the ocean. What we've been given is precious. It's majestic in its smallest details and its largest manifestations. Anyone not humbled by the power of the ocean should take a good, long look at a fifty-foot wave. If you don't have respect for a wave, it's only a matter of time before the ocean teaches you to get some. We're all equal before a wave.

PLASTICS

ED BEGLEY JR.

Plastics have betrayed us like a cheating spouse.

Early on in the dating process, we were smitten, to be sure.

He made everything so damn easy.

From feeding us, to picking up the dry cleaning, even taking out the trash, he was eager to help at every turn.

He was clearly well-to-do. He had earnings in the billions and employed workers in the millions.

It was hard not to fall in love, and we soon became wed to this new way of life.

Sure, he changed over the years. He was so controlling. He started inserting himself in every aspect of our lives, but the thought of divorcing seemed impossible.

What about the kids? They loved him and the toys he provided with every happy meal.

Some friends tried to warn us, but we accused them of being jealous. Of having their own agenda.

When they wouldn't shut up about it, we simply stopped talking to them.

And we found a way to justify it all, because we were simply in too deep.

Until that day a few years back, when we drove down to the coast to take in the view, and there he was, caught in the act.

The rain had flushed his lies out in the open and they sat there before us, as far as the eye could see. And we quickly learned that it wasn't just in our town.

Of course, he had an explanation. It was a onetime thing. What we had witnessed wasn't his fault.

It was because of the rain, or faulty storm drains. He promised he'd never do it again.

But soon we couldn't ignore the facts. It wasn't just after a rain. And it wasn't restricted to the coast.

He was cheating on us everywhere.

In our lakes, rivers, and streams. On land, and yes, even in our bloodstream.

It turned out . . . he was slowly poisoning us!

We decided we'd get away to think things over. We went out in the middle of the ocean to clear our head. See if we could not think about him for a while.

And, there he was. Caught worse than before.

Out here he was known as the Great Pacific Garbage Patch, and he was cheating on families in every corner of the globe.

He was working this same scam everywhere.

He had a gull in every port . . . choking on plastic debris.

And, countless other sea birds, fish, and marine mammals.

Clearly WE needed help as much as he did.

So what were we to do?

We formed support groups, like: www.plasticpollutioncoalition.org

And we slowly got some recovery in our lives and started to spread the word.

We hope you'll do the same.

WHAT YOU CAN DO

- **DON'T EAT FARMED SALMON.** Any salmon marked "Atlantic" on a menu is farmed and avoiding it helps ease overfishing and pollution.

- **DOWNLOAD THE MONTEREY BAY AQUARIUM'S SEAFOOD WATCH APPLICATION ON YOUR PHONE TO HELP MAKE RESPONSIBLE CHOICES.** This helpful overview of seafood will remind you what farmed seafood, like oysters or mussels, is generally OK to enjoy—and what should be avoided.

- **ASK THE SERVER FOR THEIR BEST WILD-CAUGHT DOMESTIC OR NORTH AMERICAN SALMON OR FOR "DIVER SCALLOPS" HARVESTED ONE AT AT TIME IN A TOTALLY SUSTAINABLE MANNER.**

- **PROTECT THE FOOD WEB.** Any fish farming of carnivorous fish—that's salmon, tuna, etc.—results in overfishing as forage fish must be caught to feed the farmed fish. And despite some advancements in the field, the vast majority of at-sea fish farms still produce enormous amounts of waste and pollution. We're a long way from truly sustainable at-sea aquaculture, but the industry is starting to explore better options.

- **WRITE A LETTER TO THE USDA AND FDA COMMISSIONERS, URGING THEM TO BAN ANY IMPORTS OF FISH FARMED WITH QUINOLONES AND OTHER HARMFUL ANTIBIOTICS PERMANENTLY.**

CHAPTER EIGHT

LIVING
BLUE

FOR THE PAST SEVEN CHAPTERS, WE'VE

looked at the problems that face our oceans. And we've let science lead the way. It's time to look at some solutions, but before we do, I'd like to return for a moment to the sense of awe I first felt looking at the ocean, the spirit of which imbues everything that you've read.

I've done this work for twenty-five years now, and I've never considered it a burden or something to be approached with fear. It's been a privilege, and it's also been fun. I think that's because I was raised around people who were aware of the sacredness of nature and of our responsibility to respect and protect it while always keeping a light heart. I saw this in the Hopi Indians of northwestern Arizona when I was growing up there. And I've seen it as well in many other people throughout my life. Certainly in my parents. And in the people around us who worked the land, the ranchers and farmers I knew growing up. I've also seen it in the people whose lives are tied to the seas. All of them—the Hopis, my parents, the ranchers and farmers and fishermen—they've all understood that a lot has come before us and a lot will come after us, that this time we are here on Earth is not just about us, it's also about our stewardship of what we've been given. And it's so important to approach this stewardship with that light heart, with the Hopi heart.

FOR EVERY THREAT that **FACES OUR OCEANS WE POSSESS** the **KNOWLEDGE** and the **MEANS** to **REMEDY IT.**

WE'VE DETAILED A GOOD NUMBER OF DAUNTING SCENES AND scenarios throughout these pages, but for every one of those situations, there is a solution. For every threat that faces our oceans—and, by extension, that threatens *us*—we possess the knowledge and the means to remedy it.

The question we're left with is whether we possess the *will* to do what needs to be done. Are we ready to act? Do we have what turning things around will take globally, in terms of international issues; nationally, in terms of challenges we face as a society; and individually, in terms of how we choose to live our lives and respond to this crisis?

It's easy to sit back in any situation and let someone else take care of it, to ignore the problem and hope it will go away or to outright deny that the problem exists. I hope we've made it clear by now that when it comes to our oceans, we are truly at a tipping point. Complacency is no longer an option.

With other environmental issues in America's past, we've shown how we as a people are able to answer the call when we realize we're facing a crisis. We've responded to the polluting of rivers and lakes, breathing new life into waters that were all but dead. We've brought endangered plants and animals back from the brink of extinction. We've passed laws that regulate what we can put into our soil and into our air, as well as into our rivers and lakes. We've realized that we need to protect and preserve our environment rather than simply exploit it.

Thanks to the tireless efforts of thousands of marine scientists and engaged citizens, along with those of concerned, clear-sighted fishermen who refuse to stand by and watch their way of life being destroyed, we no longer have any excuse to sit back and do nothing. These legions of men and women who are committed to saving the seas have laid out the issues and forced us to look. We can no longer sit back and say, "Hey, the oceans are so big they can handle *anything*." We can no longer use them as trash bins for our garbage, as sewers for our waste, and as a vast seafood supermarket where the supply never runs out and the bill never comes due.

We've reached a point where the fate of the oceans truly is in the balance. That said, one saving grace is how remarkably resilient the oceans can be. Given even a sliver of a chance—and that's about all we've got left—they will bounce back. They've shown that they have this capacity over and over again throughout history. Take World War II, when commercial fishing in the North Atlantic slowed down because of the presence of Germany's U-boats. Over the course of those five or so years, the fish populations in that part of the Atlantic and especially the North Sea significantly increased. We've seen the same thing more recently, on a smaller scale, in the Middle East, where artisanal fishermen have reported a leap in their catches ever since industrial fishing in that region was severely restricted because of the war in Iraq. The recent spate of pirating along the Somali coast has also had a chilling effect on commercial fishing. That's left the local fishermen in their outboard dinghies and canoes rejoicing, saying the fish have been practically jumping into their boats.

The point is, unless they're pushed over the brink to the point where they cannot be saved, fish have a tremendous ability to replenish themselves. The seawater itself, even as much as we pollute it, has that same capacity, given a chance.

Here is a list of the most important things that have to be done—and

A loggerhead turtle escaping a net with a turtle excluder device

Australian barramundi fish at a Massachusetts fish farm

done *soon*—in order to bring our oceans and the life they sustain back from the brink of total destruction. Some of these goals are already being pursued. Others are waiting for people like you to stand up and push the powers that be to follow through on the overwhelming scientific evidence and *do the right thing*.

• ENFORCE THE LAWS THAT ARE ALREADY ON THE BOOKS

Too many policy leaders, nationally and internationally, are part of the fishing-industrial complex. For one reason or another, they're beholden to the fishing industry, showing more allegiance to the short-term needs of fishing-related corporations than to the long-term needs of their constituents—*us*—and the oceans.

This has got to change. Tough times require tough action. Laws are made to be enforced, *period*—not skirted by battalions of lawyers pointing the way toward loopholes or watered down by lawmakers whose primary concern is pleasing the business interests who put them in office. In Daniel Pauly's view, it's time for laws of the sea to be treated as obligations, not mere suggestions. We need to remind our government representatives that the laws protecting our oceans must be enforced. The more we show them how much this means to us, the more it will mean to them.

THIS TIME WE ARE HERE on EARTH is NOT JUST ABOUT US

IT'S ALSO ABOUT OUR STEWARDSHIP of WHAT WE'VE BEEN GIVEN.

Left: a Baghdad fish market in 2009; *right:* an Iraqi fisherman

• ELIMINATE FISHERIES SUBSIDIES

According to Oceana, eliminating fishing subsidies is "one of the single greatest actions that can be taken to protect the world's oceans."

This is why Oceana, along with numerous other environmental organizations, has relentlessly worked for years to push through the "Doha decision"—a set of goals established by the WTO at a 2001 meeting in the Middle Eastern city of Doha, Qatar. Among those goals is substantially restricting, if not entirely eliminating, government subsidies to fisheries.

Unfortunately, the WTO has missed a series of deadlines since that time and is now six years behind schedule, making the Doha discussions the longest-running set of trade talks in history.

But WTO director-general Pascal Lamy is not deterred. At a WTO Trade Negotiations Committee meeting in November 2010, he referred to "a clear sense of urgency," "intensified engagement," and a desire for "negotiations across the board to conclude the end game" arising among the nations involved.

"In sum, we have the political signal, we have the technical expertise," he concluded, "to translate these into a comprehensive deal which you can all take back home."

In other words, if Lamy's expectations hold true, the world could finally see significant restrictions on fisheries subsidies sometime in 2011.

• REDUCE THE SIZE OF THE WORLD'S FISHING FLEET

This will be a natural by-product of cutting back subsidies. Without government backing, a huge number of those *over*fishing boats will be forced to cease operation, and we'll move closer to striking a balance between the numbers and sizes of the boats catching fish and the numbers and sizes of the fish to be caught.

In other words, we'll move that much closer to *sustainable* fishing in the oceans.

IT'S TIME for LAWS of the SEA to BE TREATED as OBLIGATIONS, NOT MERE SUGGESTIONS.

• USE SCIENCE-BASED QUOTAS TO SET FISHING LIMITS

We need to take pressure off overexploited stocks of fish in order to give them time to recover. As a marine science maxim puts it, "A reduction in fishing pressure today will yield long-term harvests tomorrow."

The fastest way to reduce that pressure is to apply catch limits to the commercial catching of fish. But too often, for a host of reasons, the governmental bodies that regulate the size of fish catches ignore the advice of scientists and set unsustainable quotas. Getting the science right and ensuring that fishermen are obliged to follow it is critical in establishing a stable, coherent system for managing fisheries.

• BATTLE DISCARDED BYCATCH WITH "CAP, COUNT, AND CONTROL"

Most fishing results in bycatch, i.e., the hauling in of animals and fish that were not targeted by the gear; this bycatch is often discarded—tossed back into the sea. To prevent this inhumane waste, a system of cap, count, and control should be implemented. It would require each fishing boat to count it as part of the boat's total catch, and—since the quotas would "cap" the catch's total weight and species—to pay a penalty for the size of its bycatch.

This system would require a network of overseers to be placed aboard a sufficient number of boats to monitor the boats' catches and counts. Under this system, fisheries would have an incentive to be more careful and selective in terms of their methods.

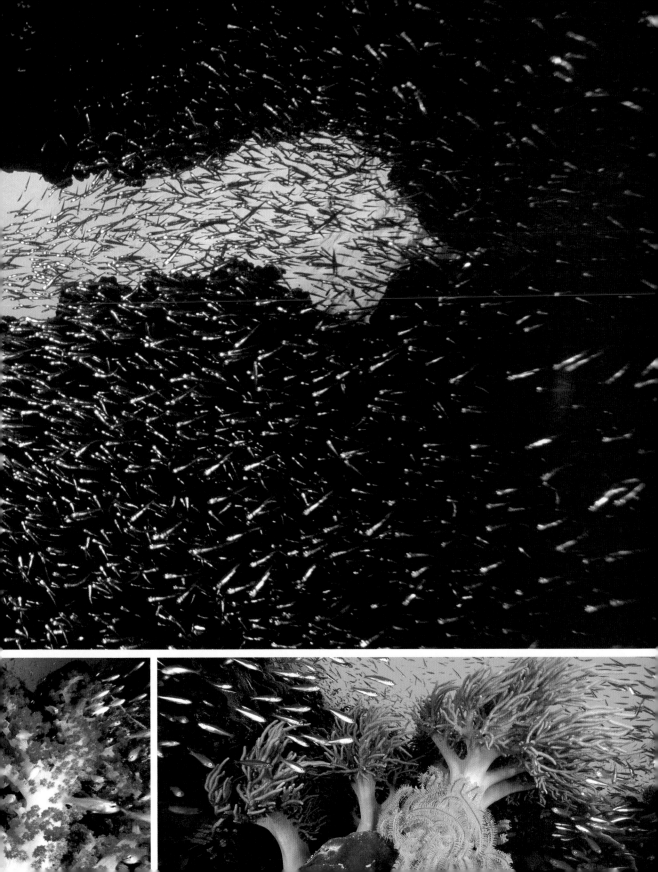

• ELIMINATE DESTRUCTIVE FISHING PRACTICES

Doing away with the most damaging and indiscriminate types of fishing practices and gear has to become a priority.

There have already been successful efforts.

- In the Atlantic Ocean and the Gulf of Mexico, the US government now requires that all American shrimp trawlers use turtle excluder devices. Sea turtle bycatch has been cut by an estimated 97 percent.

- In the Mediterranean, several EU member governments have been able to crack down significantly on the illegal use of UN-banned driftnets (so-called "walls of death"), which had been killing several thousand dolphins and other sea creatures each year.

- In Australia, prawn trawlers adjusted their devices to cut their fish bycatch by more than 60 percent without decreasing the size of their total catch.

The priority now is to end the destructive practice of bottom trawling. Oceana and other groups have succeeded in protecting more than 2 million square miles of ocean habitat from this form of fishing. In Belize—home to the second-largest barrier reef in the world—the government just banned trawling in all its waters, becoming only the third country in the world to completely prohibit this practice. In countries where bottom trawling is allowed to continue, the legal size of those rollers and rockhoppers we talked about earlier must be reduced to minimize the damage to seafloor habitat. Trawlers must also be forced to avoid areas where fish and other sea life, such as sea turtles, are actively spawning or migrating, and where there is sensitive habitat (like deep-sea corals).

• CREATE MARINE RESERVES

This is a biggie.

One of the best ways to restore our oceans—especially the sections of the seas in greatest crisis right now—is to designate specific zones as off-limits to any kind of fishing. These marine reserves are essentially oceanic national parks, protected from industrial and commercial exploitation.

Right now, nearly 12 percent of the world's land has been set aside as protected national parks. The corresponding figure for our oceans is 0.6 percent. That's terrible, and it can be easily remedied with a few strokes of some pens.

One of those pen strokes took place just last year, in 2010, when the president of Chile signed into existence an enormous marine reserve in the waters surrounding the uninhabited Pacific island of Sala y Gómez. The reserve, named for the island, is roughly the size of Greece, and unlike the waters around nearby Easter Island, which have been badly depleted by fishing, the waters around Sala y Gómez are replete with vulnerable species such as sharks and lobsters that will now be able to thrive in a protected haven.

Sylvia Earle has a great term she uses to describe protected marine reserves. She calls them "hope spots."

We can never have too much hope.

DOING AWAY with the **MOST DAMAGING** and **INDISCRIMINATE TYPES** of **FISHING PRACTICES** —— and **GEAR HAS** to **BECOME** a **PRIORITY.** ——

• PROTECT PARTICULAR SPECIES

In the same way that we've regulated or outlawed the trade of terrestrial products like ivory and furs, we need to extend "off-limits" signs to endangered species of fish and other animals in our oceans. We've already done this with some—the most obvious being whales. But many more need our protection.

The most obvious in need of protection are those "big fish" whose numbers are now 90 percent lower than they were in 1950—bluefin tuna, swordfish, marlin, king mackerel, and sharks. But just as important are prey species, those small fish whose populations have plummeted in recent decades as they've been scooped up by the billions to provide feed for fish farms. In 2002, the US government identified prey fish as an essential component of a healthy oceanic ecosystem. It's encouraging to see our government recognizing the importance of protecting sea life for the widespread effects it has throughout the entire food web, from one end to the other.

Individual states have already recognized the importance of protecting prey fish. And off the coasts of Washington, Oregon, and California, a federal ban has been instituted on the taking of krill, which are so critical to the marine life that feeds on them—especially blue whales, which survive on almost nothing *but* krill.

• STOP USING FISH AS FEED FOR FARM ANIMALS

Sticking with the subject of prey fish, it's bad enough that they are the primary source of feed for fish farms. But there is no excuse and no reason for fish to be fed to farm animals.

A recent study showed that the world's farmed pigs and chickens consume twice the amount of seafood in one year that the Japanese people consume as a nation and *six times* the amount we Americans eat.

Researchers all agree that we need to take the pressure off the world's fisheries by finding feed for farm animals from sources other than the oceans.

"We should work to eliminate the use of tasty fish for livestock production," says Daniel Pauly. "It's a waste. Plus, it is not what pigs or chickens naturally eat. When was the last time you saw a chicken fishing?"

• BUILD SMARTER FISH FARMS

In the previous chapter I referred to the need for reform of the aquaculture industry. Although many marine scientists conclude that there is no such thing as a safe, healthy fish farm, there are those who see a saving grace in what they call "smart aquaculture." The FAO agrees.

By "smart" they mean properly managed, built on a smaller scale (like the traditional Chinese method), and raising species of fish that are highly efficient in terms of reproduction and, most important, *feed.*

Aquaculturists have found what they believe are the fish of the future: freshwater fish, and vegetarian and herbivorous saltwater fish able to feed on algae, plankton, and even human waste.

Some of these "fish of the future" are tilapia (which I mentioned in the previous chapter in connection with seafood fraud), Chinese carp, Arctic char, and a fish called the barramundi.

There are ways **WE CAN ACTUALLY SAVE THE OCEANS** with **OUR OWN INDIVIDUAL ACTIONS.**

Fish of the future do not need those millions of tons of fish meal and fish oil that the currently farmed carnivorous species like salmon and tuna need to survive and grow. And, if they are raised using proper precautions to avoid endangering the surrounding wild ecosystem, farmed fish can at least partially fill the "fish gap," say proponents of this kind of aquaculture.

Even the most avid proponents of the possibilities of aquaculture acknowledge that the fish gap cannot be completely closed by fish farming in any form. The most optimistic scenarios leave us with a world in the near future—within the next 20 to 30 years—where the demand for fish simply cannot be met. So, what can we do?

Well, if we've exhausted all we can possibly do on the supply side of the equation, then our last hope is to turn to the demand side.

And that's where you come in. You, and me, and every other person around us. There are ways we can actually save the oceans with our own individual actions.

Beginning with changing the way we eat.

THE TIME IS COMING—MORE LIKELY SOONER THAN LATER—WHEN those "big fish" we savor so much—the poached salmon, the grilled swordfish, the seared tuna—will for all intents and purposes be gone from the menus of even our finest, priciest restaurants.

We'll be the last to see them go, because as Americans, we are blessed—many of us—with a higher standard of living than many other people on Earth. We live near the top of, if you will, the world's wealth web. The illusion of the oceans' abundance we talked about earlier will persist here in the United States longer than almost anywhere else. But finally, inevitably, the day will come when even the most privileged among us will have to eat lower on the food chain and give up those big fish.

But far from being a sad or tragic turn of events, that transition will actually be a good thing. It will most certainly be good for the oceans, and for the web of life those oceans are struggling right now to sustain. It will be good for us as well, in ways many of us may not realize. And it won't be nearly as difficult to make that transition as many of us might imagine.

Sardines

We're starting to hear it all the time, about so many facets of our lives: We can live better and use fewer resources. We just have to be smart. This will be the key to surviving on a planet whose resources, we now understand, are not "inexhaustible"—that term Thomas Huxley uttered so confidently, so long ago, about the numbers of fish in the sea.

If we truly care about the oceans, we can start making a change for the better this very minute by doing this one simple thing—learning to eat smaller, lower on the food chain.

Take sardines, for example. There's nothing wrong with the small, finger-size fish we're used to seeing in our supermarkets, packed in tins filled with olive oil. You can certainly live on sardines like that, even love them. But wild sardines can grow even larger—nothing like tuna or salmon, of course, but large enough to be the feature of a nice meal. My image of sardines used to be much different, but it was shattered one afternoon a few years ago when I sat down at an outdoor café in Spain and was served a single sardine close to a foot in length that was sizzling fresh off the grill.

That was an amazing experience. I haven't had the sardinella they eat in Africa, or the anchoveta they eat in Peru, or the blue whiting they eat, poached or steamed, in Russia and the Baltic states, or even menhaden flesh. I don't know if any of them are as delicious as that grilled sardine in Spain, but, prepared right, they are likely to be pretty tasty. I've heard that it's not uncommon in some parts of the world for the local people to *prefer* smaller fish, even when the big ones are available.

All over the world, many people already eat—and enjoy—smaller, more sustainable fish. And so can we. By eating them, we can help ensure that the bigger fish in the oceans have a chance to thrive again. Why not make it normal for our children, so there will be no shock of adjustment when they become adults and they face an ocean where supply simply can't meet demand.

If we do this, if we cut back on the "big fish," we'll be helping our oceans by giving them a break, taking off the pressure, easing the squeeze on the top of the marine food web, the big predators. After all, we're the biggest predators on the planet. The most powerful, anyway. We've *over*powered the oceans for far too long. It's time now to start taking responsibility for what we've done. I don't think learning to enjoy sardines and anchovies more than tuna steaks and salmon sashimi is that high a price to pay. At this point, with what the oceans are facing, eating those big fish—bluefin tuna, for example—is not just a conservation issue or a practical issue, but also a moral one. Paul Greenberg, in *Four Fish*, calls it "the seafood equivalent of driving a Hummer."

Eat small and eat smart—we can all do this.

With that in mind, here is a list of ten things each one of us can do to "live blue"—make lifestyle choices that can help preserve the oceans for ourselves and for generations to come. Starting on page 290, you'll find specific Web sites and other contact information for groups involved in each of these subjects.

EATING THOSE **BIG FISH** IS THE SEAFOOD **EQUIVALENT** OF DRIVING A **HUMMER.**

1. **JOIN A GROUP THAT SUPPORTS THE OCEANS.**
   There are a ton of great ocean conservation groups out there, like Oceana. Go online and do a Google search or go to sites like Charity Navigator to find out more. Also check out the list of recommended Web sites on page 293. The important thing is to get involved. I do heartily recommend Oceana—we really get things done. You can find out more at www.oceana.org.

2. **VOTE RESPONSIBLY. CONTACT YOUR REPRESENTATIVES.**
   Electing the right public officials is essential to having good ocean policy. Do your research and make an informed decision. Exercise your right to vote, and stay involved after Election Day. If you have concerns or questions, contact your representatives. You'll find helpful Web sites on page 293.

3. **EAT SUSTAINABLE SEAFOOD.**
   Global fisheries are on the verge of collapse. According to the FAO, 80 percent of the world's fisheries are now overexploited, fully exploited, significantly

depleted, or recovering from overexploitation. Carry a Seafood Watch card that identifies your best choices for sustainability, good alternatives, and which fish you should avoid eating. (You can print this card at the Monterey Bay Aquarium Web site listed on page 293.) Ask your seafood restaurant or fish market to buy from sustainable fisheries. Look for special terms like "line caught," "diver caught," "sustainably caught," and "sustainably harvested."

4. REDUCE ENERGY USE.

Carbon dioxide from burning fossil fuels is making our oceans more acidic. One consequence could be the loss of corals on a global scale, as their calcium skeletons are destroyed by the increasing acidity of the water. There are many simple ways you can reduce your energy use.

- Drive a hybrid or electric car.

- Maintain your vehicle properly, especially the tire inflation.

- Use mass transit, and support the installation of local light-rail systems.

- Use a bike whenever you can, for work and errands (the health benefits are a bonus).

- Combine errands to reduce trips.

- Install a programmable thermostat in your house.

- Set your thermostat a few degrees higher in the summer and lower in the winter.

- Turn off appliances when they aren't in use.

- Switch to more efficient lighting such as compact fluorescent lightbulbs in your house.

- Shop local farmers' markets for produce, cheese, meat, and other edible goods to create a robust marketplace for food that travels fewer miles, which conserves fossil fuels and reduces packaging.

- Cut down on the number of leisure air travel trips you take each year. Try a "stay-cation," such as a local hiking trip with family and good friends.

5. USE REUSABLE PLASTIC PRODUCTS.

Plastic debris in the oceans degrades marine habitats and contributes to the deaths of many marine animals. Because floating plastic often resembles food to many marine birds, sea turtles, and marine mammals, they can choke or starve because their digestive systems get blocked when they eat it. Help prevent these unnecessary deaths. Do not buy bottled water—use reusable water bottles. Use reusable cloth bags for shopping.

Left: BEACH CLEANUP, San Juan, Nicaragua; *right:* ALBATROSS CHICK full of plastic marine debris, Hawaii

6. PROPERLY DISPOSE OF HAZARDOUS MATERIALS.

Motor oil and other hazardous materials often end up washing into coastal areas because they aren't disposed of properly. This pollutes the water and hurts the overall health of our oceans. Be sure to dispose of hazardous waste in an environmentally safe way.

7. USE LESS FERTILIZER.

When fertilizers are used in gardening and agriculture, the excess eventually ends up in the ocean. One result is a "dead zone"—an area with very low levels of oxygen in the water. In fact, there's one the size of New Jersey in the Gulf of Mexico during the spring and summer. Since all marine life, including fish and shrimp, requires oxygen to live, creatures must flee the area or die. Many other coastal areas are at risk, too. So use fertilizer sparingly and remember that more usually is not better.

8. PICK UP LITTER ON BEACHES.

Much of the plastic and debris found in the ocean is first discarded on the beach. As beach crowds increase, so does the amount of trash left behind. Don't let your day at the beach contribute to the destruction of our oceans. Bring a trash bag with you for your garbage. Organize a beach cleanup party with friends and family or the local community.

9. BUY OCEAN-FRIENDLY PRODUCTS.

Avoid products produced using unsustainable or environmentally harmful methods. For example, avoid cosmetics containing shark squalene and jewelry made of coral or sea turtle shell. These products are directly linked to unsustainable fishing methods and the destruction of entire ecosystems.

10. SHARE WHAT YOU'VE LEARNED.

Spread the word via Facebook and Twitter about ongoing issues. Don't lecture, but look for opportunities to share interesting information and fun facts about the oceans with family and friends, especially when you're at the beach or near the sea. We're learning in so many ways that we—human beings—can't reengineer this planet, that it's not here as a limitless resource for us to mine, log, drill, hunt, and fish to our hearts' content.

Probably the most important lesson we've learned is that everything is connected. The things we do to harm the oceans harm so many other things by extension, like ripples that spread when a stone hits the surface of water.

The same goes for the things we do to *help.* Never feel like a problem is too large to be fixed. And never believe that one person is too small to make a difference.

Everything connects. Everyone matters.

And each of us can learn to live blue.

———

YOU'VE TAKEN A BIG FIRST STEP BY READING THIS BOOK. THANK you for that. Now, I'd like to ask you to go a step further and absorb as much as you can of what you've just read into your own life. If each of us carries an awareness, a mindfulness of the extraordinary grace and power of *water*, we will find ways, large and small, to honor its sanctity.

On these pages, I've suggested ways for all of us to get involved. But really, ultimately, you will find your own way. Your own mind and heart will lead you.

In the end, this is all about healing and health and, most important, hope. So remember to have a light heart. Imagine the oceans you want to have and then do something good for them—something that makes you feel good. If you find yourself feeling overwhelmed, then set aside what you're doing and choose something else.

Finally, don't forget the child you once were. Keep that young child's sense of wonderment, of awe.

And have fun.

EVERYTHING is CONNECTED.

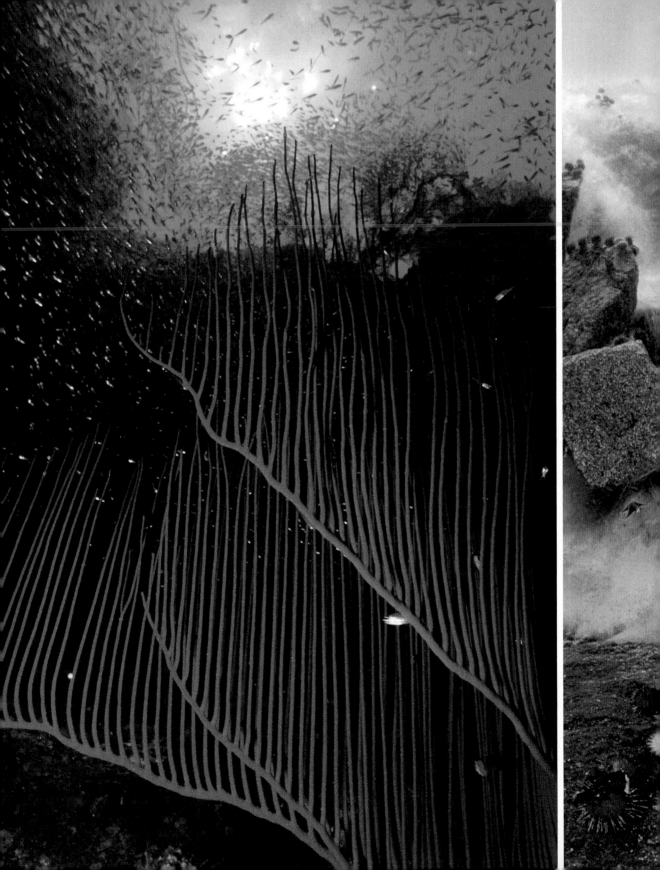

The **THINGS WE DO** that **HARM** the **OCEANS**

HARM SO MANY OTHER THINGS

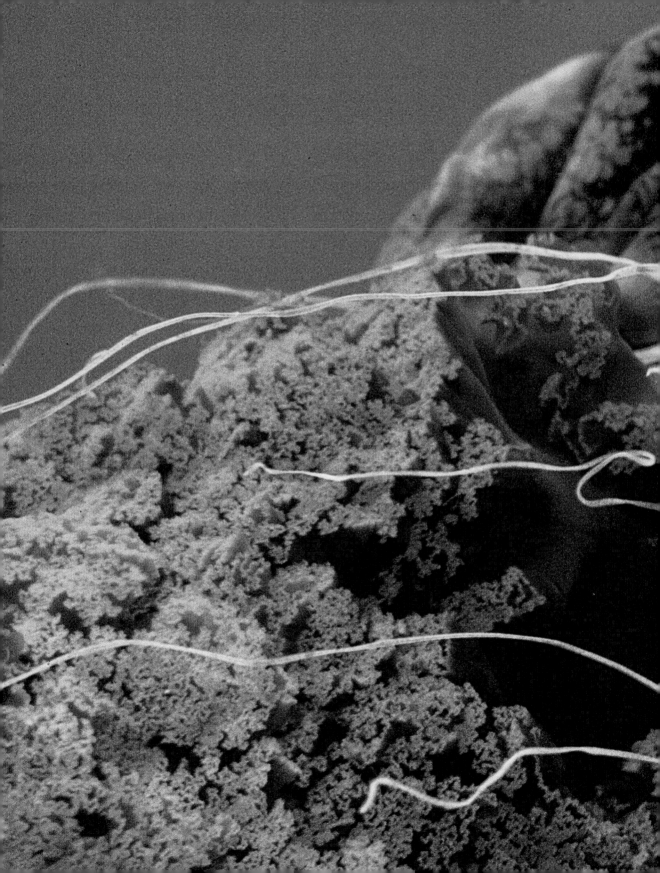

LIKE RIPPLES that SPREAD

————————— WHEN a STONE HITS the SURFACE of WATER.

NEVER BELIEVE that ONE PERSON is TOO SMALL to MAKE a DIFFERENCE.

EVERYTHING CONNECTS EVERYONE MATTERS

RECOMMENDED READING

LEARN MORE ABOUT THE IMPACT OF OIL

- Read a report about the long-term impact of oil on wildlife and public health: www.oceana.org/toxic-legacy
- Visit the International Bird Rescue Research Center—learn how birds are cleaned after an oil spill: www.ibrrc.org/
- Go to the Gulf Restoration Network Web site to learn more about impacts on the Gulf of Mexico: http://healthygulf.org/
- Learn about what happened in the past with oil spills from *Exxon Valdez* expert Dr. Jeff Short: http://oceana.org/oil-spill-facts
- Watch Tom Friedman discuss his documentary *Addicted to Oil*: http://dsc.discovery. com/convergence/addictedtooil/addictedtooil.html
- Read Oceana's wind report: "Untapped Wealth: Offshore Wind Can Deliver Cleaner, More Affordable Energy and More Jobs Than Offshore Oil": http://na.oceana.org/ sites/default/files/Offshore_Wind_Report.pdf
- Visit www.black-tides.com to learn more about oil and what it does when spilled.
- Watch the video "An Abbreviated History of Fossil Fuels" to observe a succinct story of our oil addiction: www.youtube.com/watch?v=cJ-J91SwP8w
- Watch the fascinating new "solutions" documentary *Carbon Nation* in a local theater or through Amazon.com or Netflix.
- Check out *Power Trip: The Story of America's Love Affair with Energy* (Harper Perennial, 2010), by former Grist.org and *Outside* columnist Amanda Little. This is a great and quick read about how American ingenuity led us down the path of fossil fuel dependence and how that same ingenuity can help us transform our energy future with affordable investments in clean energy.

LEARN ABOUT OCEAN ACIDIFICATION

- Watch *A Sea Change*, a documentary on ocean acidification: www.aseachange.net/ store.htm
- Watch the Natural Resources Defense Council's documentary online, narrated by Sigourney Weaver, on ocean acidification: www.nrdc.org/oceans/acidification/ aboutthefilm.asp

- Read Elizabeth Kolbert's groundbreaking article "The Darkening Sea," in the *New Yorker*, November 20, 2006, page 66.
- Review the "Acid Test," Oceana's report on ocean acidification: www.oceana.org/acid-test
- Watch Oceana's "Ocean Acid Test" with Dr. Jeffrey Short: www.google.com/landing/cop16/climatetours.html#oceana

FIND OUT MORE ABOUT AQUACULTURE AND THE CRISIS FACING THE WORLD'S FISHERIES

- *Bottomfeeder: How to Eat Ethically in a World of Vanishing Seafood* (Bloomsbury, 2008), by Taras Grescoe: www.tarasgrescoe.com/
- *Cod: The Biography of the Fish That Changed the World* (Penguin, 1997), by Mark Kurlansky: www.markkurlansky.com/books/other_non-fiction.aspx
- *The End of the Line* (New Press, 2006), film and book by Charles Clover: http://endoftheline.com/
- *The Fishes of the Sea: Commercial and Sport Fishing in New England* (Sheridan House, 2001), by Dave Preble
- *Four Fish: The Future of the Last Wild Food* (Penguin, 2010), by Paul Greenberg: www.fourfish.org/
- *Hooked: Pirates, Poaching, and the Perfect Fish* (Rodale, 2006), by G. Bruce Knecht
- *The Most Important Fish in the Sea* (Island, 2007), by H. Bruce Franklin: http://islandpress.org/mostimportantfish/
- *Song for the Blue Ocean: Encounters Along the World's Coasts and Beneath the Seas* (Holt, 1999), by Carl Safina: http://carlsafina.org/publications/books/song-for-the-blue-ocean/
- *An Unnatural History of the Sea: The Past and Future of Humanity and Fishing* (Gaia Books Ltd, 2007), by Callum Roberts: www.york.ac.uk/res/unnatural-history-of-the-sea/
- *Voyage of the Turtle: In Pursuit of the Earth's Last Dinosaur* (Holt, 2007), by Carl Safina: http://carlsafina.org/publications/books/voyage-of-the-turtle/
- Comprehensive ecology guide to the oceans by University of British Columbia and PEW Charitable Trusts: www.seaaroundus.org/
- Learn about salmon farming: www.farmedanddangerous.org/

FIND OUT MORE ABOUT BOTTOM TRAWLING
AND OTHER FORMS OF DESTRUCTIVE FISHING

- Bottom trawling primer: www.oceana.org/bottom-trawling
- FAO information on bottom trawling: www.fao.org/fishery/geartype/205/en
- Videos of the *Atlantic Dawn* Pelagic Trawler:
  www.dsi-as.com/default.aspx?m=2&i=190
- "Altered Oceans: A Five Part Series on the Crisis in the Seas," the *Los Angeles Times* series on ocean issues, by Ken Weiss and Usha Lee McFarling:
  www.latimes.com/news/local/la-oceans-series,0,7783938.special
- A series of tours of ocean and fisheries issues presented using Google Earth:
  http://earth.google.com/ocean/
- *Sea Sick: The Hidden Crisis in the Global Ocean* (Pier 9, 2008), by Alanna Mitchell. This book won the 2010 Grantham Prize for Excellence in Reporting on the Environment: www.alannamitchell.com/alanna-mitchell-books1.htm

FIND OUT MORE ABOUT SEAMOUNTS AND THE DEEP SEA

- Learn about the science of intraplate seamounts: www.mbari.org/volcanism/Seamounts/Default.htm
- Go to the global census of marine life on seamounts: censeam.niwa.co.nz/
- Learn about the creatures of the deep and the deep sea in *The Deep: The Extraordinary Creatures of the Abyss* (University of Chicago Press, 2007), by Claire Nouvian: www.thedeepbook.org/
- For public access to current information on a series of National Oceanic and Atmospheric Administration scientific and educational explorations and activities in the marine environment: http://oceanexplorer.noaa.gov/

FIND OUT MORE ABOUT SUBSIDIES, SEAFOOD FRAUD,
HUMAN RIGHTS VIOLATIONS, AND FLAGS OF CONVENIENCE

- *The End of the Line: How Overfishing Is Changing the World and What We Eat* (New Press, 2007), by Charles Clover; read the book that provided the basis for the documentary.
- Eric A. Bilsky, "Conserving Marine Wildlife through World Trade Law," *Michigan Journal of International Law* 599 (2009): http://students.law.umich.edu/mjil/article-pdfs/v30n3-Bilsky.pdf.
- *Hooked: Pirates, Poaching, and the Perfect Fish* (Rodale, 2006), by G. Bruce Knecht
- Pacific Coast Federation of Fishermen's Associations: www.pcffa.org
- The World Forum of Fish Harvesters & Fishworkers: www.alliance21.org/2003/rubrique395.html

WEB SITES

- BLUE OCEAN INSTITUTE: www.blueocean.org
- ENVIRONMENTAL JUSTICE FOUNDATION *("Protecting people and planet")*: www.ejfoundation.org
- FISH2FORK *("The campaigning restaurant guide for people who want to eat fish sustainably")*: www.fish2fork.com
- FISHBASE: www.fishbase.org
- GREENPEACE *("Inspiring action for a green and peaceful future")*: www.greenpeace.org
- MONTEREY BAY AQUARIUM *("Seafood Watch")*: www.montereybayaquarium.org
- *NATIONAL GEOGRAPHIC'S* OCEAN SITE: http://ocean.nationalgeographic.com/ocean/
- NATIONAL RESOURCES DEFENSE COUNCIL *("The Earth's best defense")*: www.nrdc.org
- OCEANA *("Protecting the world's oceans")*: www.oceana.org
- THE OCEAN CONSERVANCY: www.oceanconservancy.org
- PEW CHARITABLE TRUSTS OCEANS: www.pewtrusts.org/our_work_category.aspx?id=126
- THE PLASTIC POLLUTION COALITION: www.plasticpollutioncoalition.org
- SEA AROUND US PROJECT: www.seaaroundus.org/
- SMITHSONIAN'S OCEAN PORTAL: http://ocean.si.edu/
- WILDAID: www.wildaid.org
- WORLD WILDLIFE FUND *("Wildlife conservation; endangered species conservation")*: www.worldwildlife.org

FURTHER READING

- Bryson, Bill. *A Short History of Nearly Everything.* New York: Broadway, 2003.
- Diamond, Jared. *Collapse: How Societies Choose to Fail or Succeed.* New York: Penguin, 2005.
- Friedman, Thomas. *Hot, Flat and Crowded: Why We Need a Green Revolution—And How It Can Renew America.* New York: Farrar, Straus and Giroux, 2008.
- Koslow, Tony. *The Silent Deep: The Discovery, Ecology, and Conservation of the Deep Sea.* Chicago: University of Chicago Press, 2007.
- *Oceans: A Scientific American Reader.* Chicago: University of Chicago Press, 2007.
- Pauly, Daniel, and Jay Maclean. *In a Perfect Ocean: The State of Fisheries and Ecosystems in the North Atlantic Ocean.* Washington, DC: Island, 2003.
- Safina, Carl. *Eye of the Albatross: Visions of Hope and Survival.* New York: Henry Holt, 2002.
- Scully, Matthew. *Dominion: The Power of Man, the Suffering of Animals, and the Call to Mercy.* New York: St. Martin's, 2002.

ACKNOWLEDGMENTS

There are so many people who helped make this book possible. Let me start by acknowledging those who literally made this a book.

First, David Kuhn, who encouraged me to take on this project and then led me to the people at Rodale, whose taste and talent I trusted from the first day I met them. They include Karen Rinaldi, whose passion for oceans equals that of anyone I've ever met; Colin Dickerman, whose insight and intelligence is woven throughout these pages and who is simply the best editor an author could ask for; Gena Smith, who worked tirelessly to coordinate all the book's contributors; Nancy Elgin and Sonya Maynard, whose diligence and attention to detail made sure the right words were in the right places and that the facts were indeed facts; and Amy King, Greg Villepique, Brooke Myers, Elizabeth Krenos, and Nancy N. Bailey, who provided much-needed support during the project. Thanks as well to Don Foley, whose remarkable illustrations make complex subjects both comprehensible and beautiful, and to Paul Kepple and his team, including photo editor Susan Oyama and designers Ralph Geroni and Susan Van Horn, whose elegant design brought the book to life.

Speaking of facts, this book wouldn't exist without the support and advice of the staff and scientists at Oceana, whose high standards, I hope, are reflected on these pages. These include, especially, Andy Sharpless, the CEO, and Mike Hirshfield, Oceana's chief scientist; along with Jim Simon, Matt Littlejohn, Suzannah Evans, Jackie Savitz, Courtney Sakai, Susan Murray, Margot Stiles and, last but certainly not least, Daniel Pauly, who is a giant in the field of marine fisheries and one of my heroes.

Most of all, thanks to Mike D'Orso, to whom I am so grateful for agreeing to work with me on this book. He is a wonderful writer, and I am so honored to have spent this time with him.

On the personal front, I want to thank my parents for the unending love that came my way and the joy with which they led their lives. Thanks as well to my sister, Jan, for her wisdom and constant love.

To Robert Sulnick, whose friendship and passion to make a difference inspired me to get involved and stay involved, I can't thank you enough. Special acknowledgment to my manager, Keith Addis, who has been my partner in this environmental journey. To then-Congresswoman Barbara Boxer, who encouraged us to start AOC, thank you for being there from the beginning. Thank you as well, Theo Von Hoffman, who ran the office in those tough early days, along with all the staffs and boards of directors of AOC and Oceana, who have shared their knowledge and support with me over the years.

Finally, thanks to my wife, Mary, whose love and passion for life inspires me every day.

INDEX

Boldface page references indicate photographs and illustrations.
Underscored references indicate boxed text, charts, and graphs.